# ABSOLUTE
# BEGINNER'S
# GUIDE

### TO

# Computer Basics

Michael Miller

800 East 96th Street,
Indianapolis, Indiana 46240

# Absolute Beginner's Guide to Computer Basics

International Standard Book Number: 0-7897-2896-6

Library of Congress Catalog Card Number: 2002113709

Printed in the United States of America

First Printing: November 2002

06   05   04      9   8   7   6

## Trademarks

## Warning and Disclaimer

**Associate Publisher**
Greg Wiegand

**Managing Editor**
Thomas Hayes

**Acquisitions Editor**
Angelina Ward

**Development Editor**
Nicholas J. Goetz

**Project Editor**
Natalie Harris

**Indexer**
Kelly Castell

**Proofreader**
Kellie Cotner

**Team Coordinator**
Sharry Leigh Gregory

**Interior Designer**
Anne Jones

**Cover Designer**
Anne Jones

# Contents at a Glance

Introduction, 1

**Part I    Getting Started, 7**

1    Understanding Your Computer Hardware, 9

2    Setting Up Your New Computer System, 31

**Part II    Using Windows, 39**

3    Understanding Microsoft Windows XP, 41

4    Taking Windows for a Spin, 59

5    Personalizing Windows, 71

6    Working with Files and Folders, 83

**Part III    Using Computer Software, 97**

7    Installing New Software, 99

8    Using Microsoft Works Suite, 105

9    Working with Words, 113

10    Working with Numbers, 127

11    Working with a Database, 139

12    Managing Your Finances, 147

13    Creating Greeting Cards and Other Cool Projects, 159

14    Learning with Educational Software, 165

15    Playing Games, 171

**Part IV    Using the Internet, 177**

16    Understanding the Internet, 179

17    Getting Connected to the Internet, 183

18    Surfing the Web, 191

19    Finding Stuff Online, 199

20    Buying and Selling Online, 209

21    Sending and Receiving Email, 221

22    Using Instant Messaging and Chat, 231

23    Using Newsgroups, Message Boards, and Mailing Lists, 237

24    Downloading Files, 243

25    Creating Your Own Web Page, 247

**Part V    Working with Music and Pictures, 253**

26    Working with Pictures, 255

27    Playing CDs and DVDs, 269

28    Playing Internet Audio and Video, 277

29    Downloading and Playing Digital Music, 283

30    Burning Your Own CDs, 295

31    Editing Your Own Home Movies, 299

**Part VI    Protecting and Maintaining Your System, 307**

32    Protecting Yourself and Your Kids Online, 309

33    Adding New Hardware, 319

34    Setting Up a Home Network, 325

35    Performing Routine Maintenance, 333

36    Dealing with Common Problems, 341

Index, 351

# Table of Contents

**Introduction**    **1**

How This Book Is Organized    **2**

Conventions Used in This Book    **3**
    Menu Commands    **3**
    Shortcut Key Combinations    **4**
    Web Page Addresses    **4**
    Special Elements    **4**

Let Me Know What You Think    **5**


**I  Getting Started**

**1  Understanding Your Computer Hardware    9**

What Your Computer Can—and Can't—Do    **10**
    Good for Work    **10**
    Good for Play    **10**
    Good for Managing Your Finances    **10**
    Good for Keeping in Touch    **11**
    Good for Getting Online    **11**

Getting to Know Your Personal Computer System    **11**
    Pieces and Parts—Computer Hardware    **11**
    The Right Tools for the Right Tasks—Computer Software    **12**
    Making Everything Work—with Windows    **13**
    Don't Worry, You Can't Screw It Up—Much    **14**

Computer Hardware Basics    **14**
    Your PC's System Unit—The Mother Ship    **14**
    Microprocessors: The Main Engine    **17**
    Computer Memory: Temporary Storage    **19**

Hard Disk Drives: Long-Term Storage    **20**
Disk Drives: Portable Storage    **20**
CD-ROM Drives: Storage on a Disc    **21**
DVD Drives: Even More Storage on a Disc    **22**
Keyboards: Fingertip Input    **22**
Mice: Point-and-Click Input Devices    **23**
Modems: Getting Connected    **24**
Sound Cards and Speakers: Making Noise    **24**
Video Cards and Monitors: Getting the Picture    **25**
Printers: Making Hard Copies    **27**
Portable PCs—Lightweight All-in-One Systems    **27**

**2  Setting Up Your New Computer System    31**

Before You Get Started    **32**

Connecting the Cables    **32**

Turning It On and Setting It Up    **34**
    Powering On for the First Time    **34**
    Powering On Normally    **35**

Setting Up Additional Users    **36**


**II  Using Windows**

**3  Understanding Microsoft Windows XP    41**

What Windows Is—and What It Does    **42**

Different Versions of Windows    **42**

Working Your Way Around the Desktop    **43**

Important Windows Operations  **44**
   Pointing and Clicking  **44**
   Double-Clicking  **44**
   Right-Clicking  **44**
   Dragging and Dropping  **45**
   Hovering  **45**
   Moving and Resizing Windows  **45**
   Maximizing, Minimizing, and Closing
   Windows  **46**
   Scrolling Through a Window  **47**
   Using Menus  **47**
   Using Toolbars  **48**
   Using Dialog Boxes, Tabs, and Buttons
   **49**

Using the Start Menu  **51**
   Launching a Program  **51**
   Switching Between Programs  **52**
   Shutting Down Windows—and Your
   Computer  **52**

Understanding Files and Folders  **53**
   Managing PC Resources with My
   Computer  **54**
   Managing Files with My Documents  **55**
   Managing Windows with the Control
   Panel  **55**

All the Other Things in Windows  **56**
   Accessories  **57**
   Internet Utilities  **57**
   System Tools  **57**

Getting Help in Windows  **57**

**4 Taking Windows for a Spin  59**

Playing a Game  **60**

Launching a Program—and Printing and
Saving a Document  **63**
   Open Notepad  **63**
   Writing Your Note  **64**
   Printing Your Note  **64**

Saving Your File  **65**
Closing the Program  **65**

Viewing Your Documents  **66**

Examining Your Hard Disk  **67**

Shutting Down Your System  **69**

**5 Personalizing Windows  71**

Changing the Desktop Size  **72**

Enabling ClearType  **73**

Changing Your Desktop Theme  **73**

Personalizing the Desktop Background  **73**

Changing the Color Scheme  **75**

Activating Special Effects  **75**
   Using the Effects Dialog Box  **75**
   Using the Performance Options Dialog Box
   **76**

Changing Your Click  **77**

Changing the Way the Start Menu Works
**78**

Displaying More—or Fewer—Programs on the
Start Menu  **79**

Selecting Which Icons to Display on the Start
Menu—and How  **79**

Adding a Program to the Start Menu—
Permanently  **80**

Using a Screensaver  **80**

Changing System Sounds  **81**

Resetting the Time and Date  **82**

**6 Working with Files and Folders 83**

Viewing Folders and Files **84**
Changing the Way Files Are Displayed **84**
Sorting Files and Folders **85**
Grouping Files and Folders **85**
Saving Your Settings, Universally **86**

Navigating Folders **87**

Creating New Folders **88**

Renaming Files and Folders **88**

Copying Files **89**
The Easy Way to Copy **89**
Other Ways to Copy **90**

Moving Files **90**
The Easy Way to Move **91**
Other Ways to Move a File **91**

Deleting Files **91**
The Easy Way to Delete **91**
Restoring Deleted Files **92**
Managing the Recycle Bin **93**

Working with Compressed Folders **93**
Compressing a File **93**
Extracting Files **94**

**III Using Computer Software**

**7 Installing New Software 99**

Automatic Installation **100**

Manual Installation **101**

Installing Programs from the Internet **101**

Removing Old Programs **102**

Things to Remember **103**

**8 Using Microsoft Works Suite 105**

What's in Works **106**
Microsoft Works—Including Works
Spreadsheet, Works Database, Works
Calendar, and Address Book **106**
Microsoft Word **107**
Microsoft Money **107**
Microsoft Picture It! Photo **107**
Microsoft Encarta Encyclopedia **108**
Microsoft Streets & Trips **108**

Working Works **108**
Finding Your Way Around the Task
Launcher **108**
Launching a Program **109**
Launching a New Task **110**
Launching an Old Document **111**

**9 Working with Words 113**

Exploring the Word Interface **114**
What's Where in Word **114**
Viewing a Word Document—in Different
Ways **115**
Zooming to View **116**

Working with Documents **116**
Creating a New Document **117**
Opening an Existing Document **118**
Saving the Document **118**

Working with Text **119**
Entering Text **119**
Editing Text **119**
Formatting Text **120**
Checking Spelling and Grammar **120**

Printing a Document **121**
Previewing Before You Print **121**
Basic Printing **121**
Changing Print Options **121**

Formatting Your Document **122**
   Formatting Paragraphs **122**
   Using Word Styles **122**
   Assigning Headings **123**

Working with an Outline **124**

Working with Pictures **125**
   Inserting a Picture from the Clip Art
   Gallery **125**
   Inserting Other Types of Picture Files
   **125**
   Formatting the Picture **126**

The Absolute Minimum **126**

**10 Working with Numbers** 127

Understanding Spreadsheets **128**

Creating a New Spreadsheet **129**

Entering Data **129**

Formatting Your Spreadsheet **129**
   Applying Number Formats **129**
   Formatting Cell Contents **130**

Inserting and Deleting Rows and Columns
**130**
   Insert a Row or Column **130**
   Delete a Row or Column **130**
   Adjusting Column Width **131**

Using Formulas and Functions **131**
   Creating a Formula **131**
   Basic Operators **131**
   Working with Other Cells **132**
   Quick Addition with AutoSum **133**
   Using Functions **133**

Sorting a Range of Cells **134**

Creating a Chart **135**

The Absolute Minimum **137**

**11 Working with a Database** 139

Creating a New Database **140**
   Creating a Preformatted Database **140**
   Creating a Blank Database **140**

Changing Views **141**

Editing Your Database **142**
   Adding Data **142**
   Adding New Records **142**
   Adding New Fields **142**

Sorting and Filtering **143**
   Sorting Data **143**
   Filtering Data **143**

Creating a Report **144**
   Printing a List **144**
   Using ReportCreator to Create a Report
   **145**

**12 Managing Your Finances** 147

Configuring Microsoft Money **148**
   First-Time Setup with the Setup Assistant
   **148**
   Setting Up Your Accounts **149**
   Setting Up Your Categories **149**

Navigating Money **150**
   Home Sweet Home **150**
   Money's Financial Centers **150**

Track Your Budget **151**

Doing Your Banking—Electronically **152**
   Entering Transactions **152**
   Balancing Your Checkbook **153**
   Online Banking **154**

Paying Recurring Bills **155**
   Scheduling the Payment **155**
   Paying the Bill **156**
   Printing Checks in Money **156**
   Paying Bills Online **157**

**13 Creating Greeting Cards and Other Cool Projects  159**

Using Home Publishing Software  **160**

Sending Electronic Greeting Cards  **162**
Popular Greeting Card Sites  **162**
Sending a Card at Yahoo! Greetings  **162**

**14 Learning with Educational Software  165**

Finding the Best Educational Software  **166**
Early Learning  **166**
Elementary  **166**
High School  **167**
Continuing Education  **167**

Using Encyclopedia Programs  **168**
The Best Encyclopedia Software  **168**
Using Microsoft Encarta  **168**

**15 Playing Games  171**

Building a State-of-the-Art Gaming System  **172**

Installing and Playing PC Games  **173**

Playing Games Online  **174**

Playing Games—Against Other Players  **175**

**IV  Using the Internet**

**16 Understanding the Internet  179**

What the Internet Is—and What It Isn't  **180**

How an Internet Connection Works  **180**

The Most Important Parts of the Internet  **181**

**17 Getting Connected to the Internet  183**

Different Types of Connections  **184**

Choosing an ISP  **184**

Before You Connect  **185**

Setting Up a Completely New Account  **186**

Setting Up an Existing Account  **187**

Sharing an Internet Connection  **187**
Configuring the Host PC  **188**
Configuring the Client PCs  **189**
Configuring Non-Windows XP PCs  **189**

Connecting  **190**

**18 Surfing the Web  191**

Understanding the Web  **192**

Using Internet Explorer  **192**

Basic Web Surfing  **194**

Advanced Operations  **194**
Saving Your Favorite Pages  **195**
Revisiting History  **196**
Printing  **196**

Let's Go Surfin'!  **196**

**19 Finding Stuff Online  199**

How to Search  **200**
Constructing a Query  **200**
Using Wildcards  **200**

Where to Search  **201**
Directory Searching with Yahoo!  **201**
Index Searching with Google  **202**
Other Good Search Sites  **202**

Searching for People  **202**

Searching for News, Sports, and Weather **203**
    Searching for the Latest News **203**
    Searching for Sports Headlines and Scores **204**
    Searching for Weather Reports **204**

Searching for Financial Information **205**

Searching for Medical Information **205**

Searching—For Seniors **207**

20 **Buying and Selling Online** **209**

Shopping Online **210**
    How to Shop—Safely **210**
    The Biggest—and the Best—Online Retailers **211**

Buying a Car—Online **212**

Buying a Home—Online **213**

Making Online Reservations **214**

Buying and Selling at Online Auctions **215**
    How Online Auctions Work **215**
    Bidding—and Buying—on eBay **216**
    Selling on eBay **218**

21 **Sending and Receiving Email** **221**

Setting Up Your Email Accounts **222**

Understanding the Outlook Express Window **223**

Composing a Message **223**

Reading New Messages **224**

Replying to a Message **225**

Sending Files via Email **225**
    Attaching a File to an Email Message **225**
    Opening an Email Attachment **226**
    Watching Out for Email Viruses **227**

Listing Your Friends in an Address Book **227**
    Adding New Contacts **228**
    Editing Contacts **229**
    Sorting and Searching **229**
    Sending Email to a Contact **230**

22 **Using Instant Messaging and Chat** **231**

Sending and Receiving Instant Messages **232**
    Getting Connected **232**
    Adding New Contacts **233**
    Sending a Message **234**
    Receiving a Message **234**

Chat with Friends Online **234**
    Chatting at Yahoo! **235**
    Other Chat Sites **236**

23 **Using Newsgroups, Message Boards, and Mailing Lists** **237**

Using Good "Netiquette" **238**

Read and Post to Usenet Newsgroups **238**
    Understanding Newsgroup Names **239**
    Searching for Newsgroups and Articles **239**
    Creating and Posting Newsgroup Articles **240**

Message Boards **240**
    Using Yahoo! Message Boards **240**
    Other Web Message Boards **241**

Email Mailing Lists **242**

**24 Downloading Files** 243

Finding Files Online **244**

Downloading from a File Archive **244**

Downloading Files from Any Web Page **245**

**25 Creating Your Own Web Page** 247

Creating a Home Page at Yahoo! GeoCities
**248**

Using Page Building Software **251**

Uploading Your Pages **251**

**V Working with Music and Pictures**

**26 Working with Pictures** 255

Working with a Digital Camera **256**
Connecting Your Digital Camera **256**
Transferring Pictures to Your PC **257**
Working with Pictures in Your Camera
**258**

Scanning Your Photos **259**
Connecting and Configuring a Scanner
**259**
Making a Scan **259**

Managing Your Photos **260**

Editing Your Photos—with Microsoft Picture
It! Photo **261**
Opening a Picture for Editing **261**
Touching Up a Picture **262**
Cropping a Picture **263**
Adding Special Effects **263**
Creating Photo Albums and Other Projects
**264**

Printing Your Photos **264**
Choosing the Right Printer—and Paper
**264**
Printing from a Program **265**
Using the Photo Printing Wizard **265**

Emailing a Picture **266**

Printing Photos Online **267**
Ordering from a Photo-Processing Site
**267**
Ordering from Within Windows XP **268**

**27 Playing CDs and DVDs** 269

Play a CD on Your PC **270**

Using Windows Media Player **270**

Playing a CD **272**

Playing a DVD **272**
Using Windows Media Player to Play DVDs
**273**
Changing Display Size **273**
Navigating DVD Menus **274**
Changing Audio Options **274**
Playing in Slow Motion—or Fast Motion
**274**
Displaying Subtitles and Closed Captions
**274**

**28 Playing Internet Audio and Video** 277

Listening to Internet Radio **278**
Listening with Windows Media Player
**278**
Listening with RealAudio **279**
Finding an Internet Radio Station **280**

Watching Webcasts **280**
Using Windows Media Player **281**
Using RealOne Player **281**
Using QuickTime Player **281**
Finding Webcasts on the Internet **282**

**29  Downloading and Playing Digital Music 283**

Understanding Digital Audio   **284**
MP3 Audio   **284**
Windows Media Audio   **284**

Finding Digital Music to Download   **285**

Swapping Files with Other Users   **286**

Playing Digital Music on Your PC   **287**
Choosing a Media Player   **287**
Playing Digital Audio Files   **287**
Using Windows Media Player   **288**
Create a Playlist of Your Favorite Songs **288**

Making Copies of Your Favorite Songs   **289**
Ripping with Windows Media Player **290**
Ripping with MusicMatch Jukebox   **291**

**30  Burning Your Own CDs   295**

How to Burn a CD   **296**

Burning CDs with Windows Media Player **296**

Creating CD Labels   **297**

**31  Editing Your Own Home Movies   299**

Connecting and Configuring Your System for Video Editing   **300**

Understanding Windows Movie Maker   **300**

Importing Your Source Material   **301**

Editing Your Video   **302**
Add a Clip   **302**
Move a Clip   **302**
Remove a Clip   **303**

Trim a Clip   **303**
Split a Clip   **303**
Combine Multiple Clips   **304**

Adding Transitions   **304**

Working with Audio   **304**

Saving—and Watching—Your Movie   **305**

**VI  Protecting and Maintaining Your System**

**32  Protecting Yourself and Your Kids Online 309**

Protecting Against Inappropriate Content **310**
Using Content Filtering Software   **311**
Content Filtering with Internet Explorer **312**
Kid-Safe Searching   **312**

Dealing with Email Spam   **313**
Protecting Your Email Address   **313**
Blocking Addresses in Outlook Express **314**
Using Anti-Spam Software   **314**

Protecting Your System from Computer Viruses   **315**
How to Catch a Virus   **315**
Signs of Infection   **315**
Practicing Safe Computing   **315**
Using an Antivirus Program   **316**

Protecting Against Other Forms of Computer Attack   **317**
Using the Windows XP Internet Connection Firewall   **317**
Using Third-Party Firewall Software   **317**

**33 Adding New Hardware** 319

Most Popular Peripherals **320**

Understanding Ports **321**

Adding New External Hardware **322**

Adding New Internal Hardware **322**

Using the Add Hardware Wizard **323**

**34 Setting Up a Home Network** 325

Understanding Home Networks **326**

Different Ways to Connect **327**
  Ethernet Networks **327**
  Wireless Networks **327**
  Phone Line Networks **327**

Setting Up a Home Network **328**
  Choosing the Right Equipment **328**
  Setting Up the Network **329**
  Running the Network Setup Wizard **330**
  Sharing Files and Folders **331**

**35 Performing Routine Maintenance** 333

Cleaning Up Unnecessary Files **334**

Defragging Your Disk **335**

Performing a Hard Disk Checkup with
ScanDisk **336**

Backing Up Important Files **337**
  Making a Backup **338**
  Restoring Files from a Backup **339**

**36 Dealing with Common Problems** 341

What to Do When Windows Freezes **342**
  What Causes Windows to Freeze? **342**
  Dealing with Error Messages **342**
  Freezes Without Error Messages **343**
  Dealing with Application Freezes **343**

Dealing with a Major Crash **344**

Undoing the Damage with System Restore
**344**
  Setting System Restore Points **344**
  Restoring Your System **345**

How to Troubleshoot Computer Problems
**346**
  Using Windows Troubleshooters **348**
  Troubleshooting in Safe Mode **348**

**Index** 351

# About the Author

**Michael Miller** is a successful and prolific author with a reputation for practical advice and technical accuracy and an unerring empathy for the needs of his readers.

Mr. Miller has written more than four dozen how-to and reference books since 1989, for Que and other major publishers. His books for Que include *Special Edition Using the Internet and Web*, *The Complete Idiot's Guide to Online Search Secrets*, and, with Jim Louderback, *TechTV's Guide to Microsoft Windows XP for Home Users*. He is known for his casual, easy-to-read writing style and his practical, real-world advice—as well as his ability to explain a wide variety of complex topics to an everyday audience.

Mr. Miller is also president of The Molehill Group, a strategic consulting and authoring firm based in Carmel, Indiana. As a consultant, he specializes in providing strategic advice to and writing business plans for Internet- and technology-based businesses.

You can email Mr. Miller directly at abg@molehillgroup.com. His Web site is located at www.molehillgroup.com.

# Dedication

*To my nephews Alec and Ben Hauser—thanks for another fun summer vacation!*

# Acknowledgments

Thanks to the usual suspects at Que, including but not limited to Greg Wiegand, Angelina Ward, Nicholas J. Goetz, Natalie Harris, Kelly Castell, Kellie Cotner.

# We Want to Hear from You!

As the reader of this book, *you* are our most important critic and commentator. We value your opinion and want to know what we're doing right, what we could do better, what areas you'd like to see us publish in, and any other words of wisdom you're willing to pass our way.

As an associate publisher for Que, I welcome your comments. You can email or write me directly to let me know what you did or didn't like about this book—as well as what we can do to make our books better.

Please note that I cannot help you with technical problems related to the *topic* of this book. We do have a User Services group, however, where I will forward specific technical questions related to the book.

When you write, please be sure to include this book's title and author as well as your name, email address, and phone number. I will carefully review your comments and share them with the author and editors who worked on the book.

Email:      feedback@quepublishing.com

Mail:       Greg Wiegand
            Que
            800 East 96th Street
            Indianapolis, IN 46240 USA

For more information about this book or another Que title, visit our Web site at www.quepublishing.com. Type the ISBN (excluding hyphens) or the title of a book in the Search field to find the book's page.

# INTRODUCTION

Since this is the *Absolute Beginners Guide to Computer Basics*, let's start at the absolute beginning. Which is this:

Computers aren't supposed to be scary.

Intimidating, sometimes. Difficult to use, perhaps. Inherently unreliable, most definitely. (Although they're better than they used to be.)

But scary? Definitely not.

Computers aren't scary because there's nothing they can do to hurt you. And there's not much you can do to hurt them, either. It's kind of a wary coexistence between man and machine, but the relationship has the potential to be quite beneficial.

To you, anyway.

A lot of people think that they're scared of computers because they think they're unfamiliar with them. But that isn't really true.

You see, even if you've never actually used a computer before, you've been exposed to computers and all they can do for at least the last 20 years or so. Whenever you make a deposit at your bank, you're working with computers. Whenever you make a purchase at a retail store, you're working with computers. Whenever you watch a television show, or read a newspaper article, or look at a picture in a magazine, you're working with computers.

That's because computers are used in all those applications. Somebody, somewhere, is working behind the scenes with a computer to manage your bank account.

In fact, it's hard to imagine, here at the dawn of the twenty-first century, how we ever got by without all those keyboards, mice, and monitors. (Or, for that matter, the Internet.)

However, just because computers have been around for awhile doesn't mean that everyone knows how to use them. It's not unusual to feel a little trepidation the first time you sit down in front of that intimidating monitor and keyboard. Which keys should you press? What do they mean by "double-clicking the mouse?" And what are all those little pictures onscreen?

As foreign as all this might seem at first, computers really aren't that hard to understand—or to use. You have to learn a few basic concepts, of course (all the pressing and clicking and whatnot), and it helps to understand exactly what part of the system does what. But once you get the hang of things, computers really are fairly easy to use.

Which, of course, is where this book comes in.

*Absolute Beginner's Guide to Computer Basics* will help you figure out how to use your new computer system. You'll learn how computers work, how to connect all the pieces and parts together, and how to start using them. You'll learn about computer hardware and software, about Windows and operating systems, and about the Internet. And after you're comfortable with the basic concepts (which won't take too long, trust me), you'll learn how to actually do stuff.

You'll learn how to do useful stuff, like writing letters and balancing your checkbook and making your own picture postcards. Fun stuff, like listening to music and watching movies and playing games. Online stuff, like searching for information and sending email and chatting with friends via instant messages. And essential stuff, like copying files and troubleshooting problems and protecting against thieves and hackers.

All you have to do is sit yourself down in front of your computer, try not to be scared (there's nothing to be scared of, really), and work your way through the chapters and activities in this book. And remember that computers aren't hard to use, they don't break easily, and they let you do all sorts of fun and useful stuff once you get the hang of them.

Really!

# How This Book Is Organized

This book is organized into six main parts, as follows:

- **Part 1, Getting Started**, describes all the pieces and parts of your system, and how to connect them together to get your new PC up and running.

- **Part 2, Using Windows**, introduces the backbone of your entire system, the Microsoft Windows operating system. You'll learn how Windows works, and how to use Windows to perform basic tasks, such as copying and deleting files and folders. (You'll also learn fun stuff, like how to change the picture on your computer desktop.)

- **Part 3, Using Computer Software**, tells you everything you need to know about running the most popular computer programs. You'll learn how to use Microsoft Works Suite, Microsoft Word, Microsoft Money, and all sorts of other programs—including educational software and PC games.

■ **Part 4, Using the Internet**, is all about going online. You'll discover how to surf the Web, send and receive email, use instant messaging and chat, and download files. You'll even learn how to shop online, buy and sell at online auctions, and create your own personal Web page!

■ **Part 5, Working with Music and Pictures**, shows you how to download and play MP3-format music files, how to burn your own audio CDs, how to watch DVDs on your computer screen, and how to use your PC with your digital camera and camcorder.

■ **Part 6, Protecting and Maintaining Your System**, contains all the boring (but necessary) information you need to know to keep your new PC in tip-top shape. You'll learn how to protect your PC from computer viruses and online attacks, how to reduce the amount of spam you receive in your email inbox, how to add new pieces of hardware to your system, how to set up a simple home network, how to perform routine maintenance, and how to deal with (and troubleshoot) common PC problems.

Taken together, the 36 chapters in this book will help you progress from absolute beginner to experienced computer user. Just read what you need, and before long you'll be using your computer like a pro!

# Conventions Used in This Book

I hope that this book is easy enough to figure out on its own, without requiring its own instruction manual. As you read through the pages, however, it helps to know precisely how I've presented specific types of information.

## Menu Commands

Most computer programs operate via a series of pull-down menus. You use your mouse to pull down a menu and then select an option from that menu. This sort of operation is indicated like this throughout the book:

Select File, Save

*or*

Click the Start button and select All Programs, Accessories, Notepad.

All you have to do is follow the instructions in order, using your mouse to click each item in turn. When there are submenus tacked onto the main menu (as in the All Programs, Accessories, Notepad example), just keep clicking the selections until you come to the last one—which should open the program or activate the command you wanted!

## Shortcut Key Combinations

When you're using your computer keyboard, sometimes you have to press two keys at the same time. These "two-key" combinations are called *shortcut keys* and are shown as the key names joined with a plus sign (+).

For example, Ctrl+W indicates that you should press the W key while holding down the Ctrl key. It's no more complex than that.

## Web Page Addresses

There are a lot of Web page addresses in this book. (That's because you'll probably be spending a lot of time on the Internet.) They're noted as such:

www.molehillgroup.com

Technically, a Web page address is supposed to start with http:// (as in http://www.molehillgroup.com). Because Internet Explorer and other Web browsers automatically insert this piece of the address, however, you don't have to type it—and I haven't included it in any of the addresses in this book.

## Special Elements

This book also includes a few special elements that provide additional information not included in the basic text. These elements are designed to supplement the text to make your learning faster, easier, and more efficient.

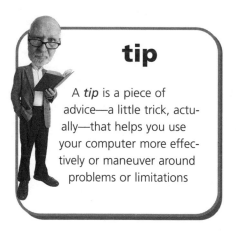

# tip

A *tip* is a piece of advice—a little trick, actually—that helps you use your computer more effectively or maneuver around problems or limitations

# note

A *note* is designed to provide information that is generally useful but not specifically necessary for what you're doing at the moment. Some are like extended tips—interesting, but not essential.

A *caution* will tell you to beware of a potentially dangerous act or situation. In some cases, ignoring a caution could cause you significant problem—so pay attention to them!

## Let Me Know What You Think

I always love to hear from readers. If you want to contact me, feel free to email me at abg@molehillgroup.com. I can't promise that I'll answer every message, but I will promise that I'll read each one!

If you want to learn more about me and any new books I have cooking, check out my Molehill Group Web site at www.molehillgroup.com. Who knows—you might find some other books there that you'd like to read.

# PART 1

# GETTING STARTED

1   Understanding Your Computer
    Hardware . . . . . . . . . . . . . . . . . . . . . 9

2   Setting Up Your New Computer
    System . . . . . . . . . . . . . . . . . . . . . 31

## IN THIS CHAPTER

- What Your Computer Can—and Can't—Do
- Getting to Know Your Personal Computer System
- Computer Hardware Basics

1

# UNDERSTANDING YOUR COMPUTER HARDWARE

Chances are you're reading this book because you just bought a new computer, are thinking about buying a new computer, or maybe even had someone give you their old computer. (Nothing wrong with high-tech hand-me-downs!) At this point you might not be totally sure what it is you've gotten yourself into. Just what is this mess of boxes and cables, and what can you—or *should* you—do with it?

This chapter serves as an introduction to the entire concept of personal computers in general—what they do, how they work, that sort of thing—and computer hardware in particular. It's a good place to start if you're not that familiar with computers, or want a brief refresher course in what all those pieces and parts are, and what they do.

Of course, if you want to skip the background and get right to using your computer, that's okay, too. For step-by-step instructions on how to connect and configure your new PC, go directly to Chapter 2, "Setting Up Your New Computer System."

# What Your Computer Can—and *Can't*—Do

What good is a personal computer, anyway?

Everybody has one, you know. (Including you, now!) In fact, it's possible you bought your new computer just so you wouldn't feel left out. But now that you have your very own personal computer, what do you do with it?

## Good for Work

A lot of people use their home PCs for work-related purposes. You can bring your work (reports, spreadsheets, you name it) home from the office and finish it on your home PC, at night or on weekends. Or, if you work at home, you can use your computer to pretty much run your small business—you can use it to do everything from typing memos and reports to generating invoices and setting budgets.

In short, anything you can do with a normal office PC, you can probably do on your home PC.

## Good for Play

All work and no play makes Jack a dull boy, so there's no reason not to have a little fun with your new PC. Not only can you use your PC to play some really cool games, you can also use it to track your favorite hobby, create interesting crafts projects, print pictures from your latest family vacation, listen to your favorite songs, and watch your favorite videos. In fact, with the right software and hardware, you can even use your PC to edit movies you take with your video camcorder!

## Good for Managing Your Finances

You don't have to be a professional accountant to use your PC to manage your finances. Software programs, such as Microsoft Money and Quicken, let you create budgets, write checks, and balance your accounts, right from your computer screen. You can even set up your system to automatically pay bills and do other banking online—no paper checks necessary.

## Good for Keeping in Touch

Want to send a letter to a friend? With your new PC (and a word processor program, such as Microsoft Word), it's a cinch. Even better, save a stamp and send that friend an electronic letter—called an *email*—over the Internet. And if that person's online the same time you are, you can chat with him in real time via an instant messaging program. Many families use their PCs for almost all their communications!

## Good for Getting Online

Speaking of email, chances are one of the main reasons you got a PC was to get connected to the Internet. The Internet's a great tool; in addition to email and instant messaging, you can join online message boards, participate in public chat rooms, and browse the World Wide Web—which is chock full of interesting and informative content and services. Now you won't feel left out when people start talking about "double-you double-you double-you" this and "dot-com" that—because you'll be online, too.

# Getting to Know Your Personal Computer System

Now that you know *why* you have that brand-new personal computer sitting on your desk, you might be interested in just *what* it is that you have. It's important to know what each part of your system is, what it does, and how to hook it all together.

## Pieces and Parts—Computer Hardware

We'll start by looking at the physical components of your system—the stuff we call computer *hardware*. As you can see in Figure 1.1, there are a lot of different pieces and parts that make up a typical computer system. You should note, however, that no two computer systems are identical, since you can always add new components to your system—or disconnect other pieces you don't have any use for.

**note**

This book is written for users of relatively new personal computers—in particular, PCs running the Windows XP operating system. If you have an older PC, most of the advice here is still good, although not all the step-by-step instructions will apply.

**FIGURE 1.1**

A typical per-
sonal computer
system.

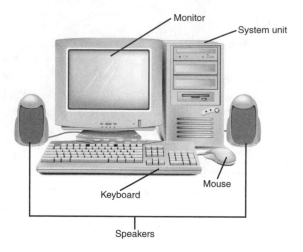

These items are the basic elements you'll find in
almost all computer systems. Of course, you can add
lots of other items to your personal system, including *printers* (to make printouts of documents and
pictures), *scanners* (to change a hardcopy document or picture to electronic format), *PC cameras*
(to send live video of yourself to friends and family), *digital cameras* (to transfer your snapshots to
electronic format), and *joysticks* (to play the most
challenging games). You can even add the appropriate items to connect multiple PCs together in a
*network*.

## The Right Tools for the Right Tasks— Computer Software

By themselves, all those little beige boxes really
aren't that useful. You can connect them and set
them in place, but they won't do anything until
you have some *software* to make things work.

> **note**
>
> Learn more about
> these pieces and parts in
> "Computer Hardware Basics,"
> later in this chapter. If you need
> help connecting all the pieces and
> parts, turn to Chapter 2. And if
> you want to add a new piece of
> hardware to your basic system,
> check out Chapter 33, "Adding
> New Hardware to Your System."

Computer *hardware* are those things you can touch—your system unit, monitor, and
the like. Computer *software*, on the other hand, is something you *can't* touch,
because it's nothing more than a bunch of electronic bits and bytes. These bits and
bytes, however, combine into computer programs—sometimes called *applications*—
that provide specific functionality to your system.

For example, if you want to crunch some numbers, you need a piece of software called a *spreadsheet* program. If you want to write a letter, you need a *word processing* program. If you want to make changes to some pictures you took with your digital camera, you need *graphics editing* software.

In other words, you need separate software for each task you want to do with your computer. Fortunately, most new computer systems come with a lot of this software already installed, for free.

If you want or need any additional software, you'll have to buy and install it yourself—as described in Chapter 7, "Installing New Software."

## Making Everything Work—with Windows

When you're not using a specific piece of application software, you interface with your computer via a special piece of software called an *operating system*. As the name implies, this program makes your system operate; it's your gateway to the hardware part of your system.

The operating system is also how your application software interfaces with your computer hardware. When you want to print a document from your word processor, that software works with the operating system to send the document to your printer.

You can learn more about Windows in Chapter 3, "Understanding Microsoft Windows XP."

Most computers today ship with an operating system called Windows. This operating system has been around for about 15 years and is published by Microsoft Corporation. Computers manufactured by Apple Computing use a different operating system, called the Mac OS. Therefore, computers running Windows and computers by Apple aren't totally compatible with each other.

There have been several different versions of Windows over the years. The current version is called Windows XP, and if you have a new PC, this is probably the version you're using. (Older versions—which look a little different but work pretty much the same—include Windows 95, Windows 98, and Windows Me.) You use Windows to launch specific programs and to perform various system maintenance functions, such as copying files and turning off your computer.

## Don't Worry, You Can't Screw It Up—Much

The balance of this chapter goes into a bit more detail about the hardware components of your PC system. Before you proceed, however, there's one other important thing you need to know about computers.

A lot of people are afraid of their computers. They think if they press the wrong key or click the wrong button that they'll break something or will have to call in an expensive repairperson to put things right.

This really isn't true.

The important thing to know is that it's really, really difficult to break your computer system. Yes, you can drop something and break it easily enough, but in terms of breaking your system through normal use, it just doesn't happen that often.

It *is* possible to make mistakes, of course. You can click the wrong button and accidentally delete a file you didn't want to delete or turn off your system and lose a document you forgot to save. You can even take inadequate security precautions and find your system infected by a computer virus. But in terms of doing serious harm just by clicking your mouse, it's unlikely.

So don't be afraid of the thing. Your computer is a tool, just like a hammer or a blender or a camera. After you learn how to use it, it can be a very useful tool. But it's *your* tool, which means *you* tell *it* what to do—not vice versa. Remember that you're in control and that you're not going to break anything, and you'll have a lot of fun—and maybe even get some real work done!

# Computer Hardware Basics

As you just read, computer hardware are those parts of your system you can actually see and touch. This includes your system unit and everything connected to it, including your monitor, keyboard, mouse, and printer.

The balance of this chapter presents all the various pieces of hardware you can have in a computer system—including those parts you can't always see because they're built in to your system unit. So, if you're curious about microprocessors and memory and modems and monitors, read on—this is the chapter for you!

Vertical system units often are called *towers* or *mini-towers*.

## Your PC's System Unit—The Mother Ship

The most important piece of hardware in your computer system is the *system unit*. This is the big, ugly box that houses your disk drives and many other components. You can find system units that lie horizontally on your desk (like the one in Figure 1.2) or ones that stand straight up (like the one in Figure 1.3). You can even find some computers that build the system unit into the monitor!

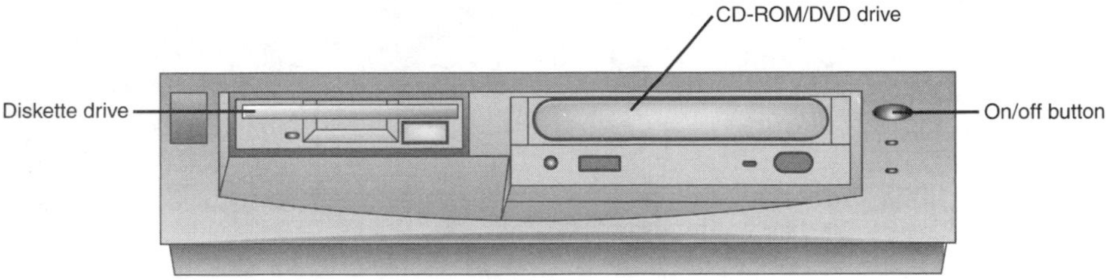

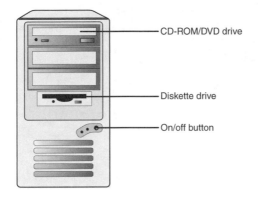

**FIGURE 1.2**

A desktop-type computer system unit.

**FIGURE 1.3**

A system unit in a mini-tower configuration.

The back of the system unit typically is covered with all types of connectors. This is because all the other parts of your computer system connect to your system unit, and they all have to have a place to plug in. And, because each component has its own unique type of connector, you end up with the assortment of jacks (called *ports* in the computer world) that you see in Figure 1.4.

All the good stuff in your system unit is inside the case. With most system units, you can remove the case to peek and poke around inside.

To remove your system unit's case, look for some big screws or thumbscrews on either the side or back of the case. (Even better—read your PC's instruction manual for instructions specific to your unit.) With the screws loosened or removed, you should then be able to either slide off the entire case, or pop open the top or back.

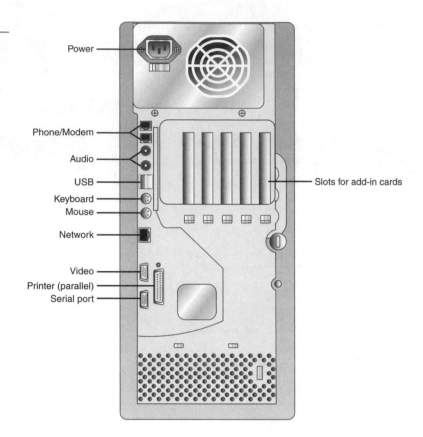

When you open the case on your system unit, you see all sorts of computer chips and circuit boards. The really big board located at the base of the computer (to which everything else is plugged into) is called the *motherboard*, because it's the "mother" for your microprocessor and memory chips, as well as for the other internal components that enable your system to function. This motherboard contains several slots, into which you can plug additional *boards* (also called *cards*) that perform specific functions.

As you can see in Figure 1.5, most PC motherboards contain six or more slots for add-on cards. For example, a video card enables your microprocessor to transmit video signals to your monitor. Other available cards enable you to add sound and modem/fax capabilities to your system.

**caution**

Always turn off your computer before attempting to remove the system unit's case—and be careful about touching anything inside! If you have any built-up static electricity, you can seriously damage the sensitive chips and electronic components with an innocent touch.

## Microprocessors: The Main Engine

We're not done looking at the system unit just yet. Buried somewhere on that big motherboard is a specific chip that controls your entire computer system. This chip is called a *microprocessor* or a *central processing unit (CPU)*.

The microprocessor is the brains inside your system. It processes all the instructions necessary for your computer to perform its duties. The more powerful the microprocessor chip, the faster and more efficiently your system runs.

Microprocessors carry out the various instructions that let your computer compute. Every input and output device hooked up to a computer—the keyboard, printer, monitor, and so on—either issues or receives instructions that the microprocessor then processes. Your software programs also issue instructions that must be implemented by the microprocessor. This chip truly is the workhorse of your system; it affects just about everything your computer does.

Desktop computer systems are composed of all these separate components. Portable PCs, on the other hand, have all that stuff crammed into a single case. So, you don't have a separate system unit, monitor, keyboard, and mouse—they're part of one very compact unit. Learn more about personal computers in the section "Portable PCs—Lightweight All-in-One Systems," later in this chapter.

**FIGURE 1.5**

What your PC looks like on the inside—a big motherboard with lots of add-on boards attached.

Different computers have different types of microprocessor chips. Many IBM-compatible computers use chips manufactured by Intel. Some use Intel-compatible chips manufactured by AMD and other firms. But all IBM-compatible computers that run the Windows operating system use Intel-compatible chips.

In addition to having different chip manufacturers (and different chip families from the same manufacturer), you'll also run into microprocessor chips that run at different speeds. CPU speed is measured in megahertz (MHz); a CPU with a speed of 1MHz can run at one million clock ticks per second! The higher the megahertz, the faster the chip runs. If you're still shopping for a new PC, look for one with the combination of a powerful microprocessor and a high clock speed for best performance.

If you want to know which microprocessor is installed in your system, Windows can tell you. If your computer is running Windows XP, all you have to do is follow these steps:

1. Click the **Start** button to display the **Start** menu.

2. Select **Control Panel** to open the Control Panel folder.

3. Select the **System** icon to open the System Properties dialog box, shown in Figure 1.6.

4. Select the **General** tab.

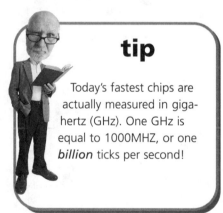

**note**

The Apple Macintosh uses chips made by Motorola that are totally different from the Intel-compatible chips. It's because of the different processor configurations that software written for the Macintosh won't run on IBM-compatible computers—and vice versa.

**tip**

Today's fastest chips are actually measured in giga-hertz (GHz). One GHz is equal to 1000MHZ, or one *billion* ticks per second!

The System section of this dialog box tells you which version of Windows you're running; the Registered To section tells you who you are (or, rather, how your version of Windows is registered); and the Computer section tells which processor you have and how much memory (RAM) you have installed.

**FIGURE 1.6**

Use the System Properties dialog box to find out what processor your computer is running.

## Computer Memory: Temporary Storage

Speaking of memory, before your CPU can process any instructions you give it, your instructions must be stored somewhere, in preparation for access by the microprocessor. These instructions—along with other data processed by your system—are temporarily held in the computer's *random access memory (RAM)*. All computers have some amount of memory, which is created by a number of memory chips. The more memory that's available in a machine, the more instructions and data that can be stored at one time.

Memory is measured in terms of *bytes*. One byte is equal to approximately one character in a word processing document. A unit equaling approximately one thousand bytes (1,024, to be exact) is called a *kilobyte (KB)*, and a unit of approximately one thousand (1,024) kilobytes is called a *megabyte (MB)*. A thousand megabytes is a *gigabyte (GB)*.

Most computers today come with at least 256MB of memory, and it's not uncommon to find machines with 512MB or more. To enable your computer to run as many programs as quickly as possible, you need as much memory installed in your system as it can accept—or that you can afford. Extra memory can be added to a computer by installing a new memory module, which is as easy as plugging a "stick" directly into a slot on your system's motherboard.

If your computer doesn't possess enough memory, its CPU must constantly retrieve data from permanent storage on its hard disk. This method of data retrieval is slower than retrieving instructions and data from electronic memory. In fact, if your machine doesn't have enough memory, some programs will run very slowly (or you might experience random system crashes), and other programs won't run at all!

## Hard Disk Drives: Long-Term Storage

Another important physical component inside your system unit is the *hard disk drive*. The hard disk permanently stores all your important data. Some hard disks can store more than 50 gigabytes of data. (Contrast this to your system's random access memory, which stores only a few hundred megabytes of data, temporarily.)

A hard disk consists of numerous metallic platters. These platters store data *magnetically*. Special read/write *heads* realign magnetic particles on the platters, much like a recording head records data onto magnetic recording tape.

Before data can be stored on any disk, including your system's hard disk, that disk must first be *formatted.* A disk that has not been formatted cannot accept any data. When you format a hard disk, your computer prepares each track and sector of the disk to accept and store data magnetically.

**caution**

If you try to reformat your hard disk, you'll erase all the programs and data that have been installed—so don't do it!

Of course, when you buy a new PC, your hard disk is already formatted for you. (And, in most cases, your operating system and key programs also are preinstalled.)

## Disk Drives: Portable Storage

Along with a hard disk drive, most computers have a *removable disk drive*. Removable disks—often called *floppy disks* or *diskettes*—work much like hard disks except that they consist of thin sheets of a magnetic-tape–like material instead of hard metallic platters. (Figure 1.7 shows a typical 3 1/2" floppy disk.)

**FIGURE 1.7**

Transfer files from PC to PC via removable disk.

Because removable disks are more portable than hard disks, they're typically used to store data that's transported physically from PC to PC. And disks are useful, too, for storing backup copies of the data on your PC's hard disk.

In addition to standard 3 1/2" disks, your computer system might include other types of portable storage media—most of which offer much more capacity than the 1.44MB found on a standard disk. For example, Iomega's Zip drive offers up to 250MB of portable storage on a removable disk that's slightly larger than a floppy. Sony's Superdisc can store up to 120MB on a disk that is physically compatible with—and can thus fully replace—traditional 3 1/2" drives.

It's not uncommon these days to find PCs equipped with removable *hard* disks. With hard disk prices becoming more affordable by the day, some users like to install a second, removable, hard disk on their systems. That way they can store key data on the removable hard disk, then pull it out of their machines and take it with them—to another PC.

## CD-ROM Drives: Storage on a Disc

There's a third type of disk that is now standard on personal computer systems. This disc is called a *CD-ROM*. (The initials stand for *compact disc—read-only memory*.)

CD-ROM discs, such as the one in Figure 1.8, look just like the compact discs you play on your audio system. They're also very similar in the way they store data (audio data in the case of regular CDs; computer data in the case of CD-ROMs).

**FIGURE 1.8**

Store tons of data, digitally, on a shiny CD-ROM disc.

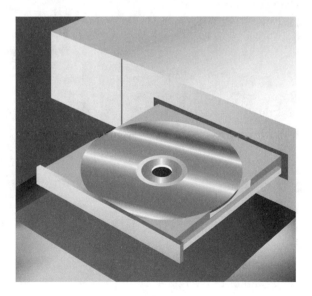

Information is encoded at a disc-manufacturing plant, using an industrial-grade laser. This information takes the form of microscopic pits (representing the 1s and 0s of computer binary language) below the disc's surface. Similar to hard and floppy disks, the information is arranged in a series of tracks and sectors, but the tracks are so close together that the disk surface is highly reflective.

Data is read from the CD-ROM disc via a drive that uses a consumer-grade laser. The laser beam follows the tracks of the disc and reads the pits, translating the data into a form your system can understand.

By the way, the *ROM* part of CD-ROM means that you can only read data from the disk; unlike normal hard disks and disks, you can't write new data to a standard CD-ROM. However, recordable (CD-R) and rewritable (CD-RW) drives are available that *do* let you write data to CD discs—although they're a bit more expensive than standard CD-ROM drives.

## DVD Drives: Even More Storage on a Disc

Beyond the CD-ROM is the new *DVD* medium. DVDs can contain up to 4.7GB of data (compared to 650MB for a typical CD-ROM), and therefore are ideally suited for large applications or games that otherwise would require multiple CDs. Similar to standard CD-ROMs, most DVDs are read-only—although all DVD drives can also read CD-ROM discs. In addition, most DVD drives play full-length DVD movies, which turns your PC into a mini movie machine.

DVD really isn't an acronym for anything in particular. Some manufacturers claim that it stands for *digital versatile disc* or *digital video disc*, but it's really just a bunch of initials with no real meaning.

And, just as there are recordable CD-ROM drives, you can also find recordable DVD drives. These DVD-R drives are a little expensive ($500 or more), but the prices are coming down—and they let you record an entire movie on a single disc.

## Keyboards: Fingertip Input

Computers receive data by reading it from disk, accepting it electronically over a modem, or receiving input directly from you, the user. You provide your input by way of what's called, in general, an *input device*; the most common input device you use to talk to your computer is the keyboard.

A computer keyboard, similar to the one in Figure 1.9, looks and functions just like a typewriter keyboard, except that computer keyboards have a few more keys. Some of these keys (such as the arrow, PgUp, PgDn, Home, and End keys) enable you to move around within a program or file. Other keys provide access to special program features. When you press a key on your keyboard, it sends an electronic signal to your system unit that tells your machine what you want it to do.

**FIGURE 1.9**

A standard PC
keyboard.

Most PC keyboards look like the one in Figure 1.9. Some keyboards, however, have
an ergonomic design that splits the keyboard into right and left parts and twists and
tilts each side for maximum comfort. In addition, some manufacturers make *wireless*
keyboards that connect to your system unit via radio signals—thus eliminating one
cable from the back of your system.

## Mice: Point-and-Click Input Devices

It's a funny name, but a necessary device.

A computer *mouse*, like the one shown in Figure 1.10, is a small handheld device.
Most mice consist of an oblong case with a roller underneath and two or three buttons on top. When you move the mouse along a desktop, an onscreen pointer
(called a *cursor*) moves in response. When you click (press and release) a mouse button, this motion initiates an action in your program.

**FIGURE 1.10**

Roll the mouse
back and forth
to move the
onscreen cursor.

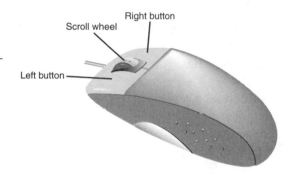

Mice come in all shapes and sizes. Some have wires, and some are wireless. Some
are relatively oval in shape, and others are all curvy to better fit in the palm of your
hand. Some have the typical roller ball underneath, and others use an optical sen-
sor to determine where and how much you're rolling. Some even have extra buttons
that can be programmed for specific functions or a scroll wheel you can use to scroll
through long documents or Web pages.

Of course, a mouse is just *one* type of input device you can hook up to your PC.
Trackballs, joysticks, game controllers, and pen pads all count as input devices,

whether they work in conjunction with a mouse or replace it. You can use one of these alternative devices to replace your original mouse or (in some cases) to supplement it.

If you have a portable PC, you don't have a separate mouse, but rather a built-in pointing device of some sort—a touchpad, rollerball, or TrackPoint (the thing that looks like a little rubber eraser). Fortunately, you don't have to use the built-in pointing device on a portable PC; most portables let you attach an external mouse, which then overrides the internal device.

## Modems: Getting Connected

Almost all PC systems today include a *modem*. A modem enables your computer to connect to telephone lines and transmit data to and from the Internet and commercial online services (such as America Online).

Modems come in either internal (card-based) or external (hooking up to an open port on the back of your system) models. *Internal* modems usually fit into a slot on your motherboard and connect directly to a telephone line. *External* modems are free-standing devices that connect to your system unit by cable and hook directly to a phone line.

If you connect to the Internet via a broadband connection, you probably have an external cable or DSL modem. These devices work just like traditional phone line modems, but are specifically designed to work with the data transmitted over digital cable and DSL lines.

**note**

The word "modem" stands for "modulate-demodulate," which is how digital data is sent over traditional analog phone lines. The data is "modulated" for transmittal, and "demodulated" upon receipt.

## Sound Cards and Speakers: Making Noise

Every PC comes with its own built-in speaker. In fact, some systems come with multiple-speaker audio systems, complete with subwoofers and so-called "3D" sound. (Figure 1.11 shows a typical right-left-subwoofer speaker system.)

All speaker systems are driven by a sound card that is installed inside your system unit. If you upgrade your speaker system, you also might need to upgrade your sound card accordingly.

**FIGURE 1.11**

A typical set of right and left external speakers, complete with subwoofer.

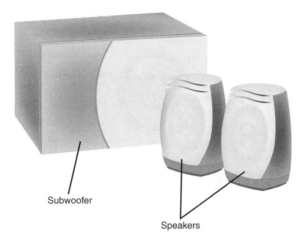

Subwoofer

Speakers

## Video Cards and Monitors: Getting the Picture

Operating a computer would be difficult if you didn't constantly receive visual feedback showing you what your machine is doing. This vital function is provided by your computer's monitor.

The traditional monitor, similar to the one shown in Figure 1.12, is a lot like a little television set. Your microprocessor electronically transmits words and pictures (*text* and *graphics*, in PC lingo) to your monitor, in some approximation of how these visuals would appear on paper. You view the monitor and respond according to what you see onscreen.

**FIGURE 1.12**

A traditional tube-type video monitor.

Although the traditional monitor uses a picture tube (similar to the one in a normal television set) to display its picture, another type of monitor does away with the tube. A so-called *flat-screen* monitor, such as the one in Figure 1.13, uses an LCD display instead—which is not only flat, but also very thin. (These are the same types of displays used in portable PCs.)

You measure the size of a monitor by measuring from corner to corner, diagonally. The traditional desktop monitor is normally a 14" or 15" monitor; larger 17" and 19" monitors are becoming more common as they become more affordable.

The monitor itself does not generate the images it displays. These images are electronically crafted by a *video card* installed inside your system unit. To work correctly, both video card and monitor must be matched to display images of the same resolution.

*Resolution* refers to the size of the images that can be displayed onscreen and is measured in pixels. A *pixel* is a single dot on your screen; a full picture is composed of thousands of pixels. The higher the resolution, the sharper the resolution— which lets you display more (smaller) elements onscreen.

**tip**

The measurement is different for tube-type monitors than it is for flat-screen monitors. This is because a flat-screen monitor displays its images all the way to the edge of the screen, and traditional tube-type monitors don't. For that reason, a 15" flat-screen monitor has the same size picture as a 17" tube-type monitor.

Resolution is expressed in numbers of pixels, in both the horizontal and vertical directions. The lowest-price video cards and monitors have a 640×480 or 800×600 pixel resolution; you probably want a card/monitor combination that can display at the 1024×768 resolution.

## Printers: Making Hard Copies

Your monitor displays images in real time, but they're fleeting. For permanent records of your work, you must add a printer to your system. Printers create hard copy output from your software programs.

You can choose from various types of printers for your system, depending on your exact printing needs. The two main types of printers today are laser and inkjet printers.

*Laser* printers work much like copying machines, applying toner (powdered ink) to paper by using a small laser. *Inkjet* printers, on the other hand, shoot jets of ink to the paper's surface to create the printed image. Inkjet printers are typically a little lower priced than laser printers, although the price difference is shrinking.

You also can choose from either black-and-white or color printers. Black-and-white printers are faster than color printers and better if you're printing memos, letters, and other single-color documents. Color printers, however, are great if you have kids, and they're essential if you want to print pictures taken with a digital camera.

By the way, there's a new type of "combination" printer available that combines a printer with a scanner and a fax machine. If you need all these devices and are short on space, these are pretty good deals.

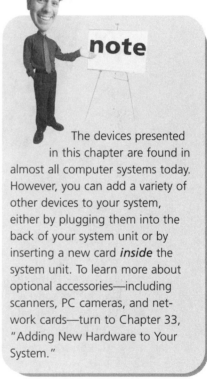

**note**

The devices presented in this chapter are found in almost all computer systems today. However, you can add a variety of other devices to your system, either by plugging them into the back of your system unit or by inserting a new card *inside* the system unit. To learn more about optional accessories—including scanners, PC cameras, and network cards—turn to Chapter 33, "Adding New Hardware to Your System."

## Portable PCs—Lightweight All-in-One Systems

Before we wrap up this chapter, we need to discuss a slightly different type of computer. This type of PC combines all the various elements (except for a printer) into a single case and then adds a battery so you can use it on the go. This type of PC is called a *portable computer*—or, depending on its size, a *laptop* or *notebook* PC.

Most portable PCs, like the one in Figure 1.14, feature a flip-up LCD screen. When the screen is folded down, the PC is very portable; when the screen is flipped up, the keyboard is exposed.

**FIGURE 1.14**

A typical portable PC—all those components in a single package.

All portable PCs include some sort of built-in pointing device—but typically not a standalone mouse. A portable might have a touchpad, rollerball, or Trackpoint (which looks like a miniature joystick in the middle of the keyboard). Speakers typically are built into the base of the unit, and various types of disk drives are located on the sides or underneath.

The key thing about portable PCs—in addition to their small sizes and light weights—is that they can operate on battery power. Depending on the PC (and the battery), you might be able to operate a portable for up to four hours before switching batteries or plugging the unit into a wall outlet. That makes portables great for use on airplanes, in coffeshops, or anywhere plugging in a power cord is inconvenient.

The only bad thing about portable PCs is that they're more expensive than a similarly equipped desktop PC. Expect to pay almost twice as much for the same features in a portable because all the normal components have to be shrunk down to a more compact size.

# THE ABSOLUTE MINIMUM

Here are the key points to remember from this chapter:

- Your computer system is composed of various pieces of hardware, almost all of which plug into that big beige box called the system unit.

- You interface with your computer hardware via a piece of software called an operating system. The operating system on your new computer is probably some version of Microsoft Windows.

- You use specific software programs to perform specific tasks, such as writing letters and editing digital photos.

- The brains and engine of your system is the system unit, which contains the microprocessor, memory, disk drives, and all the connections for your other system components.

- To make your system run faster, get a faster microprocessor or more memory.

- Data is temporarily stored in your system's memory; you store data permanently on some type of disk drive—either a hard disk, floppy disk, or CD-ROM.

## IN THIS CHAPTER

- Before You Get Started
- Connecting the Cables
- Turning It On and Setting It Up
- Setting Up Additional Users

2

# SETTING UP YOUR NEW COMPUTER SYSTEM

Chapter 1, "Understanding Your Computer Hardware," gave you the essential background information you need to understand how your computer system works. Now it's time to put that information to work—and get your system up and running!

This chapter tells you how to connect all the various pieces and parts of your computer system. In most cases, it's as simple as plugging the right cables into the right connectors—and many manufacturers make it even easier by color-coding all the cables. In any case, as long as you can figure out which cable goes where, you'll be ready to start computing in no time.

# Before You Get Started

It's important to prepare the space where you'll be putting your new PC. Obviously, the space has to be big enough to hold all the components—though you don't have to keep all the components together. You can, for example, spread out your left and right speakers, place your subwoofer on the floor, and separate the printer from the system unit. Just don't put anything so far away you can't plug it in! (And make sure you have a spare power outlet—or even better, a mutli-outlet power strip—nearby.)

You also should consider the ergonomics of your setup. You want your keyboard at or slightly below normal desktop height, and you want your monitor at or slightly below eye level. Make sure your chair is adjusted for a straight and firm sitting position with your feet flat on the floor, and then place all the pieces of your system in relation to that.

Wherever you put your system, you should make sure that it's in a well-ventilated location free of excess dust and smoke. (The moving parts in your computer don't like dust and dirt or any other such contaminants that can muck up the way they work.) Because your computer generates heat when it operates, you must leave enough room around the system unit for the heat to dissipate. *Never* place your computer in a confined, poorly ventilated space; your PC can overheat and shut down if it isn't sufficiently ventilated.

For extra protection to your computer, connect the power cable on your system unit to a surge suppressor rather than directly into an electrical outlet. A *surge suppressor*—which looks like a power strip with multiple outlets—protects your PC from power-line surges that could damage its delicate internal parts. When a power surge temporarily *spikes* your line voltage (causes the voltage to momentarily increase above normal levels), a surge suppressor shuts down power to your system, acting like a circuit breaker or fuse.

**tip**

When you unpack your PC, be sure you keep all the manuals, CD-ROMs, disks, and cables. Put the ones you don't use in a safe place, in case you need to reinstall any software or equipment at a later date.

**caution**

Before you connect *any-thing* to your system unit, make sure that it's turned off.

# Connecting the Cables

Now it's time to get connected. Position your system unit so you easily can access all the connections on the back, and carefully run the cables from each of the other components so that they're hanging loose at the rear of the system unit.

Now start connecting the cables, in the order shown in Table 2.1. (Some manufacturers color-code the cables and connectors to make the connection even easier—just plug the blue cable into the blue connector, and so on.)

## Table 2.1—Connecting Your System Components

| Order | Connection | Looks Like |
|---|---|---|
| 1. | Connect your mouse to the mouse connector. | |
| 2. | Connect your keyboard to the keyboard connector. | |
| 3. | Connect your video monitor to the video connector. | |
| 4. | Connect your printer to the parallel connector. (This connector is sometimes labeled "printer" or "LPT1.") | |
| 5. | Connect a cable from your telephone line to the "line in" connector on your modem or modem board. Connect a cable from the "line out" connector on your modem to your telephone. | |
| 6. | Connect the phono jack from your speaker system to the "audio out" or "sound out" connector. | |
| 7. | Connect any other devices to the appropriate USB, parallel, or serial connector. | |
| 8. | Plug the power cable of your video monitor into a power outlet. | |
| 9. | If your system includes powered speakers, plug them into a power outlet. | |
| 10. | Plug any other powered external component into a power outlet. | |
| 11. | Plug the power cable of your system unit into a power outlet. | |

# Turning It On and Setting It Up

Now that you have everything connected, sit back and rest for a minute.

Next up is the big step—turning it all on.

It's important that you turn things on in the proper order. Follow these steps:

1. Turn on your video monitor.

2. Turn on your speaker system—but make sure the speaker volume knob is turned down (towards the left).

3. Turn on any other system components that are connected to your system unit— such as your printer, scanner, external modem, and so on.

4. Turn on your system unit.

**caution**

Make sure that every cable is *firmly* connected—both to the system unit and the specific piece of hardware. Loose cables can cause all sorts of weird problems, so be sure they're plugged in really good.

Note that your system unit is the *last* thing you turn on. That's because when it powers on, it has to sense the other components of your system—which it can do only if the other components are plugged in and turned on.

## Powering On for the First Time

The first time you turn on your PC is a unique experience. A brand-new, out-of-the-box system will have to perform some basic configuration operations, which include asking you to input some key information.

This first-time startup operation differs from manufacturer to manufacturer, but typically includes some or all of the following steps:

- **Windows Product Activation**—You may be asked to input the long and nonsensical product code found on the back of your Windows installation CD (or someplace else in the documentation that came with your new PC). Your system then phones into the Microsoft mother ship, registers your system information, and unlocks Windows for you to use. (Many manufacturers "pre-activate" Windows at the factory, so you might not have to go through this process.)

**note**

Windows registration is optional; product activation is mandatory.

- **Windows Registration**—A slightly different process from product activation, registration requires you to input your name and other personal information, along with the Windows product code. This information then is phoned into the Microsoft mother ship to register your copy of Windows with the company, for warranty purposes.

- **Windows Configuration**—During this process Windows asks a series of questions about your location, the current time and date, and other essential information. You also might be asked to create a username and password.

- **System Configuration**—This is where Windows tries to figure out all the different components that are part of your system, such as your printer, scanner, and so on. Enter the appropriate information when prompted; if asked to insert a component's installation CD, do so.

Some computer manufacturers supplement these configuration operations with setup procedures of their own. It's impossible to describe all the different options that might be presented by all the different manufacturers, so watch the screen carefully and follow all the onscreen instructions.

After you have everything configured, Windows finally starts, and then *you* can start using your system.

Some installation procedures require your computer to be restarted. In most cases, this happens automatically; then the installation process resumes where it left off.

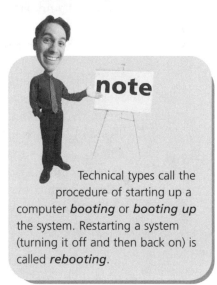

Technical types call the procedure of starting up a computer *booting* or *booting up* the system. Restarting a system (turning it off and then back on) is called *rebooting*.

## Powering On Normally

After everything is installed and configured, starting your computer is a much simpler affair. When you turn on your computer, you'll notice a series of text messages flash across your screen. These messages are there to let you know what's going on as your computer *boots up*.

After a few seconds (during which your system unit beeps and whirrs a little bit), the Windows Welcome screen appears. All registered users are listed on this screen. Click your username or picture, enter your password (if necessary), and then press the **Enter** key or click the **green right-arrow** button. After you're past the Welcome screen, you're taken directly to the Windows desktop, and your system is ready to run.

# Setting Up Additional Users

If you're using your personal computer at home, chances are you're not the only person using it; it's likely that you'll be sharing your PC to some degree with your spouse and kids. Fortunately, you can configure Windows so that different people using your computer signs on with their own custom settings—and access to their own personal files.

You should assign each user in your household his own password-protected *user account*. Anyone trying to access another user's account and files without the password will then be denied access.

There are three different types of user accounts you can establish on your computer—computer administrator, limited, and guest. You'll want to set yourself up as the computer administrator because only this account can make system-wide changes to your PC, install software, and access all the files on the system. Set up other household members with limited accounts; they'll be able to use the computer and access their own files but won't be able to install software or mess up the main settings. Any guests to your household, then, can sign on via the guest account.

**note**

If you have only a single user on your PC and that user doesn't have a password assigned, Windows moves past the Welcome screen with no action necessary on your part.

**tip**

For most users, Windows is ready to run right out of the box. You might, however, want to tweak a few of the configuration settings. The most common settings to configure are discussed in Chapter 5, "Personalizing Windows."

Only the computer administrator can add a new user to your system. To set up a new account on your machine, be sure you're logged on via an administrator account and then follow these steps:

1. Click the **Start** button to open the **Start** menu.
2. Select **Control Panel** to open the Control Panel folder.
3. Select **User Accounts** to open the User Accounts utility, shown in Figure 2.1.
4. Select **Create a New Account**.

**FIGURE 2.1**

Use the User Accounts utility to create and change user accounts.

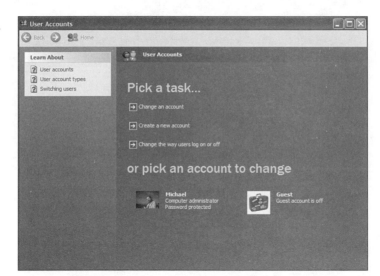

5. When the next screen appears, enter a name for the account and click **Next**.
6. On the next screen, check either the **Computer Administrator** or **Limited** option; then click the **Create Account** button.

Windows XP now creates the new account and randomly assigns a picture that will appear next to the username. You or the user can change this picture at any time by returning to the User

Accounts utility, selecting the account, and then selecting the Change My Picture option.

By default, no password is assigned to the new account. If you want to assign a password, return to the User Accounts utility, select the account, and then select the **Create a Password** option.

# The Absolute Minimum

Here are the key points to remember when connecting and configuring your new computer:

- Most cables plug into only a specific connector—and on some new systems, they're color-coordinated for easier hookup.

- Make sure your cables are *firmly* connected; loose cables are the cause of many computer problems.

- Connect all the cables to your system unit *before* you turn on the power.

- Remember to turn on your printer and monitor before you turn on the system unit.

- If you have multiple users in your household, create a user account for each person—and assign each user his own password.

- You better remember your password—or you won't be able to log in to Windows!

# PART

# Using Windows

3 Understanding Microsoft Windows XP . . 41

4 Taking Windows for a Spin . . . . . . . . . . 59

5 Personalizing Windows . . . . . . . . . . . . 71

6 Working with Files and Folders . . . . . . . 83

## In This Chapter

- What Windows Is—and What It Does
- Different Versions of Windows
- Working Your Way Around the Desktop
- Important Windows Operations
- Using the Start Menu
- Understanding Files and Folders
- All the Other Things in Windows
- Getting Help in Windows

# 3

# Understanding Microsoft Windows XP

As you learned back in Chapter 1, "Understanding Your Computer Hardware," it's the software and operating system that make your hardware work. The operating system for most personal computers is Microsoft Windows, and you need to know how to use Windows to use your PC system.

This chapter gives you a brief overview of what Windows does and how it works and tells you a little bit about software programs in the bargain.

# What Windows Is—and What It Does

Before you can use your computer to do *anything*, you need to know how to use Windows. This is because Windows pretty much runs your computer for you; if you don't know your way around Windows, you won't be able to do much of anything on your new PC.

Windows is a piece of software called an *operating system*. An operating system does what its name implies—it *operates* your computer *system*, working in the background every time you turn on your PC.

Equally important, Windows is what you see when you first turn on your computer, after everything turns on and boots up. The "desktop" that fills your screen is part of Windows, as is the taskbar at the bottom of the screen and the big menu that pops up when you click the **Start** button.

# Different Versions of Windows

The version of Windows installed on your new PC is probably Windows XP. Microsoft has released different versions of Windows over the years, and XP is the latest—which is why it comes preinstalled on most new PCs.

If you've used a previous version of Windows—such as Windows 95, Windows 98, or Windows Me—on another PC, Windows XP probably looks and acts a little differently to you. (It's even different from the version of Windows found in most large corporations—Windows 2000.) Don't worry; everything that was in the old Windows is still in the new Windows—it's probably just in a slightly different place.

Some new PCs come with a slightly different version of Windows XP called Windows XP Media Center Edition. The Media Center is an optional interface that sits on the top of the normal Windows XP desktop and allows one-button access to key multimedia functions, including My TV, My Music, My Pictures, and My Videos. In fact, PCs equipped with Media Center come with

**note**

There are actually two different retail versions of Windows XP available. Home Edition (which is the version that probably came with your new PC) is the version of XP for home and small-business users. Professional Edition is designed for larger businesses and corporate users. They both share the same basic functionality; XP Professional just has a few more features specially for large corporate networks.

a handheld remote control for quick switching from across the room! If you have Windows XP Media Center, don't panic; underneath the Media Center is the same Windows XP we all know and love, and that is described in this chapter.

# Working Your Way Around the Desktop

As you can see in Figure 3.1, the Windows XP desktop includes a number of elements. Get to know the desktop; you're going to be seeing a lot of it from now on!

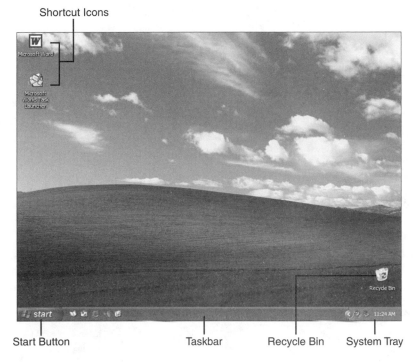

Shortcut Icons

**FIGURE 3.1**

The Windows XP desktop—click the **Start** button to get going!

Start Button          Taskbar          Recycle Bin     System Tray

The major parts of the Windows desktop include:

- **Start button**—Opens the **Start** menu, which is what you use to open all your programs and documents.
- **Taskbar**—Displays buttons for your open applications and windows, as well as different toolbars for different tasks.
- **System Tray**—The part of the taskbar that holds the clock, volume control, and icons for other utilities that run in the background of your system.

- **Shortcut Icons**—These are links to software programs you can place on your desktop; a "clean" desktop includes just one icon, for the Windows Recycle Bin.
- **Recycle Bin**—This is where you dump any files you want to delete.

# Important Windows Operations

To use Windows efficiently, you must master a few simple operations, such as pointing and clicking, dragging and dropping, and right-clicking. You perform all these operations with your mouse.

## Pointing and Clicking

The most common mouse operation is *pointing and clicking.* Simply move the mouse so that the cursor is pointing to the object you want to select, and then click the left mouse button once. Pointing and clicking is an effective way to select menu items, directories, and files.

## Double-Clicking

If you're using Windows XP's default operating mode, you'll need to *double-click* an item to activate an operation. This involves pointing at something onscreen with the cursor and then clicking the left mouse button twice in rapid succession. For example, to open program groups or launch individual programs, simply double-click a specific icon.

## Right-Clicking

When you select an item and then click the *right* mouse button, you'll often see a pop-up menu. This menu, when available, contains commands that directly relate to the selected object. Refer to your individual programs to see whether and how they use the right mouse button.

**tip**

This classic double-click mode is activated by default on most new PCs. Windows XP also includes a new single-click mode, which makes Windows act more like a Web page. In this mode, you hover over an object to select it and single-click to activate it. To learn how to switch to single-click mode, see Chapter 5, "Personalizing Windows."

## Dragging and Dropping

*Dragging* is a variation of clicking. To drag an object, point at it with the cursor and then press and hold down the left mouse button. Move the mouse without releasing the mouse button, and drag the object to a new location. When you're done moving the object, release the mouse button to drop it onto the new location.

You can use dragging and dropping to move files from one folder to another or to delete files by dragging them onto the Recycle Bin icon.

## Hovering

When you position the cursor over an item without clicking your mouse, you're *hovering* over that item. Many operations require you to hover your cursor and then perform some other action.

## Moving and Resizing Windows

Every software program you launch is displayed in a separate onscreen window. When you open more than one program, you get more than one window—and your desktop can quickly get cluttered.

There are many ways to deal with desktop clutter. One way to do this is to move a window to a new position. You do this by positioning your cursor over the window's title bar (shown in Figure 3.2) and then clicking and holding down the left button on your mouse. As long as this button is depressed, you can use your mouse to drag the window around the screen. When you release the mouse button, the window stays where you put it.

**FIGURE 3.2**

The various parts of a window.

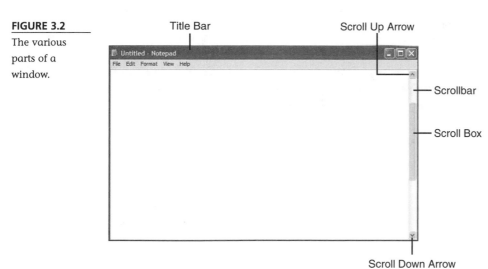

You also can change the size of most windows. You do this by positioning the cursor over the very edge of the window—any edge. If you position the cursor on either side of the window, you can resize the width. If you position the cursor on the top or bottom edge, you can resize the height. Finally, if you position the cursor on a corner, you can resize the width and height at the same time.

After the cursor is positioned over the window's edge, press and hold the left mouse button; then drag the window border to its new size. Release the mouse button to lock in the newly sized window.

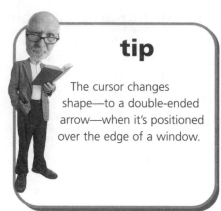

**tip**

The cursor changes shape—to a double-ended arrow—when it's positioned over the edge of a window.

## Maximizing, Minimizing, and Closing Windows

Another way to manage a window in Windows is to make it display full-screen. You do this by maximizing the window. All you have to do is click the **Maximize** button at the upper-right corner of the window, as shown in Figure 3.3.

**FIGURE 3.3**
Use the **Maximize**, **Minimize**, and **Close** buttons to manage your desktop windows.

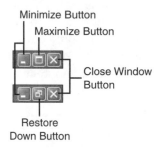

Minimize Button
Maximize Button
Close Window Button
Restore Down Button

If the window is already maximized, the **Maximize** button changes to a **Restore Down** button. When you click the **Restore Down** button, the window resumes its previous (pre-maximized) dimensions.

If you'd rather hide the window so it doesn't clutter your desktop, click the **Minimize** button. This shoves the window off the desktop, onto the Taskbar. The program in the window is still running, however—it's just not on the desktop. To restore a minimized window, all you have to do is click the window's button on the Windows Taskbar (at the bottom of the screen).

If what you really want to do is close the window (and close any program running within the window), just click the window's **Close** button.

## Scrolling Through a Window

Many windows contain more information than can be displayed at once. When you have a long document or Web page, only the first part of the document or page is displayed in the window. To view the rest of the document or page, you have to scroll down through the window, using the various parts of the scroll bar (shown in Figure 3.4).

There are several ways to scroll through a window. To scroll up or down a line at a time, click the up or down arrow on the window's scrollbar. To move to a specific place in a long document, use your mouse to grab the scroll box (between the up and down arrows) and drag it to a new position. You can also click on the scroll bar between the scroll box and the end arrow, which scrolls you one screen at a time.

> **caution**
>
> If you try to close a window that contains a document you haven't saved, you'll be prompted to save the changes to the document. Because you probably don't want to lose any of your work, click **Yes** to save the document and then close the program.

If your mouse has a scroll wheel, you can use it to scroll through a long document. Just roll the wheel back or forward to scroll down or up through a window.

**FIGURE 3.4**

Use the scrollbar to scroll through long pages.

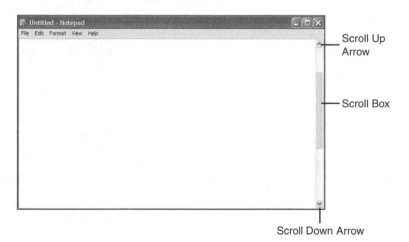

Scroll Up Arrow

Scroll Box

Scroll Down Arrow

## Using Menus

Most windows in Windows use a set of pull-down menus to store all the commands and operations you can perform. The menus are aligned across the top of the window, just below the title bar, in what is called a *menu bar*.

You open (or pull down) a menu by clicking the menu's name. The full menu then appears just below the menu bar, as shown in Figure 3.5. You activate a command or select a menu item by clicking it with your mouse.

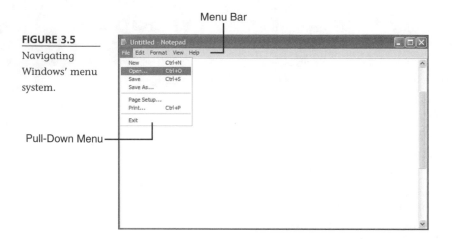

Menu Bar

**FIGURE 3.5**
Navigating Windows' menu system.

Pull-Down Menu

Some menu items have a little black arrow to the right of the label. This indicates that additional choices are available, displayed on a submenu. Click the menu item or the arrow to display the submenu.

Other menu items have three little dots (called an *ellipsis*) to the right of the label. This indicates that additional choices are available, displayed in a dialog box. Click the menu item to display the dialog box.

The nice thing is, after you get the hang of this menu thing in one program, the menus should be very similar in all the other programs you use. For example, almost all programs have a **File** menu that lets you open, save, and close documents, as well as an **Edit** menu that lets you cut, copy, and paste. While each program has menus and menu items specific to its own needs, these common menus make it easy to get up and running when you install new software programs on your system.

**tip**

If an item in a menu, toolbar, or dialog box is dimmed (or grayed), that means it isn't available for the current task.

## Using Toolbars

Some Windows programs put the most frequently used operations on one or more *toolbars*, typically located just below the menu bar. (Figure 3.6 shows a typical

Windows toolbar.) A toolbar looks like a row of buttons, each with a small picture (called an *icon*) and maybe a bit of text. You activate the associated command or operation by clicking the button with your mouse.

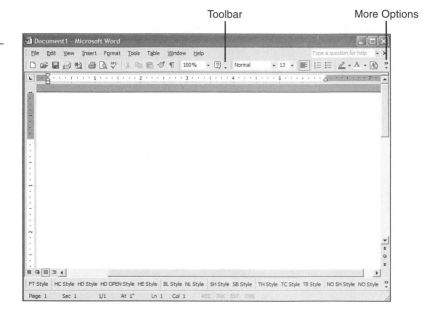

Toolbar                                     More Options

**FIGURE 3.6**

Using a typical Windows toolbar.

If the toolbar is too long to display fully on your screen, you'll see a right arrow at the far-right side of the toolbar. Click this arrow to display the buttons that aren't currently visible.

## Using Dialog Boxes, Tabs, and Buttons

When Windows or an application requires a complex set of inputs, you are often presented with a *dialog box*. A dialog box is similar to a form in which you can input various parameters and make various choices—and then register those inputs and choices when you click the **OK** button. (Figure 3.7 shows the Print dialog box, found in most Windows applications.)

**tip**

If you're not sure which button does what, you can hover the cursor over the button to display a *tool tip*. A tool tip is a small text box that displays the button's label or other useful information.

**FIGURE 3.7**

**FIGURE 3.7**

Use dialog boxes to control various aspects of your Windows applications.

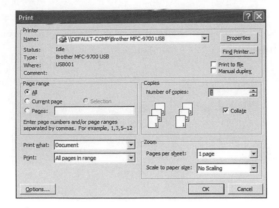

There are several different types of dialog boxes, each one customized to the task at hand. However, most dialog boxes share a set of common features, which include the following:

- **Buttons**—Most buttons either register your inputs or open an auxiliary dialog box. The most common buttons are OK (to register your inputs and close the dialog box), Cancel (to close the dialog box without registering your inputs), and Apply (to register your inputs without closing the dialog box). Click a button once to activate it.

- **Tabs**—These allow a single dialog box to display multiple "pages" of information. Think of each tab, arranged across the top of the dialog box, as a "thumbtab" to the individual page in the dialog box below it. Click the top of a tab to change to that particular page of information.

- **Text boxes**—These are empty boxes where you type in a response. Position your cursor over the empty input box, click your left mouse button, and begin typing.

- **Lists**—These are lists of available choices; lists can either scroll or drop down from what looks like an input box. Select an item from the list with your mouse; you can select multiple items in some lists by holding down the **Ctrl** key while clicking with your mouse.

- **Check boxes**—These are boxes that let you select (or deselect) various stand-alone options.

- **Sliders**—These are sliding bars that let you select increments between two extremes, similar to a sliding volume control on an audio system.

# Using the Start Menu

All the software programs and utilities on your computer are accessed via Windows' **Start** menu. You display the **Start** menu by using your mouse to click the **Start** button, located in the lower-left corner of your screen.

As you can see in Figure 3.8, the Windows XP **Start** menu consists of two columns of icons. Your most frequently used programs are listed in the left column; basic Windows utilities and folders are listed in the right column. To open a specific program or folder, just click the icon.

Frequently Used Programs

**FIGURE 3.8**

Access all the programs on your system from the Start menu.

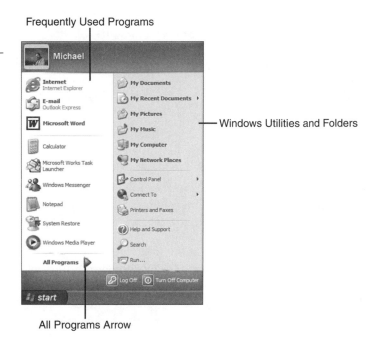

Windows Utilities and Folders

All Programs Arrow

To view the rest of your programs, click the **All Programs** arrow. This displays a new menu called the **Programs** menu. From here you can access various programs, sorted by type or manufacturer. (When more programs are contained within a master folder, you'll see an arrow to the right of the title; click this arrow to display additional choices. )

## Launching a Program

Now that you know how to work the **Start** menu, it's easy to start any particular software program. All you have to do is follow these steps:

1. Click the **Start** button to display the **Start** menu.

2. If the program is displayed on the **Start** menu, click the program's icon.

3. If the program isn't visible on the main **Start** menu, click the **All Programs** button, find the program's icon, and then click it.

## Switching Between Programs

After you've launched a few programs, it's easy to switch between one program and another. To switch to another program (and send all other open programs to the background), you can do one of the following:

- Click the application's button in the taskbar, as shown in Figure 3.9.

**FIGURE 3.9**

Use the taskbar buttons to switch between applications.

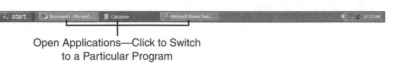

Open Applications—Click to Switch
to a Particular Program

- Click any visible part of the application's window—including its title bar.
- Hold down the **Alt** key and then press the **Tab** key repeatedly until the application window you want is selected. (This cycles through all open windows.) When you're at the window you want, release the **Alt** key.

If you have multiple windows open at the same time, you can determine which is currently the active window by its title bar. The title bar for the active program is brighter, and the title bar text is bright white. An inactive title bar is more dull, with off-white text. If you have overlapping windows on your desktop, the window on top is always the active one. The active application's **Taskbar** button looks like it's pressed in.

## Shutting Down Windows—and Your Computer

Windows starts automatically every time you turn on your computer. Although you will see lines of text flashing onscreen during the initial startup, Windows loads automatically and goes on to display the Windows desktop.

**caution**

Do *not* turn off your computer without shutting down Windows. You could lose data and settings that are temporarily stored in your system's memory.

When you want to turn off your computer, you do it through Windows. In fact, you don't want to turn off your computer any other way—you *always* want to turn things off through the official Windows procedure.

To shut down Windows and turn off your PC, follow these steps:

1. Click the **Start** button to display the **Start** menu.
2. Click the **Turn Off Computer** button.
3. When the Turn Off Computer dialog box appears, click the **Turn Off** button.

# Understanding Files and Folders

All the information on your computer is stored in *files*. A file is nothing more than a collection of data of some sort. Everything on your computer's hard drive is a separate file, with its own name, location, and properties. The contents of a file can be a document from an application (such as a Works worksheet or a Word document), or they can be the executable code for the application itself.

Every file has its own unique name. A defined structure exists for naming files, and its conventions must be followed for Windows to understand exactly what file you want when you try to access one. Each filename must consist of two parts, separated by a period—the *name* (to the left of the period) and the *extension* (to the right of the period). A filename can consist of letters, numbers, spaces, and characters and looks something like this: `this is a filename.ext`.

Windows stores files in *folders*. A folder is like a master file; each folder can contain both files and additional folders. The exact location of a file is called its *path* and contains all the folders leading to the file. For example, a file named `filename.doc` that exists in the `system` folder, that is itself contained in the `windows` folder on your `c:\` drive, has a path that looks like this: `c:\windows\system\filename.doc`.

Learning how to use files and folders is a necessary skill for all computer users. You might need to copy files from one folder to another or from your hard disk to a floppy disk. You certainly need to delete files every now and then. To do this, you use either My Computer or My Documents—two important utilities, discussed next.

**tip**

By default, Windows XP hides the extensions when it displays filenames. To display extensions, use the Control Panel to open the Folder Options dialog box; then select the **View** tab. In the Advanced Settings list, *uncheck* the **Hide Extensions for Known File Types** option, and then click **OK**.

## Managing PC Resources with My Computer

The My Computer utility lets you access each major component of your system and perform basic maintenance functions. For example, you can use My Computer to "open" the contents of your hard disk, and then copy, move, and delete individual files.

To open My Computer, follow these steps:

1. Click the **Start** button to display the **Start** menu.

2. Select **My Computer**.

As you can see in Figure 3.10, the My Computer folder contains icons for each of the major components of your system—your hard disk drive, floppy disk drive, CD-ROM or DVD drive, and so on.

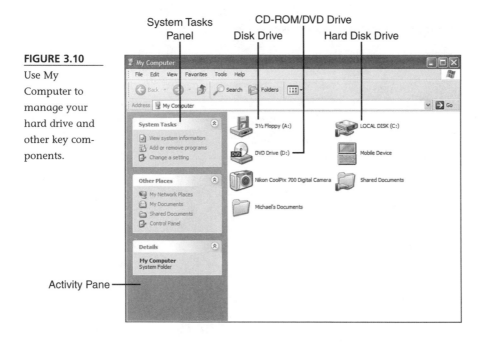

**FIGURE 3.10**

Use My Computer to manage your hard drive and other key components.

Each folder in Windows XP contains an *activity pane* (sometimes called a *task pane*) on the left side of the window. This pane lets you view relevant information about and perform key operations on the selected item.

You can also use **My Computer** to view the contents of a specific drive. When you double-click the icon for that drive, you'll see a list of folders and files located on that drive. To view the contents of any folder, just double-click the icon for that folder.

## Managing Files with My Documents

The documents you create with Microsoft Word and other software programs are actually separate computer files. By default, all your documents are stored somewhere in the My Documents folder.

Windows lets you access the contents of your My Documents folder with a few clicks of your mouse. Just follow these steps:

1. Click the **Start** button to display the **Start** menu.
2. Click **My Documents**.

As you can see in Figure 3.11, the My Documents folder not only contains individual files, it also contains a number of other folders (sometimes called *subfolders*), such as My Pictures and My Music. Double-click a subfolder to view its contents, or use the options in the Files and Folders Tasks panel to perform specific operations—including moving, copying, and deleting.

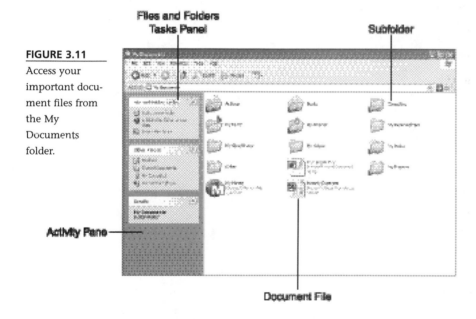

**FIGURE 3.11**
Access your important document files from the My Documents folder.

## Managing Windows with the Control Panel

There's one more Windows utility, similar to My Computer and My Documents, that you need to know about. This utility, the Control Panel, is used to manage most (but not all) of Windows' configuration settings. The Control Panel is actually a system folder (like My Computer and My Documents) that contains a number of individual utilities that let you adjust and configure various system properties.

To open the Control Panel, follow these steps:

1. Click the **Start** button to display the **Start** menu.

2. Click **Control Panel**.

When the Control Panel opens, as shown in Figure 3.12, you can select a particular category you want to configure. When the Pick a Task page appears, either click a task or click an icon to open a specific configuration utility. (When you click a task, the appropriate configuration utility is launched.)

**FIGURE 3.12**

The Windows
XP Control
Panel—configu-
ration tasks
organized by
category.

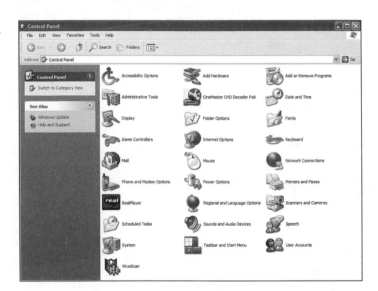

When you open a configuration utility, you'll see a dialog box for that particular item. You can then change the individual settings within that dialog box; click the **OK** button to register your new settings.

# All the Other Things in Windows

Windows is more than just a pretty desktop and some configuration utilities. Windows also includes a large number of accessory programs and system tools you can use to perform other basic system operations.

note

To learn more about
configuring various
Windows settings, see Chapter 5,
"Personalizing Windows."

## Accessories

Windows includes a number of single-function accessory programs, all accessible from the **Start** menu. These programs include a calculator, some games, two basic word processors (Notepad and WordPad), a drawing program (Paint), a player for audio and video files (Windows Media Player), and a digital video editing program (Windows Movie Maker). You access most of these accessories by clicking the **Start** button and selecting **All Programs**, **Accessories**.

## Internet Utilities

In addition to the aforementioned Windows accessories, Windows XP also gives you three important Internet utilities. These include a Web browser (Internet Explorer), an email program (Outlook Express), and an instant messaging program (Windows Messenger). You access these three utilities by clicking the Start button and selecting All Programs.

## System Tools

Windows XP includes a handful of technical tools you can use to keep your system running smoothly. You can access all these tools by clicking the **Start** button and selecting **All Programs**, **Accessories**, **System Tools**.

# Getting Help in Windows

When you can't figure out how to perform a particular task, it's time to ask for help. In Windows XP, this is done through the Help and Support Center.

note

To learn about the practical uses of these and other system tools, turn to Chapter 35, "Performing Routine PC Maintenance."

To launch the Help and Support Center, follow these steps:

1. Click the **Start** button to display the **Start** menu.
2. Click **Help and Support**.

The Help and Support Center lets you search for specific answers to your problems, browse the Help contents by topic, connect to another computer for remote assistance, go online for additional help, and access Windows's key system tools. Click the type of help you want, and follow the onscreen instructions from there.

# The Absolute Minimum

This chapter gave you a lot of background about Windows and the other software programs installed on your PC system. Here are the key points to remember:

- You use Windows to manage your computer system and run your software programs.

- Most functions in Windows are activated by clicking or double-clicking an icon or a button.

- All the programs and accessories on your system are accessed via the **Start** menu, which you display by clicking the **Start** button.

- Use **My Computer** to manage the main components of your system.

- Use **My Documents** to manage your document files and folders.

- Use the **Control Panel** to manage Windows' configuration settings.

- When you can't figure out how to do something, click the **Start** button and select **Help and Support**.

## IN THIS CHAPTER

- Playing a Game
- Launching a Program—and Printing and Saving a Document
- Viewing Your Documents
- Examining Your Hard Disk
- Shutting Down Your System

**4**

# TAKING WINDOWS FOR A SPIN

Now that you have everything connected, configured, and powered up—and you know a little about how Windows works—it's time to take your new computer for a test drive. Just to get the feel of things, you know—open a few documents, print a few pages, that sort of thing.

That's what this chapter is about.

# Playing a Game

Let's assume you followed the instructions in Chapter 2, "Setting Up Your New Computer System," and that you have all the components connected and your system up and running. You should now be looking at an empty Windows desktop, similar to the one shown in Figure 4.1.

Let's have a little fun—and play a simple computer game.

Windows XP comes with a handful of computer games already installed. The game you're probably most familiar with is Solitaire, so let's launch Solitaire and play a game or two.

All you have to do is follow these steps:

1. Click the **Start** button, in the lower-left corner of the screen.

2. When the **Start** menu appears, as shown in Figure 4.2, click the **All Programs** button.

note

If you want to take a spin around the Internet, turn to Chapter 18, "Surfing the Web." This chapter is just about the computer hardware and software sitting in front of you right now.

**FIGURE 4.1**

Start with the Windows desktop.

**FIGURE 4.2**
Click the **Start** button to display the **Start** menu.

3. When the **Programs** menu appears, as shown in Figure 4.3, click the item labeled **Games**.

**FIGURE 4.3**
Click the **All Programs** button to display all the programs installed on your system.

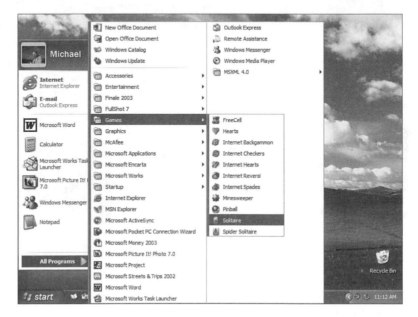

4. This displays a submenu listing all the games available in Windows. Move your cursor down to the one labeled Solitaire, and then click it.

5. Windows now launches the Solitaire program and displays it in a small window on your desktop, as shown in Figure 4.4.

**FIGURE 4.4**

Playing Solitaire on your new PC—window original size.

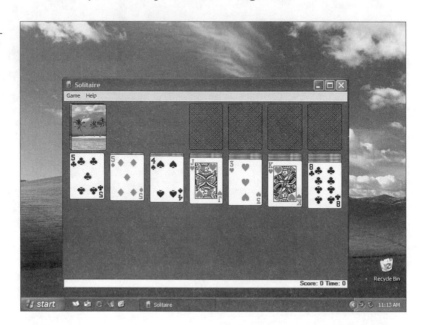

6. Before you start playing, you probably should resize the window. Move your cursor to the lower-right corner of the Solitaire window, and then drag the window border down and to the right. When the window is large enough for you, release the mouse button.

7. That was good, but maybe the game would be easier to play if it were displayed full-screen, as shown in Figure 4.5. Click the **Maximize** button (upper-right corner of the window, in the middle) to maximize the Solitaire window.

8. Now it's time to play. To move a card, grab it with your mouse and drag it onto another card. To turn over cards from the main deck, click the deck. To start a new game, pull down the **Game** menu and select **Deal**.

**tip**

Solitaire is also a good way to practice your mouse skills. You get to practice dragging and dropping (by moving cards from stack to stack) and double-clicking (to move cards to the top rows).

9. When you're done playing, close the **Solitaire** window by either clicking the window's **Close** button or pulling down the **Game** menu and selecting **Exit**.

**FIGURE 4.5**
Playing Solitaire, full-screen.

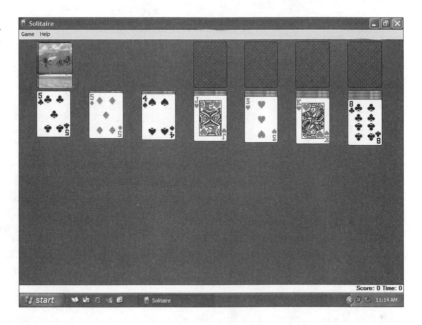

# Launching a Program—and Printing and Saving a Document

That was fun. Now let's try something a little more productive—like creating a short note. We'll use Notepad, which is a basic word processor that's part of Microsoft Windows.

## Open Notepad

To open the Notepad program, follow these steps:

1. Click the **Start** button to display the **Start** menu.

2. Click the **All Programs** button to display the **Programs** menu.

3. Click the item labeled **Accessories**, then click the item labeled **Notepad**.

4. The Notepad program now launches in its own window, as shown in Figure 4.6.

**note**

Throughout the rest of this chapter and the book, this type of operation will be combined into a single action, as in "select All Programs, Accessories, Notepad."

**FIGURE 4.6**
Writing a note
with Notepad.

## Writing Your Note

The blank white space in the middle of the screen is a new Notepad document—
kind of like a blank sheet of paper. To write a note, position the cursor within the
window and type the following text, using your computer keyboard:

`This is my very first note in Notepad.`

## Printing Your Note

Now let's print a copy of your note. Make sure your printer is connected to your
computer, and then follow these steps:

1. Pull down the **File** menu and select **Print**.
2. When the Print dialog box appears (shown in Figure 4.7), make sure the correct printer is selected in the Select Printer section; then click the **Print** button.

Your printer should now come to life and, after a few moments, spit out a piece of
paper. When you look at the paper, you should see your note printed at the top!

**FIGURE 4.7**
Printing a docu-
ment.

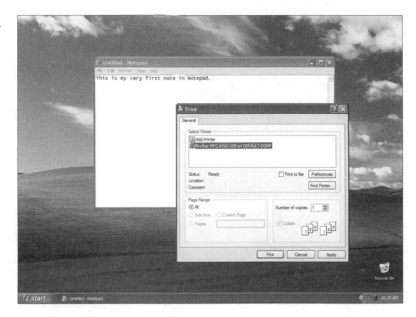

## Saving Your File

Any document you create needs to be saved to your hard disk; otherwise, it won't
exist after you close the program. To save your current note as a new file, follow
these steps:

1. Pull down the **File** menu and select **Save As**.
2. When the Save As dialog box appears (shown in Figure 4.8), click the **My
   Documents** button on the left side of the dialog box; then type `my new file`
   in the File Name box.
3. Click the **Save** button.

What you've done here is saved your document as a file named `my new file`. You
saved it in the My Documents folder, which is where Windows stores all new documents by default.

## Closing the Program

To close Notepad, pull down the **File** menu and select **Exit**.

**FIGURE 4.8**

Saving a new file in the My Documents folder.

# Viewing Your Documents

Now that you've created a document, let's take a look at it. If you remember, you saved the file in the My Documents folder, so let's open that folder and take a peek around.

Follow these steps:

1. Click the **Start** button to display the **Start** menu.

2. Select **My Documents** to open the My Documents folder, shown in Figure 4.9.

3. Hover your cursor over the my new file icon.

4. Information about your file is displayed in the Details panel of the activity pane, and basic tasks are displayed in the File and Folder Tasks panel.

   To open this file for further editing, double-click the file icon. This launches Notepad with the my new file file already loaded and ready to edit.

# Examining Your Hard Disk

Before we finish our quick spin around the desktop, let's examine the My Computer
folder and see what's on your hard disk. Follow these steps:

1. Click the **Start** button to display the **Start** menu.

2. Select **My Computer** to open the My Computer folder, shown in Figure 4.10.

3. Hover your cursor over your local hard disk drive—typically labeled drive C.

4. Information about your hard disk is displayed in the Details panel of the
   activity pane, and basic operations are displayed in the System Tasks panel.

5. Position your cursor over the hard disk icon, and click your *right* mouse button (in other words, *right-click* the icon).

6. This displays a pop-up menu. Select **Properties** from this menu.

7. When the Properties dialog box appears, select the **General** tab. As you can
   see in Figure 4.11, this tab displays a pie chart that represents how much of
   your hard disk is currently used and how much free space is available.

8. Click **OK** to close the dialog box.

**FIGURE 4.10**
The contents of
your My
Computer folder.

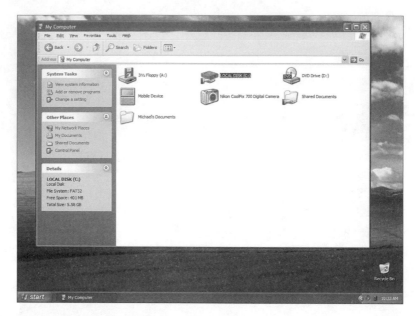

**FIGURE 4.11**
Viewing inter-
esting informa-
tion about your
hard disk.

## Shutting Down Your System

Now that our test drive is over, let's turn things off and settle in for the day. While you *could* turn off your system by pressing the big button on the front of your system unit, this isn't the *proper* way to shut off your system. The proper procedure uses Windows to shut everything down, nice and orderly.

**tip**

To turn your computer back on, press the power button on the front of your PC's system unit.

Just follow these steps:

1. Click the **Start** button to display the **Start** menu.
2. Select **Turn Off Computer**.
3. When the Turn Off Computer box appears, select **Turn Off**.

Windows will now do what it needs to do to properly close all of its system files. When the screen goes blank and your system unit stops making noise, your system is all shut down.

# THE ABSOLUTE MINIMUM

That was a fun little trip of discovery, wasn't it? Here are the key points to remember:

- Just about everything you could want to launch or open is somewhere on the **Start** menu.
- After you have a window open on your desktop, you can use your mouse to resize it—or you can maximize it to display full-screen.
- When you want to print a file in a Windows application, pull down the **File** menu and select **Print**.
- When you want to save a file in a Windows application, pull down the **File** menu and select **Save As**.
- When you want to close a Windows application, pull down the **File** menu and select **Exit**—or just click the window's **Close** button.
- To turn off your computer, use the **Turn Off Computer** command on the Windows **Start** menu.

## IN THIS CHAPTER

- Changing the Desktop Size
- Enabling ClearType
- Changing Your Desktop Theme
- Personalizing the Desktop Background
- Changing the Color Scheme
- Activating Special Effects
- Changing Your Click
- Changing the Way the Start Menu Works
- Displaying More—or Fewer—Programs on the Start Menu
- Selecting Which Icons to Display on the Start Menu—and How

5

# PERSONALIZING WINDOWS

When you first turn on your new computer system, you see the Windows desktop as Microsoft set it up for you.

Fortunately, you don't have to keep it that way.

Windows presents a lot of different ways to personalize the look and feel of your desktop. In fact, one of the great things about Windows is how quickly you can make the desktop look like *your* desktop, different from anybody else's.

# Changing the Desktop Size

You can configure your computer's display so that the desktop is larger or smaller than normal. A larger desktop lets you view more things onscreen at the same time—even though each item is smaller than before.

Changing the size of the desktop is accomplished by changing Windows's *screen resolution*. You do this by following these steps:

**tip**

You can also open the Display Properties dialog box from the Windows Control panel; just open the Control Panel folder and double-click the **Display** icon.

1. Right-click anywhere on the desktop to display a pop-up menu.

2. Select **Properties** from the pop-up menu; this displays the Display Properties dialog box.

3. Select the **Settings** tab (shown in Figure 5.1).

**FIGURE 5.1**

Use the Display Properties dialog box to configure Windows' display settings.

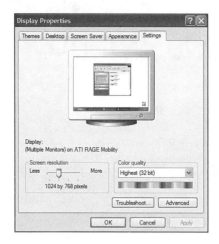

4. Adjust the Screen Resolution slider. (The sample display changes to reflect your new settings.)

While you're on this tab, you can also change the number of colors displayed. (More is better.) Just choose the desired setting from the Color Quality drop-down list, and then click **OK** when done.

# Enabling ClearType

ClearType is a new display technology in Windows XP that effectively triples the horizontal resolution on LCD displays. (In other words, it makes things look sharper—and smoother.) If you have a flat-panel monitor or a portable PC, you definitely want to turn on ClearType.

To turn on ClearType, follow these steps:

1. Open the Display Properties dialog box and select the **Appearance** tab.
2. Click the **Effects** button to display the Effects dialog box.
3. Check the **Use the Following Method to Smooth Edges of Screen Fonts** option.
4. Select **ClearType** from the pull-down list.
5. Click **OK** when done.

**tip**

To best use all the features of Windows XP, go for a 1024×768 resolution. If this setting makes things look too small (a problem if you have a smaller monitor), try the 800×600 resolution. As for color, 16-bit is my recommended minimum for Windows XP, but 32-bit looks a lot better.

# Changing Your Desktop Theme

Desktop *themes* are specific combinations of background wallpaper, colors, fonts, cursors, sounds, and screensavers—all arranged around a specific look or topic. When you choose a new theme, the look and feel of your entire desktop changes.

**caution**

Many add-on themes will cause Windows to revert to its pre-XP look; try to install XP-specific themes, when possible.

To change desktop themes, follow these steps:

1. Open the Display Properties dialog box and select the **Themes** tab.
2. Select a new theme from the Theme pull-down list.
3. Click **OK** when done.

You can find additional themes in the Microsoft Plus! for Windows add-on (www.microsoft.com/Windows/Plus/), or online at ThemeWorld.com (www.themeworld.com) and TopThemes.com (www.topthemes.com).

# Personalizing the Desktop Background

Although changing themes is the fastest way to change the look of all your desktop elements, you can also change each element separately.

For example, you can easily change your desktop's background pattern or wallpaper. You can choose from the many patterns and wallpapers included with Windows or select a graphic of your own choosing.

Just follow these steps:

1. Open the Display Properties dialog box and select the **Desktop** tab, shown in Figure 5.2.

**FIGURE 5.2**

Use the Display Properties dialog box to select a new desktop background.

2. To choose one of Windows's built-in backgrounds, make a selection from the Background list.

3. To select your own graphics file, click the **Browse** button and navigate to the file you want to use. Click the **Open** button to add this file to the Background list.

4. To determine how the image file is displayed on your desktop, select one of the items from the Position pull-down list: **Center**, **Tile**, or **Stretch**.

5. If you'd rather display a solid background color with no graphic, select **None** from the **Background** list and select a color from the **Color** list.

6. Click **OK** to register your changes.

**tip**

If you find a picture on the Web that you want to use as your desktop background, right-click the picture and select **Set as Wallpaper** from the pop-up menu.

# Changing the Color Scheme

The default Windows XP desktop uses a predefined combination of colors and fonts. If you don't like this combination, you can choose from several other predefined schemes.

To change to a new color scheme, follow these steps:

1. Open the Display Properties dialog box and select the **Appearance** tab.
2. Pull down the **Color Scheme** list, and select a new theme.
3. Click **OK** when done.

# Activating Special Effects

Windows XP includes all sorts of special effects, not all of which are turned on by default. These effects are applied to the way certain elements look or the way they pull down or pop up onscreen.

## Using the Effects Dialog Box

Some of these special effects are activated from the Effects dialog box, which you access via the Display Properties dialog box. To change these special effects, follow these steps:

1. Open the Display Properties dialog box and the **Appearance** tab.
2. Click the **Effects** button to display the Effects dialog box, shown in Figure 5.3.

**FIGURE 5.3**

Activating special effects via the Effects dialog box.

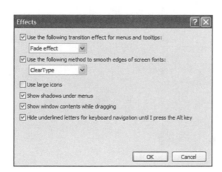

3. Make the appropriate choices from the options available.
4. Click **OK**.

The Effects dialog box offers a variety of special effects. You can choose to add transition effects for menus, display drop shadows under menus, display large icons on the desktop, display the contents of windows when they're dragged, and hide the underlined letters on menu items.

## Using the Performance Options Dialog Box

Even more special effects are activated from the Systems Property dialog box. You access these effects by following these steps:

1. Click the **Start** button to display the **Start** menu.
2. Select **Control Panel** to open the Control Panel folder.
3. Select **System** to open the Systems Properties dialog box.
4. Select the **Advanced** tab and click the **Settings** button in the Performance section.
5. When the Performance Options dialog box appears, click the **Visual Effects** tab, as shown in Figure 5.4.

**FIGURE 5.4**

Use the Performance Options dialog box to select more subtle display effects.

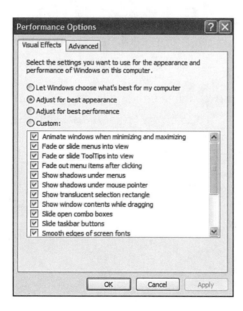

6. Choose which effects you want to activate.
7. Click **OK** when done.

Most of the effects in the Performance Options dialog box are self-explanatory, although some are extremely subtle. If you're not sure which effects to choose, select either the **Adjust for Best Appearance** or **Adjust for Best Performance** option. The first option turns on all the special effects, and the second option turns them all off. Even better is the **Let Windows Choose What's Best for My Computer** option, which activates a select group of effects that won't slow down your system's performance.

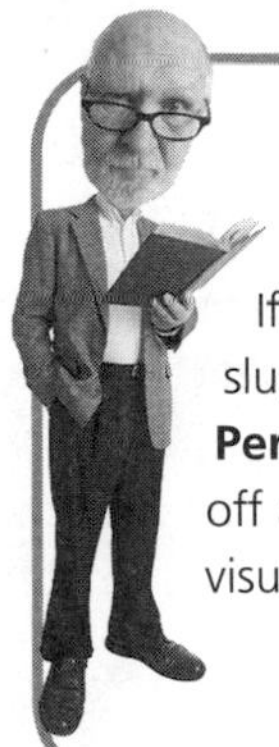

**tip**

If your system is running sluggishly, click the **Best Performance** button to turn off all the resource-draining visual effects.

## Changing Your Click

How do you click? Do you like to double-click the icons on your desktop? Would you prefer to single-click your icons, the same way you click hyperlinks on a Web page? Should the names of your icons be plain text or underlined like a hyperlink?

Windows XP comes from the factory set up for traditional double-clicking. (This is where you single-click an item to select it and double-click to open it.) To change Windows's click mode, just follow these steps:

1. Click the **Start** button to display the **Start** menu.
2. Select **Control Panel** to open the Control Panel folder.
3. Select **Folder Options** to display the Folder Options dialog box, shown in Figure 5.5.

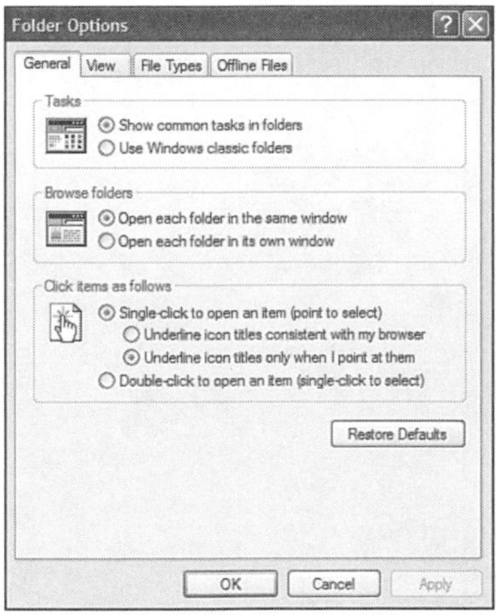


**FIGURE 5.5**
Change Windows XP to single-click operation.

4. Select the **General** tab.

5. If you want to use traditional double-clicking, check the **Double-Click to Open an Item** option. If you want to use Web-like single-clicking, check the **Single-Click to Open an Item** option. (In this mode, you select an item by hovering your cursor over it and open items with a single click.)

6. Click **OK**.

## tip

If you select single clicking, you can choose to underline the titles of all desktop icons or only underline titles when an item is hovered over.

# Changing the Way the Start Menu Works

Windows XP applies a handful of special effects to the **Start** menu. You can animate the **Start** menu when it opens, force submenus to open when you hover over them, and highlight new applications.

To change these special effects, follow these steps:

1. Right-click the **Start** button and select **Properties** from the pop-up menu; this displays the Taskbar and Start Menu Properties dialog box.

2. Select the **Start Menu** tab.

3. Click the **Customize** button to display the Customize Start Menu dialog box.

4. Select the **Advanced** tab, as shown in Figure 5.6.

**FIGURE 5.6**

Use the Customize Start Menu dialog box to change the way the **Start** menu works.

5. To make submenus open when you point at them, check the Open Submenus When I Pause On Them With My Mouse option.

6. To highlight the newest applications, check the **Highlight Newly Installed Programs** option.

7. Click **OK** when done.

# Displaying More—or Fewer—Programs on the Start Menu

By default, the **Start** menu displays the five most-recent applications you've run. You can reconfigure the Start menu to display more (up to nine) or fewer (as few as zero!) applications at a time.

To display more or fewer programs, follow these steps:

1. Right-click the **Start** button and select **Properties** from the pop-up menu to display the Taskbar and Start Menu Properties dialog box.

2. Select the **Start Menu** tab.

3. Click the **Customize** button to display the Customize Start Menu dialog box.

4. Select the **General** tab.

5. Select a new number from the **Number of Programs on Start Menu** list.

6. Click **OK** when done.

# Selecting Which Icons to Display on the Start Menu—and How

The default **Start** menu also displays icons for the **Control Panel**, **My Computer**, **My Documents**, **My Pictures**, **My Music**, **Network Connections**, **Help and Support**, and the **Run** command. You can configure Windows XP to not display any of these icons—or to display some of the icons as expandable menus. Just follow these steps:

1. Right-click the **Start** button and select **Properties** from the pop-up menu to display the Taskbar and Start Menu Properties dialog box.

2. Select the **Start Menu** tab.

3. Click the **Customize** button to display the Customize Start Menu dialog box.

4. Select the **Advanced** tab.

5. In the Start Menu Items list, click **Display As a Link** to display an icon as a link to the main item (in a separate window), **Display As a Menu** to display a pop-up menu when an icon is clicked, or **Don't Display This Item** to not display an item.

6. Repeat Step 5 for each of the items listed.

7. Click **OK** when done.

# Adding a Program to the Start Menu—Permanently

If you're not totally comfortable with the way programs come and go from the **Start** menu, you can add any program to the **Start** menu—*permanently*. All you have to do is follow these steps:

1. Click the **Start** button to display the Start menu.

2. Click the **All Programs** button to open the **Programs** menu.

3. Navigate to a specific program.

4. Right-click that program to display the pop-up menu.

5. Select **Pin to Start Menu**.

To remove a program you've added to the **Start** menu, right-click its icon and select **Unpin from Start Menu**.

The program you selected now appears on the **Start** menu, just below the browser and email icons.

# Using a Screensaver

Screensavers display moving designs on your computer screen when you haven't typed or moved the mouse for a while. This prevents static images from burning into your screen—and provides some small degree of entertainment if you're bored at your desk.

To activate one of the screensavers included with Windows XP, follow these steps:

1. Open the Display Properties dialog box and select the **Screen Saver** tab.

2. Select a screensaver from the Screen Saver drop-down list.

3. Click the **Settings** button to configure that screensaver's specific settings (if available).

4. Return to the Display Properties dialog box and select the number of minutes you want the screen to be idle before the screensaver activates.

5. Click **OK** when done.

# Changing System Sounds

Every operation in Windows can or does have a sound associated with it. When you take all the sounds together, you have a *sound scheme*—and Windows lets you change the entire sound scheme or individual sounds within the scheme. Follow these steps:

1. Click the **Start** button to display the **Start** menu.
2. Select **Control Panel** to open the Control Panel folder.
3. Select **Sounds and Audio Devices** to open the Sounds and Audio Devices Properties dialog box.
4. Select the **Sounds** tab, shown in Figure 5.7.

**FIGURE 5.7**

Change the way Windows sounds—in the Sounds and Audio Devices Properties dialog box.

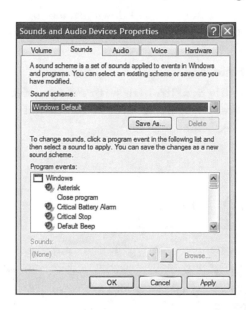

5. To change sound schemes, pull down the **Sound Scheme** list and select a new scheme.
6. To change an individual sound, select an item in the **Program Events** list and then select a new sound from the **Sounds** list.
7. Click **OK** when done.

# Resetting the Time and Date

The time and date for your system should be automatically set when you first turn on your computer. If you find that you need to change or reset the time or date settings, all you have to do is follow these steps:

1. Double-click the time display in the Windows Tray (at the bottom right of your screen) to display the Date and Time Properties dialog box.

2. Select the **Date & Time** tab.

3. Select the correct month and year from the pull-down lists, click the correct day of the month on the calendar, and set the correct time on the clock.

4. Select the **Time Zone** tab.

5. Select the correct time zone from the pull-down list. (For most states, you should also select **Automatically Adjust Clock for Daylight Saving Changes**.)

6. Select the **Internet Time** tab.

7. Check the **Automatically Synchronize with an Internet Time Server** option. (This automatically synchronizes your PC's internal clock with an ultra-accurate time server on the Internet.)

8. Click **OK** when done.

# The Absolute Minimum

Here are the key points to remember from this chapter:

- To change most display options (color, resolution, and so on), right-click anywhere on the desktop to display the Display Options dialog box.

- If you're using a laptop PC or a desktop with an LCD flat-screen display, make sure you activate the **ClearType** option.

- To change the way the **Start** menu looks and acts, right-click the **Start** button and select Properties from the pop-up menu.

- To change your PC's time or date, double-click the time display at the bottom right of your screen.

## IN THIS CHAPTER

- Viewing Folders and Files
- Navigating Folders
- Creating New Folders
- Renaming Files and Folders
- Copying Files
- Moving Files
- Deleting Files
- Working with Compressed Folders

**6**

# WORKING WITH FILES AND FOLDERS

As you learned in Chapter 3, "Understanding Microsoft Windows XP," all the documents and programs on your computer are stored in electronic files. These files are then arranged into a series of folders and sub-folders—just as you'd arrange paper files in a series of file folders in a filing cabinet.

Since all your important data is stored in files, it's important that you learn how to work with Windows' files and folders. Every user needs to know how to copy, move, and delete files—none of which, fortunately, are that hard to do.

# Viewing Folders and Files

In Windows XP you use either My Computer or My Documents (both accessible from the Windows **Start** menu) to view the folders and files on your system. Both of these tools work similarly and enable you to customize the way they display their contents.

As you can see in Figure 6.1, the My Documents folder contains not only individual files, but also other folders—called *subfolders*—that themselves contain other files. Most of the file-related operations you want to undertake are accessible directly from the File and Folder Tasks section in the Tasks pane, located at the left of the My Documents window.

**FIGURE 6.1**

Manage your folders and files with the My Documents folder.

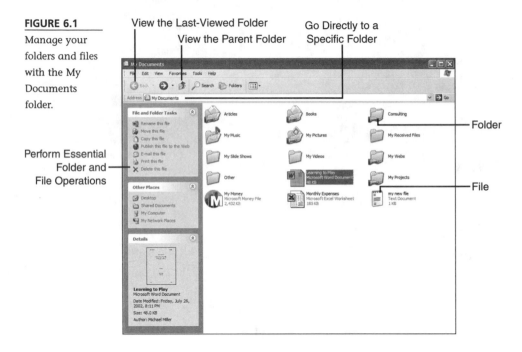

View the Last-Viewed Folder

View the Parent Folder

Go Directly to a Specific Folder

Perform Essential Folder and File Operations

Folder

File

## Changing the Way Files Are Displayed

You can choose to view the contents of a folder in a variety of ways. Just follow these steps:

1. Click the Views button on the My Documents toolbar; this displays a pop-up menu, shown in Figure 6.2.

2. Select from Thumbnails, Tiles, Icons, List, or Details views.

**FIGURE 6.2**

Click the Views button to change the way files are displayed.

The default view is the Tiles view, shown in Figure 6.1; experiment with each view to determine which you like best.

## Sorting Files and Folders

When viewing files in My Computer or My Documents, you can sort your files and folders in a number of ways. To do this, follow these steps:

1. Pull down the **View** menu and select **Arrange Icons By**.
2. Choose to sort by **Name**, **Size**, **Type**, or **Modified**.

**tip**

Thumbnails view is best for working with graphics files. Details view is best if you're looking for files by date or size.

If you want to view your files in alphabetical order, choose to sort by **Name**. If you want to see all similar files grouped together, choose to sort by **Type**. If you want to sort your files by the date and time they were last edited, choose the **Modified** option.

## Grouping Files and Folders

You can also configure Windows XP to group the files in your folder, which can make it easier to identify particular files. For example, if you sorted your files by time and date modified, they'll now be grouped by date (Today, Yesterday, Last Week, and so on), as shown in Figure 6.3. If you sorted your files by type, they'll be grouped by file extension. And so on.

To turn on grouping, follow these steps:

1. Pull down the **View** menu and select **Arrange Icons By**.
2. Check the **Show in Groups** option.

Windows now groups your files and folders by the criteria you used to sort those items.

**FIGURE 6.3**

Files grouped by date.

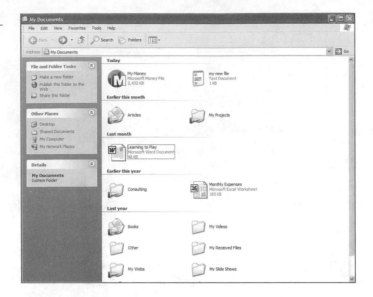

## Saving Your Settings, Universally

By default, when you customize a folder, that view is specific to that folder. To apply a folder view to all the folders on your system, follow these steps:

1. Start by configuring the current folder the way you want.

2. Select Tools, Folder Options to display the Folder Options dialog box, shown in Figure 6.4.

3. Select the View tab.

4. Click the Apply to All Folders button, and then click OK.

**FIGURE 6.4**

Use the Folder Options dialog box to make all your folders look alike.

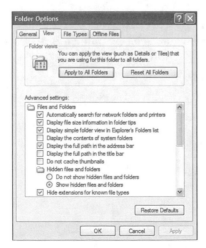

# Navigating Folders

You can navigate through the folders and sub-folders in My Computer, My Documents, and other folders in several ways:

**tip**

To return your folders to their original states, click the Reset All Folders button.

- ▓ To view the contents of a disk or folder, double-click the selected item.

- ▓ To move up the hierarchy of folders and subfolders to the next highest item, click the Up button on the toolbar.

- ▓ To move back to the disk or folder previously selected, click the Back button on the toolbar.

- ▓ To choose from the history of disks and folders previously viewed, click the down arrow on the Back button (shown in Figure 6.5) and select a disk or folder.

**FIGURE 6.5**

View a list of previously viewed folders by clicking the down arrow on the Back button.

- ▓ If you've moved back through multiple disks or folders, you can move forward to the next folder by clicking the Forward button.

- ▓ Go directly to any disk or folder by entering the path in the Address Bar (in the format *x:\folder\subfolder*) and pressing Enter or clicking the Go button.

You can also go directly to any folder by clicking the Folders button to display the Folders pane, shown in Figure 6.6. You can then select the folder you want from the Folders list.

**FIGURE 6.6**

Display the Folders pane to go directly to any folder on your computer's hard disk.

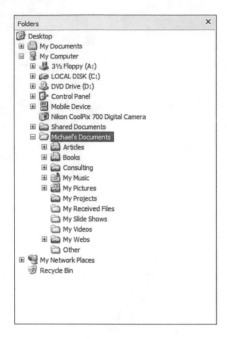

# Creating New Folders

The more files you create, the harder it is to organize and find things on your hard disk. When the number of files you have becomes unmanageable, you need to create more folders—and subfolders—to better categorize your files.

To create a new folder, follow these steps:

1. Navigate to the drive or folder where you want to place the new folder.

2. Select Make a New Folder from the File and Folder Tasks panel; a new, empty folder now appears, with the filename New Folder highlighted.

3. Type a name for your folder (which overwrites the New Folder name), and press Enter.

# Renaming Files and Folders

When you create a new file or folder, it helps to give it a name that somehow describes its contents. Sometimes, however, you might need to change a file's name. Fortunately, Windows makes it relatively easy to rename an item.

To rename a file (or folder), follow these steps:

1. Select the file or folder you want to rename.

2. Select Rename This File from the File Tasks list, or press F2; this highlights the filename.

3. Type a new name for your folder (which overwrites the current name), and press Enter.

# Copying Files

Now it's time to address the most common things you do with files—copying and moving them from one location to another. These operations, like most file operations, can be accessed directly from the Tasks pane in any Windows folder.

It's important to remember that copying is different from moving. When you *copy* an item, the original item remains in its original location—plus you have the new copy. When you *move* an item, the original is no longer present in the original location—all you have is the item in the new location.

## The Easy Way to Copy

To copy a file or a folder with Windows XP, follow these steps:

1. Select the item you want to copy.

2. Select Copy This File from the File Tasks list; this opens the Copy Items dialog box, shown in Figure 6.7.

3. Navigate to and select the new location for the item.

4. Click the Copy button.

That's it. You've just copied the file from one location to another.

**caution**

Folder and filenames can include up to 255 characters—including many special characters. Some special characters, however, are "illegal," meaning that you *can't* use them in folder or filenames. Illegal characters include the following: \ / : * ? " < > |.

**caution**

The one part of the filename you should never change is the extension—the part that comes after the "dot." That's because Windows and other software programs recognize different types of program files and documents by their extension. For example, program files always have an .EXE extension, and Microsoft Word documents always have a .DOC extension. Change the extension, and Windows won't know what to do with a file!

**FIGURE 6.7**

Use the Copy Items dialog box to copy a file or folder.

## Other Ways to Copy

The method just presented is just one of many ways to copy a file. Windows XP provides several other methods, including:

- Pull down the File menu and select Copy (or Copy to Folder), then paste to the new location.

- Right-click a file and select Copy from the pop-up menu, then paste to the new location.

- Right-click a file and select Send To from the pop-up menu, then select a location from the choices listed.

- Hold down the **Ctrl** key and then use your mouse to drag the file or folder from one location to another within the My Documents or My Computer folders.

- Drag the file or folder while holding down the *right* mouse button. When you drop the file into a new location, you see a pop-up menu that asks whether you want to move it or copy it. Select the copy option.

**tip**

If you want to copy the item to a new folder, click the New Folder button before you click the Copy button.

# Moving Files

Moving a file (or folder) is different from copying it. Moving cuts the item from its previous location and places it in a new location. Copying leaves the original item where it was *and* creates a copy of the item elsewhere.

In other words, when you copy something you end up with two of it. When you move something, you only have the one thing.

## The Easy Way to Move

To move a file, follow these steps:

1. Select the item you want to move.

2. Select Move This File from the File Tasks list.

3. When the Move Items dialog box appears (looks just like the Copy Items dialog box), navigate to and select the new location for the item.

4. Click the Move button.

**tip**

If you want to move the item to a new folder, click the New Folder button before you click the Move button.

## Other Ways to Move a File

Just as Windows provides several other ways to copy a file, you also have a choice of alternative methods for moving a file, including:

- Pull down the File menu and select Move (or Move to Folder), then paste it to the new location.

- Right-click a file name and select Cut from the pop-up menu, then paste it to the new location.

- Use your mouse to drag the file from one location to another.

- Drag the file or folder while holding down the *right* mouse button. When you drop the file into a new location, you see a pop-up menu that asks whether you want to move it or copy it. Select the move option.

# Deleting Files

Too many files eat up too much hard disk space—which is a bad thing, since you only have so much disk space. (Music and video files, in particular, can chew up big chunks of your hard drive.) Because you don't want to waste disk space, you should periodically delete those files (and folders) you no longer need.

## The Easy Way to Delete

Deleting a file is as easy as following these two simple steps:

1. Select the file.

2. Select Delete This File from the File Tasks list.

This simple operation sends the file to the Windows Recycle Bin, which is kind of a trash can for deleted files. (It's also a trash can that periodically needs to be dumped—as discussed later in this activity.)

## Restoring Deleted Files

Have you ever accidentally deleted the wrong file? If so, you're in luck. For a short period of time, Windows stores the files you delete in the Recycle Bin. The Recycle Bin is actually a special folder on your hard disk; if you've recently deleted a file, it should still be in the Recycle Bin folder.

To "undelete" a file from the Recycle Bin, follow these steps:

1. Double-click the Recycle Bin icon on your desktop to open the Recycle Bin folder (shown in Figure 6.8).
2. Select the file you want to restore.
3. Select Restore This Item from the Recycle Bin Tasks list.

**note**

You can also delete a file by dragging it from the folder window onto the Recycle Bin icon on the desktop, or by highlighting it and pressing the Del key.

This copies the deleted file back to its original location, ready for continued use.

**FIGURE 6.8**

The Recycle Bin, where all your deleted files end up.

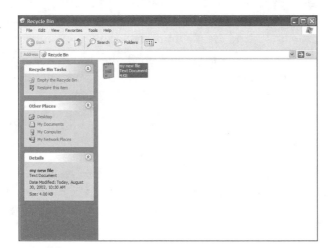

## Managing the Recycle Bin

Deleted files do not stay in the Recycle Bin indefinitely.

By default, the deleted files in the Recycle Bin can occupy 10% of your hard disk space. When you've deleted enough files to exceed this 10%, the oldest files in the Recycle Bin are automatically and permanently deleted from your hard disk.

If you'd rather dump the Recycle Bin manually (and thus free up some hard disk space), follow these steps:

1. Double-click the Recycle Bin icon on your desktop to open the Recycle Bin folder.
2. Select Empty the Recycle Bin from the Recycle Bin Tasks list.
3. When the Confirm File Delete dialog box appears, click Yes to completely erase the files, or click No to continue storing the files in the Recycle Bin.

# Working with Compressed Folders

Really big files can be difficult to move or copy. They're especially hard to transfer to other users, whether by floppy disk or email.

Fortunately, Windows XP includes a way to make big files smaller. *Compressed folders* take big files and compress them down in size, which makes them easier to copy or move. After the file has been transferred, you can then uncompress the file back to its original state.

## Compressing a File

Compressing one or more files is a relatively easy task from within any Windows folder. Just follow these steps:

1. Select the file(s) you want to compress.
2. Right-click the file(s) to display the pop-up menu.
3. Select Send to, Compressed (zipped) Folder.

Windows now creates a new folder that contains compressed versions of the file(s) you selected. (This folder is distinguished by a little zipper on the folder icon, as shown in Figure 6.9.) You can now copy, move, or email this folder, which is a lot smaller than the original file(s).

**FIGURE 6.9**

A compressed folder containing one or more files.

## Extracting Files

The process of decompressing a file is actually an *extraction* process. That's because you *extract* the original file(s) from the compressed folder.

In Windows XP, this process is eased by the use of the Extraction Wizard. Follow these steps:

1. Right-click the compressed folder to display the pop-up menu.

2. Select Extract All.

3. When the Extraction Wizard launches, as shown in Figure 6.10, click the Next button.

note

The compressed folder is actually a file with a .ZIP extension, so it can be used with other compression/decompression programs, such as WinZip.

**FIGURE 6.10**

Use the Extraction Wizard to decompress compressed files.

4. Select which folder you want to extract the files to and click Next.

5. The wizard now extracts the files and displays the Extraction Complete page.

6. Click the Finish button to view the files you've just extracted.

# THE ABSOLUTE MINIMUM

Here are the key points to remember from this chapter:

- You can use either the My Documents or My Computer folders to work with your files and folders.

- Most of the operations you'll want to perform are listed in the Tasks pane, on the left side of the My Documents folder.

- There are many ways to copy and move files, but the easiest is to select the file, then select either **Copy This File** or **Move This File** from the Tasks pane.

- You can delete a file by selecting Delete This File from the Tasks pane, or by pressing the **Del** key on your keyboard.

- If you accidentally delete a file, you may be able to recover it by opening the Recycle Bin window.

- If you need to share a really big file, consider compressing it into a compressed folder (also called a .ZIP file).

# PART III

# Using Computer Software

7   Installing New Software . . . . . . . . . . . . 99

8   Using Microsoft Works Suite . . . . . . . . 105

9   Working with Words . . . . . . . . . . . . . 113

10  Working with Numbers . . . . . . . . . . . 127

11  Working with a Database . . . . . . . . . . 139

12  Managing Your Finances . . . . . . . . . . 147

13  Creating Greeting Cards and Other
    Cool Projects . . . . . . . . . . . . . . . . . . . 159

14  Learning with Educational Software . . . 165

15  Playing Games . . . . . . . . . . . . . . . . . 171

## In This Chapter

- Automatic Installation
- Manual Installation
- Installing Programs from the Internet
- Removing Old Programs
- Things to Remember

7

# Installing New Software

Your new computer system came with a bunch of programs preinstalled on your hard disk. As useful as these programs are, at some point you're going to want to add something new. Maybe you want to upgrade from Microsoft Works Suite to the more full-featured Microsoft Office. Maybe you want to add some educational software for the kids or a productivity program for yourself. Maybe you just want to play some new computer games.

Whatever type of software you're considering, installing it on your computer system is easy. In most cases software installation is so automatic you don't have to do much more than stick a disc in the CD-ROM drive and click a few onscreen buttons. Even when it isn't that automatic, Windows will walk you through the installation process step-by-step—and you'll be using your new software in no time!

# Automatic Installation

Almost all software programs have their own built-in installation programs. Installing the software is as easy as running this built-in program.

If the program you're installing comes on a CD-ROM, just insert the program's main or installation CD in your computer's CD-ROM drive. The program's installation program should then start automatically, and all you have to do is follow the onscreen instructions.

If the installation program *doesn't* start automatically, you have to launch it manually. To do this, follow these steps:

1. Click the **Start** button to display the **Start** menu.
2. Select **Run**.
3. When the Run dialog box appears, as shown in Figure 7.1, enter `x:\setup` in the Open box. (Replace *x* with the letter of your CD-ROM drive; if your CD-ROM is drive D, you'd enter `d:\setup`.)
4. Click **OK**.

**FIGURE 7.1**

Enter the location and name of the installation program in the Run dialog box.

If the program you're installing comes on floppy disk instead of CD-ROM, you launch the setup program by inserting the first floppy disk into your PC's disk drive and then following the preceding instructions—with one small exception. Instead of entering the letter of your CD-ROM drive in the Run dialog box, just enter `a:\setup`. (The floppy disk drive is always drive A. )

**tip**

If this process doesn't work, try entering **install** instead of **setup**. (Some older programs have this different name for their installation programs.)

# Manual Installation

If the program you're installing doesn't have an automated setup program, you can install the program by using Windows's Add or Remove Programs utility.

Follow these steps:

1. Click the **Start** button to display the **Start** menu.
2. Select **Control Panel** to open the Control Panel folder.
3. Select **Add** or **Remove Programs** to display the Add or Remove Programs dialog box.
4. Click the **Add New Programs** button.
5. When the next screen appears, as shown in Figure 7.2, click the **CD** or **Floppy** button.
6. Insert the program's installation disc or disk, and then follow the onscreen instructions to complete the installation.

**FIGURE 7.2**

Use the Add or Remove Programs utility to manually install a new program.

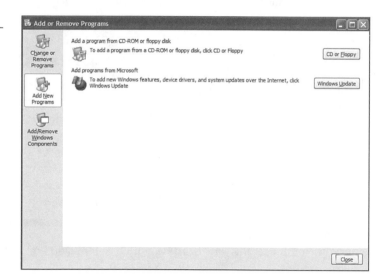

# Installing Programs from the Internet

Nowadays, many software publishers make their products available via download from the Internet. Some users like this because they can get their new programs immediately. However, downloading software like this can take quite a long time, especially if you have a normal dial-up Internet connection, because the program files are so big.

When you download a program from a major software publisher, the process is generally easy to follow. You probably have to read a page of do's and don'ts, agree to the publisher's licensing agreements, and then click a button to start the download. After you specify where (which folder on your hard disk) you want to save the downloaded file, the download begins.

When the download is complete, you should be notified via an onscreen dialog box. From this point, installing the program is almost identical to installing from CD or floppy disk—except that you have to enter the complete path to the installation file in the Run dialog box. (And even this is easy—just click the Browse button to find the folder where you saved the file. )

> **tip**
>
> Check the file size of the program before you download. If the size is larger than 2MB, you probably want to order the CD-ROM version of the program instead of trying to download it—unless you have a broadband cable or DSL connection.

## Removing Old Programs

Chances are you got a *lot* of different software programs with your new PC. Chances are also that some of these are programs you'll never use—and are just taking up space on your hard disk.

For example, your new computer might have come with both Microsoft Money and Quicken installed—and you'll only use one of these two programs. Or your system might include multiple applications for accessing the Internet, from different ISPs. Again, you'll use only one of these, which means you can delete the ones you *don't* use.

> **caution**
>
> Unless you're downloading a program from a trusted download site, the downloaded file could contain a computer virus. See Chapter 32, "Protecting Your PC Online," for more information.

If you're sure you won't be using a particular program, you can use Windows's Add or Remove Programs utility to remove the software from your hard disk. This frees up hard disk space for other programs you might install in the future.

To remove a software program from your PC, follow these steps:

1. Click the **Start** button to display the **Start** menu.
2. Select **Control Panel** to open the Control Panel folder.

3. Select **Add** or **Remove Programs** to display the Add or Remove Programs dialog box.

4. Click the **Change** or **Remove Programs** button.

5. The next screen, shown in Figure 7.3, displays a list of all the currently installed programs on your PC. Select the program's name from the Currently Installed Programs list, and then click either the **Change/Remove** or **Remove** button.

**FIGURE 7.3**

Choose a program to remove from your system.

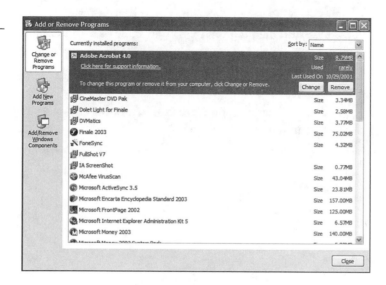

6. If prompted, confirm that you want to continue to uninstall the application. Answer any other prompts that appear onscreen; then the uninstall process will start.

After the uninstall routine is complete, click the **Close** button to close the Add or Remove Programs utility.

**note**

Some programs, such as Microsoft Word, might require you to insert the original installation disks or CD to perform the uninstall.

# THE ABSOLUTE MINIMUM

When you want to add a new software program to your computer, here's what you need to remember:

- Most programs come with their own built-in installation programs. The installation should start automatically when you insert the program's installation CD.

- If the program doesn't come with its own self-starting installation program, you can install the program by using Windows's Add or Remove Programs utility.

- The Add or Remove Programs utility can also be used to remove unused programs from your system.

- You also can download some programs from the Internet—just be careful about catching a computer virus!

**8**

# USING MICROSOFT WORKS SUITE

If you just purchased a new PC, chances are it came with a program called Microsoft Works Suite pre-installed. As its name implies, Works Suite is actually a "suite" of programs, all of which work together through a common interface. You can use the programs in Works Suite to handle just about any task you can think of performing on your personal computer.

With all the parts of Works Suite installed, you can now write letters and memos, perform spreadsheet calculations, store all sorts of data, manage your schedules and contacts, manage your checkbook and bank online, work with digital photographs, look up facts and figures, plan your next road trip, send and receive email, and surf the Internet—all from a single interface, called the Task Launcher.

It's also possible that, instead of Works Suite, your computer came with the more fully featured Microsoft Office suite or a competing software suite, such as Corel WordPerfect Productivity Pack. Office is a little like Works Suite, in that it includes a word processor, spreadsheet, and database program. But Office goes beyond Works Suite to include some very high end, very sophisticated programs—including Microsoft Excel and Microsoft Access. WordPerfect Productivity Pack is a collection of programs similar to some of the programs in Microsoft Works Suite, including the WordPerfect word processor and Quattro Pro spreadsheet.

This chapter, then, deals with Microsoft Works Suite—in particular, the most recent version, Microsoft Works Suite 2003.

# What's in Works

If you have all of Works Suite installed, you now have a dozen different programs—or program components—installed on your personal computer. Let's take a quick look at each of these programs.

## Microsoft Works—Including Works Spreadsheet, Works Database, Works Calendar, and Address Book

Microsoft Works is the core of Works Suite. Works is centered around the Task Launcher (discussed later in this chapter), and includes four different pieces of component software:

- **Works Spreadsheet** is a simple spreadsheet program, kind of like an easier-to-use version of Microsoft Excel. Works Spreadsheet lets you enter rows and columns of numbers and other data, and then perform basic calculations and analysis on those numbers. You can sort and graph your data, and use the program to create all sorts of lists and logs. (Learn more about Works Spreadsheet in Chapter 10, "Working with Numbers."

**note**

Different PC manufacturers install different versions of Works on their PCs. You might find that some **components** of Works Suite are installed, while others aren't—even though they may be available for installation from the accompanying CD-ROMs. Check with your PC's documentation to determine which components are preinstalled on your system—and which components are available for installation.

- **Works Database** is a simple database program that functions more-or-less like a giant electronic filing cabinet. You create the database files (the "drawers" in the filing cabinet), and then manage individual records (the "index cards" in each "drawer") within each file. You can use Works Database to keep track of all sorts of household records—from your favorite recipes to the names on your Christmas card list. (Learn more about Works Database in Chapter 11, "Working with a Database.")

- **Works Calendar** is a schedule management program. You see a simple calendar onscreen, and to that calendar you add your appointments and other important dates. Works Calendar then alerts you to important meetings and events.

- **Address Book** is an all-purpose contact manager. You store names, addresses, phone numbers, email addresses, and other information in the Address Book, and then import that data into other applications—into Outlook Express for email addressing, for example, or into Word for merged mailings.

## Microsoft Word

Microsoft Word is the most popular word processing program in the world—and the most powerful. With Word you can create anything from simple memos and letters to complex newsletters and reports. Word even integrates with other Works Suite programs to create merged mailings and sophisticated documents. If you're like most users, you'll find that you use Word almost every day—it's that essential! (Learn more about Microsoft Word in Chapter 9, "Working with Words.")

## Microsoft Money

When you want to computerize your personal finances, turn to Microsoft Money. This program lets you do everything from writing checks and balancing your checkbook to creating financial reports and tracking your investments online. (Learn more about Microsoft Money in Chapter 12, "Managing Your Finances.")

## Microsoft Picture It! Photo

If you're getting into digital photography—or just want to put some pictures on your Web site, or send them via email—then you need the simple picture editing tools of Picture It! Photo. This program lets you import pictures from digital cameras and scanners, take the red(eye) out, crop out unwanted parts of your pictures, and organize your pictures into collages, calendars, and photo albums. Plus, you can take the pictures you edit with Picture It! Photo and import them into other Works Suite applications. (Learn more about Picture It! Photo in Chapter 26, "Working with Pictures.")

## Microsoft Encarta Encyclopedia

Encarta is an electronic version of a traditional encyclopedia—with the added benefit of multimedia audio and video! If you have children, this application will get a lot of use—it's great for researching homework and reports, or just answering all your kids' questions. (Learn more about Encarta in Chapter 14, "Learning with Educational Software.")

## Microsoft Streets & Trips

Never get lost again with the detailed driving directions generated by Microsoft Streets & Trips. Find addresses, print out maps, and generate turn-by-turn driving directions—all from your own computer!

# Working Works

You start Microsoft Works Suite by following these steps:

1. Click the **Windows Start** button to display the **Start** menu.
2. Select **All Programs** to open the **Programs** menu.
3. Select **Microsoft Works Task Launcher**.

This launches the Works Task Launcher, which is the "home base" for all your Works applications and tasks. You can start the individual Works Suite applications either from within Works (using the Task Launcher, discussed next) or from the Windows Start menu.

## Finding Your Way Around the Task Launcher

When you launch Works Suite, the Works Task Launcher appears onscreen. Along the top of the Task Launcher are links to four different pages; each page represents a different way to enter a program or document.

Here are the four pages you can link to from the Task Launcher:

- **Home.** The Home page, shown in Figure 8.1, is what you see when you first launch Works Suite. You can use the Home page to create new projects, or to open previously created projects. The Home page also includes direct links to the most popular Works applications (Word, Money, Picture It! Photo, and Encarta), as well as a current-month calendar and to-do list.

**FIGURE 8.1**

The Home page
of the Works
Suite Task
Launcher.

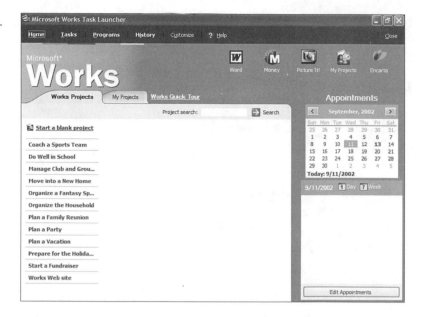

- **Tasks.** Use the Tasks page to identify a certain task you want to perform—select the task, and the Task Launcher will launch the appropriate program, with the appropriate template or wizard already loaded.

- **Programs.** Use the Programs page to launch a specific Works Suite program—then select the task you want that program to perform.

- **History.** Use the History page to reload any document you've recently edited with any Works Suite application.

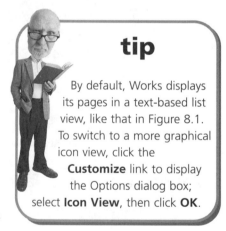

**tip**

By default, Works displays its pages in a text-based list view, like that in Figure 8.1. To switch to a more graphical icon view, click the **Customize** link to display the Options dialog box; select **Icon View**, then click **OK**.

When Task Launcher is launched, select a page, select a program or task, and then you're ready to work!

## Launching a Program

You use the Programs page to launch individual Works Suite applications. Just follow these steps:

**FIGURE 8.2**

Use the
Programs page
to launch a spe-
cific Works Suite
program.

1. From the Works Task Launcher, select the **Programs** page (shown in Figure 8.2).

2. From the Programs list, select a program.

3. From the tasks list for that program, select a task.

4. Click **Start This Task**.

The Task Launcher now launches the program you selected, with the appropriate task-based template or wizard loaded.

## Launching a New Task

To start a specific task —and have Works load the right program for that task, auto-matically—you use the Tasks page, as shown in Figure 8.3. Just follow these steps:

1. From the Works Task Launcher, select the **Tasks** page.

2. From the Tasks list, select a task category.

3. From the tasks list for that category, select a specific task.

4. Click **Start This Task**.

The Task Launcher now launches the appropriate program for your selected task—and, in most cases, presents you with a task-based template or wizard for getting started automatically.

**FIGURE 8.3**
Click the **Tasks** page to get started with a specific task— and let Works Suite figure out which program to launch!

## Launching an Old Document

If you've been working with Works for awhile, you can use the History page to reopen documents you previously created.

**FIGURE 8.4**
Click the **History** page to view a list of recent files— click a column header to sort items by that column.

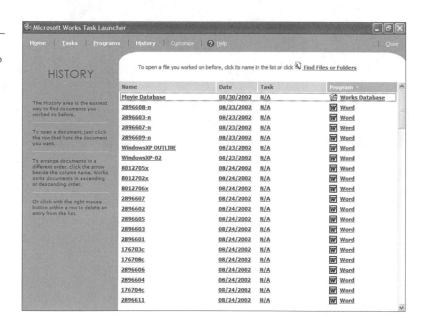

The History page lists all your recently used files, in reverse chronological order. (That's newest files first, for those of you who are vocabulary impaired.) For each file, the Task Launcher includes the file Name, the Date it was last worked on, the type of Task is was (when this is knowable), and the Program associated with that file. You can resort the list of files by any column by clicking on the column header. For example, if you wanted to sort files by name, you'd click on the Name header; click a second time to sort in the reverse order.

To open a file listed in the History pane, just click its name. Task Launcher will launch the program associated with that file, and then load the selected file into the program.

**tip**

If the file you want isn't listed on the History tab, Task Launcher lets you search for that file. When you click the Find Files or Folders link (in the top-left corner of the screen), Task Launcher displays the Find: All Files dialog box. This neat little tool lets you search your entire system for specific files.

# THE ABSOLUTE MINIMUM

Here are the key points to remember from this chapter:

- Microsoft Works Suite is a collection of many different applications and components.

- You launch applications and create new tasks from the Works Task Launcher.

- Create new tasks—and launch the associated application—from Task Launcher's Task page; launch Works Suite's applications directly from the Programs page; or open a previously created file from the History page.

- Most—but not all—Works Suite applications share the same interface, menu structure, and context-sensitive pop-up menus.

## IN THIS CHAPTER

- Exploring the Word Interface
- Working with Documents
- Working with Text
- Printing a Document
- Formatting Your Document
- Working with an Outline
- Working with Pictures
- The Absolute Minimum

9

# WORKING WITH WORDS

When you want to write a letter, fire off a quick memo, create a report, or create a newsletter, you use a type of software program called a *word processor*. While Windows XP comes with two very basic word processing programs built-in—Notepad and WordPad—you probably want a more fully featured program, one that enables you to create longer, more sophisticated documents.

For most computer users, Microsoft Word is the word processing program of choice. Word is a full-featured word processor, and it's included with both Microsoft Works Suite and Microsoft Office. You can use Word for all your writing needs—from basic letters to fancy newsletters, and everything in between.

You start Word either from the Windows Start menu (select Start, All Programs, Microsoft Word) or, if you're using Microsoft Works Suite, from the Works Task Launcher. When Word launches, a blank document appears in the Word workspace.

# Exploring the Word Interface

Before we get started, let's take a quick tour of the Word workspace—so you know what's what and what's where.

## What's Where in Word

**FIGURE 9.1**

The Word work-space—to per-form most tasks, just pull down a menu or click a toolbar button.

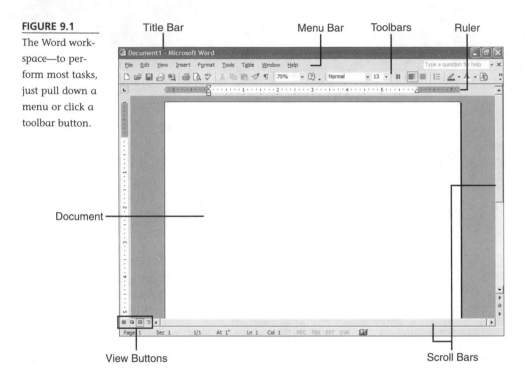

Title Bar     Menu Bar    Toolbars    Ruler

Document

View Buttons     Scroll Bars

The Word workspace, shown above, is divided into seven main parts:

- **Title bar.** This is where you find the filename of the current document, as well as buttons to minimize, maximize, and close the window for the current Word document.

- **Menu bar.** This collection of pull-down menus contains virtually all of Word's commands. Use your mouse to click a menu item, and then the menu pulls down to display a full range of commands and options.

- **Toolbars.** By default, two toolbars—Standard and Formatting— are docked at the top of the workspace, just underneath the menu bar. Word includes a number of different toolbars that you can display anywhere in the Word workspace. Click a button on any toolbar to initiate the associated command or operation. (To display additional toolbars, pull down the View menu and select Toolbars; when the list of toolbars appears, check those toolbars you want to display, and uncheck those you want to hide.)

- **Ruler.** This allows you to measure the width of a document—and set tabs and margins.
- **Document.** This main space displays your current Word document.
- **View buttons.** The View buttons let you switch between different document views.
- **Scroll bars.** The scroll bar at the bottom of the page lets you scroll left and right through the current page; the scroll bar along the side of the workspace lets you scroll through a document from top to bottom.
- **Status bar.** This provides information about your current document—including what page you're on.

There's one more part of the Word workspace that can be displayed at appropriate times. That's the Task Pane, which is similar to the Task pane found in Windows XP's My Documents and My Computer folders. In Word, the Task Pane appears on the right side of the workspace, and contains commands related to what you're currently doing in the application. You display the Task Pane by selecting View, Task Pane.

**note**

This book focuses on Microsoft Word 2002, also known as Word XP or Word 10.0, which is the version of Word included in both Works Suite 2003 and Office XP.

**tip**

If two toolbars docked side-by-side are longer than the available space, buttons at the end of one or both of the toolbars will not be displayed. Instead, you'll see a **More Buttons** arrow; click this double-arrow to display a submenu of the leftover buttons.

## Viewing a Word Document—in Different Ways

Word can display your document in one of four different *views*. Each view is a particular way of looking at your document:

- **Normal View.** This is primarily a text-based view, because certain types of graphic objects—backgrounds, headers and footers, and some pictures—aren't displayed. This is *not* a good view for laying out the elements on your page.

- **Web Layout View**. This is the view you use when you're creating a document to be displayed on the Web. In this view all the elements in your document (including graphics and backgrounds) are displayed pretty much as they would be if viewed by a Web browser.

- **Print Layout View**. This is the view you use to lay out the pages of your document—with *all* elements visible, including graphics and backgrounds.

- **Outline View.** This is a great view for looking at the structure of your document, presenting your text (but *not* graphics!) in classic outline fashion. In this view you can collapse an outlined document to see only the main headings, or expand a document to show all (or selected) headings and body text.

> **tip**
>
> If you're not sure just what button on which toolbar does what, you're not alone—those little graphics are sometimes hard to decipher. To display the name of any specific button, just hover your cursor over the button until the descriptive *ScreenTip* appears.

## Zooming to View

It's easy to change the size of the document displayed in the Word workspace. The Standard toolbar includes a pull-down Zoom list, from which you can select a pre-set zoom level (from 10 percent to 500 percent). You can also choose to have your document automatically fill up the entire width of your screen by selecting the Page Width option.

Another way to change the onscreen size of your document is to pull down the **View** menu and select **Zoom** to display the Zoom dialog box. This dialog box lets you choose from both pre-selected and custom zoom levels—and previews your selected zoom level.

# Working with Documents

Anything you create with Word is called a *document*. A document is nothing more than a computer file, that can be copied, moved, and deleted—or edited, from within Word.

# Creating a New Document

Any new Word document you create is based on what Word calls a *template*. A template combines selected styles and document settings—and, in some cases, prewritten text or calculated fields—to create the building blocks for a specific type of document. You can use templates to give yourself a head start on specific types of documents.

To create a new Word document based on a specific template, follow these steps:

1. Pull down Word's **File** menu and select **New** to display the New Document pane, shown in Figure 9.2.

2. From the New Template section of the New Document pane, click **General Templates** to open the Templates dialog box, shown in Figure 9.3.

3. Select one of the prepared templates.

4. Click **OK**.

If your version of Word is installed as part of Works Suite, you can view additional Works-related templates by selecting **File**, **New Works Template**.

**FIGURE 9.2**

Use the New Document pane to open new and existing Word documents.

**FIGURE 9.3**

Select a tab to select templates of a specific type.

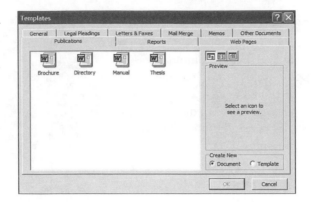

## Opening an Existing Document

To open a previously created document, follow these steps:

1. Select **File**, **Open** to display the Open dialog box.

2. Navigate to and select the file you want to open.

3. Click **Open**.

## Saving the Document

Every document you make— that you want to keep—must be saved to a file.

The first time you save a file, you have to specify a filename and location. Do this by following these steps:

1. Pull down the **File** menu and select **Save As** to display the Save As dialog box.

2. Navigate to the folder where you want to save the file.

3. Enter a name for the new file.

4. Click the **Save** button.

When you make additional changes to a document, you must save those changes. Fortunately, after you've saved a file once, you don't need to go through the whole Save As routine again. To "fast save" an existing file, all you have to do is click the **Save** button on Word's Standard toolbar—or pull down the **File** menu and select **Save**.

# Working with Text

Now that you know how to create and save Word documents, let's examine how you put specific words on paper—or, rather, on screen.

## Entering Text

You enter text in a Word document at the *insertion point*, which appears onscreen as a blinking cursor. When you start typing on your keyboard, the new text is added at the insertion point.

You move the insertion point with your mouse by clicking on a new position in your text. You move the insertion point with your keyboard by using your keyboard's arrow keys.

## Editing Text

After you've entered your text, it's time to edit. With Word you can delete, cut, copy, and paste text—or graphics—to and from anywhere in your document, or between documents.

Before you can edit text, though, you have to *select* the text to edit. The easiest way to select text is with your mouse; just hold down your mouse button and drag the cursor over the text you want to select. You also can select text using your keyboard; use the Shift key—in combination with other keys—to highlight blocks of text. For example, **Shift+Left Arrow** selects one character to the left; **Shift+End** selects all text to the end of the current line.

Any text you select appears as white text against a black highlight. After you've selected a block of text, you can then edit it in a number of ways, as detailed in Table 9.1.

**TABLE 9.1**   Word Editing Operations

| Operation | Keystroke | Menu Location |
| --- | --- | --- |
| Delete | Del | Edit, Clear |
| Copy | Ctrl+Insert | Edit, Copy |
| Cut | Shift+Del or Ctrl+X | Edit, Cut |
| Paste | Shift+Ins | Edit, Paste |

## Formatting Text

After your text is entered and edited, you can use Word's numerous formatting options to add some pizzazz to your document. It's easiest to edit text when you're working in Print Layout view because this displays your document as it will look when printed. To switch to this view, pull down the **View** menu and select **Print Layout**.

Formatting text is easy—and most achievable from Word's Formatting toolbar. This toolbar, located at the top of the screen, includes buttons for bold, italic, and underline, as well as font, font size, and font color. To format a block of text, highlight the text and then click the desired format button.

More text formatting options are available in the Font dialog box. To display this dialog box, pull down the **Format** menu and select **Font**. From here, you can perform both basic formatting (font, font style, font color, and so on) and advanced formatting (strikethrough, superscript, subscript, shadow, outline, emboss, engrave, character spacing, and text animation). Just select the formatting you want and click **OK**.

## Checking Spelling and Grammar

If you're not a great speller, you'll appreciate Word's automatic spell checking. You can see it right on screen; just deliberately misspell a word, and you'll see a squiggly red line under the misspelling. That's Word telling you you've made a spelling error!

When you see that squiggly red line, position your cursor on top of the misspelled word, then right-click your mouse. Word now displays a pop-up menu with its suggestions for spelling corrections. You can choose a replacement word from the list, or return to your document and manually change the misspelling.

Sometimes Word meets a word it doesn't recognize, even though the word is spelled correctly. In these instances, you can add the new word to Word's spelling dictionary by right-clicking the word and selecting **Add** from the pop-up menu.

Word also includes a built-in grammar checker. When Word identifies bad grammar in your

Not all people like to use Word's grammar checker; some find it overly intrusive. You can turn off grammar checking by selecting **Tools**, **Options** to display the Options dialog box. Select the **Spelling & Grammar** tab, uncheck the **Check Grammar As You Type** option, then click **OK**.

document, it underlines the offending passage with a green squiggly line. Right-click anywhere in the passage to view Word's grammatical suggestions.

# Printing a Document

When you've finished editing your document, you can instruct Word to send a copy to your printer.

## Previewing Before You Print

It's a good idea, however, to preview the printed document onscreen before you print it—so you can make any last-minute changes without wasting a lot of paper.

To view your document with Word's Print Preview, click the **Print Preview** button on Word's Standard toolbar (or pull down the **File** menu and select **Print Preview**).

The to-be-printed document appears onscreen with each page of the document presented as a small thumbnail. To zoom in or out of the preview document, click the **Magnifier** button and then click the magnifier cursor anywhere on your document. When you're done previewing your document, click the **Close** button.

## Basic Printing

The fastest way to print a document is with Word's fast print option. You activate a fast print by clicking the **Print** button on Word's Standard toolbar.

When you do a fast print of your document, you send your document directly to your default printer. This bypasses the Print dialog box (discussed next) and all other configuration options.

## Changing Print Options

Sometimes fast printing isn't the best way to print. For example, you might want to print multiple copies, or print to a different (nondefault) printer. For these and similar situations, you need to use Word's Print dialog box.

You open the Print dialog box, shown in Figure 9.4, by pulling down the **File** menu and selecting **Print**.

After you have the Print dialog box displayed, you can choose any one of a number of options specific to this particular print job. After you've made your choices, click the **OK** button to start printing.

Select What Part(s) of
Your Document to Print    Select Your Printer

**FIGURE 9.4**

Print your docu-
ment—with
options.

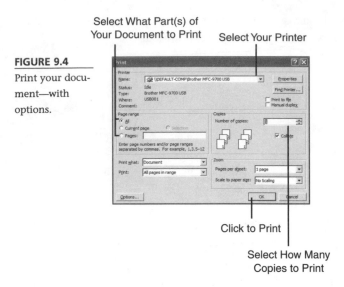

Click to Print

Select How Many
Copies to Print

# Formatting Your Document

When you're creating a complex document, you need to format more than just a few words here and there.

## Formatting Paragraphs

When you need to format complete paragraphs, you use Word's Paragraph dialog box.

You open the Paragraph dialog box by positioning your cursor within a paragraph and then pulling down the **Format** menu and selecting **Paragraph**. From here, you can precisely adjust how the entire paragraph appears, including indentation, line spacing, and widow/orphan control.

## Using Word Styles

If you have a preferred paragraph formatting you use over and over and over, you don't have to format each paragraph individually. Instead, you can assign all your formatting to a paragraph *style* and then assign that style to specific paragraphs throughout your document. Most templates come with a selection of pre-designed styles; you can modify these built-in styles or create your own custom styles.

Styles include formatting for fonts, paragraphs, tabs, borders, numbering, and more.

To apply a style to a paragraph, position the insertion point anywhere in the para-graph and then pull down the **Style** list (in the Formatting toolbar) and select a style. (You don't have to select the entire paragraph; just having the insertion point in the paragraph does the job.)

To modify a style, follow these steps:

1. Pull down the **Format** menu and select Styles and Formatting; this displays the Styles and Formatting pane, shown in Figure 9.5.

**FIGURE 9.5**

Use the Styles and Formatting pane to modify and assign Word styles.

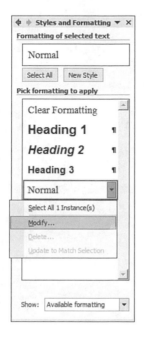

2. Hover your cursor over which style you want to edit; this displays a down button.

3. Click the **Down** button and select **Modify**; this displays the Modify Style dialog box.

4. Change basic properties from this dialog box, or click the **Format** button to select other properties to modify.

5. Click **OK** when done.

## Assigning Headings

When you're creating a long document, you probably want to separate sections of your document with headings. Headings appear as larger, bolder text, like mini-headlines.

Word includes several built-in heading styles—Heading 1, Heading 2, Heading 3, and Heading 4. Assign these styles to your document's headings, as appropriate. (And if you don't like the way they look, edit the styles to your liking—as described previously.)

# Working with an Outline

If you have a really long document, you might find it easier to work with the various sections in the form of an outline. For this purpose, Word lets you view your document in Outline view, as shown in Figure 9.6. Just pull down the **View** menu and select **Outline**.

**tip**

To force a manual page break in your document—as you might if you want a new section to start on a new page—position the cursor at the front of the line and then press **Ctrl+Enter**. You can also select **Insert**, **Break** to display the Break dialog box, select **Page Break**, then click **OK**.

**FIGURE 9.6**

Use Outline view to reorganize the sections of your document.

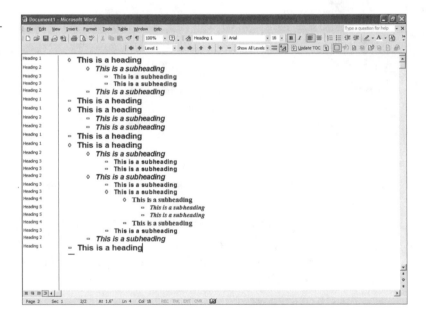

When you're in Outline view, Word displays your headings as different outline levels. Text formatted with the Heading 1 style appears as Level 1 headings in your outline, text formatted as Heading 2 appears as Level 2 headings, and so on.

To make your outline easier to work with, you can select how many levels of headings are displayed. (Just pull down the Show Level list and select the appropriate level number.) You also can choose to expand or contract various sections of the outline by clicking the plus and minus icons to the side of each Level text in your outline.

Outline view makes rearranging sections of your document extremely easy. When you're in Outline view, you can move an entire section from one place to another by selecting the Level heading and then clicking the up and down arrow buttons. (You also can drag sections from one position to another within the outline.)

# Working with Pictures

Although memos and letters might look fine if they contain nothing but text, other types of documents—newsletters, reports, and so on—can be jazzed up with pictures and other graphic elements.

## Inserting a Picture from the Clip Art Gallery

The easiest way to add a graphic to your document is to use Word's built-in Clip Art Gallery. The Clip Art Gallery is a collection of ready-to-use illustrations and photos, organized by topic, that can be pasted directly into your Word documents.

To insert a piece of clip art, follow these steps:

1. Position your cursor where you want the picture to appear.

2. Select **Insert**, **Picture**, **Clip Art**; this displays the Insert Clip Art pane.

3. Enter one or more keywords into the Search For box, then click **Search**.

4. Pictures matching your criteria are now displayed in the pane; double-click a graphic to insert it into your document.

> **tip**
>
> If you'd rather browse through available clip art, select **Insert**, **Picture**, **Clip Collection** to display the Insert Clip Art dialog box; select a specific category to display all matching pictures.

## Inserting Other Types of Picture Files

You're not limited to using graphics from the Clip Art Gallery. Word lets you insert any type of graphics file into your document—including GIF, JPG, BMP, TIF, and other popular graphic formats.

To insert a graphics file into your document, follow these steps:

1. Position your cursor where you want the picture to appear.

2. Select **Insert**, **Picture**, **From File**; this displays the Insert Picture dialog box.

3. Navigate to and select the picture you want to insert.

4. Click the **Insert** button to insert that picture into your document.

## Formatting the Picture

After you've inserted a picture in your document, you might need to format it for best appearance.

To format the picture itself, double-click the picture. This displays the Format Picture dialog box, which lets you format colors, line, size, layout, brightness, contrast, and other settings.

To move your picture to another position in your document, use your mouse to drag it to its new position. You also can resize the graphic by clicking the picture and then dragging a selection handle to resize that side or corner of the graphic.

To change the way text flows around the graphic, double-click the graphic to display the Format Picture dialog box and then select the **Layout** tab. You can choose to display the picture inline with the text, wrap around the text as a square, flow in front of the text, or display behind the text.

# The Absolute Minimum

Here are the key points to remember from this chapter:

- Microsoft Word is a powerful word processing program included with both Works Suite and Microsoft Office.

- Most editing commands are found on Word's **Edit** menu; most formatting commands are found on the **Format** menu.

- There are several different ways you can view a Word document, selectable from the small buttons at the lower left corner of the workspace. The most useful views are the Normal and Print Layout views; you can also use the Outline view to display your document as a hierarchical outline.

- If you reuse similar formatting throughout your document, consider using a Word style to apply similar formatting to multiple paragraphs.

- Insert clip art or graphics files by selecting **Insert**, **Picture**, and then selecting the appropriate type of picture.

## IN THIS CHAPTER

- Understanding Spreadsheets
- Creating a New Spreadsheet
- Entering Data
- Formatting Your Spreadsheet
- Inserting and Deleting Rows and Columns
- Using Formulas and Functions
- Sorting a Range of Cells
- Creating a Chart
- The Absolute Minimum

**10**

# WORKING WITH NUMBERS

When you're on your computer and want to crunch some numbers, you use a program called a *spreadsheet*.

A spreadsheet is nothing more than a giant list. Your list can contain just about any type of data you can think of—text, numbers, and even dates. You can take any of the numbers on your list and use them to calculate new numbers. You can sort the items on your list, pretty them up, and print the important points in a report. You can even graph your numbers in a pie, line, or bar chart!

There are several different spreadsheet programs available for your personal computer. Heavy-duty number crunchers go for full-featured spreadsheet programs, such as Microsoft Excel, Quattro Pro, or Lotus 1-2-3. More casual users don't necessarily need all the sophisticated analytical capabilities of these two spreadsheet powerhouses, and often gravitate to the spreadsheet included with Microsoft Works Suite—called, appropriately enough, Works Spreadsheet. Works Spreadsheet is easier to learn than either Excel or 1-2-3, and will do just about anything the average home user needs to do.

This chapter, then, shows you how to use Works Spreadsheet—so limber up those fingers and get ready for some heavy-duty number crunching!

# Understanding Spreadsheets

Whether you're using Works Spreadsheet, Excel, or 1-2-3, all spreadsheet programs work in pretty much the same fashion. In a spreadsheet, everything is stored in little boxes called *cells*. Your spreadsheet is divided into lots of these cells, each located in a specific location on a giant grid made of *rows* and *columns*. Each single cell represents the intersection of a particular row and column.

As you can see in Figure 10.1, each column has an alphabetic label (A, B, C, and so on). Each row, on the other hand, has a numeric label (1, 2, 3, and so on). The location of each cell is the combination of its column and row locations. For example, the cell in the upper-left corner of the spreadsheet is in column A and row 1; therefore, its location is signified as A1. The cell to the right of it is B1, and the cell below A1 is A2.

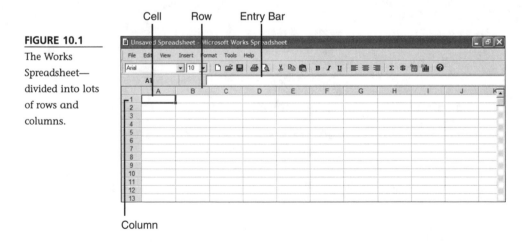

**FIGURE 10.1**

The Works Spreadsheet— divided into lots of rows and columns.

The Entry bar at the top of the workspace echoes the contents of the selected, or *active*, cell. You can type data directly into the active cell or into the Entry bar.

# Creating a New Spreadsheet

As with most Works Suite applications, you can start Works Spreadsheet either from Windows (select **Start**, **All Programs**, **Microsoft Works**, **Microsoft Works Spreadsheet**) or from the Works Task Launcher.

To open a blank spreadsheet in the Works Spreadsheet workspace, click the **New** button on the toolbar. A blank spreadsheet is now loaded into the workspace, ready to accept any text or numbers you want to enter.

The instructions in this chapter are specific to Works Spreadsheet. If you're using another spreadsheet program, such as Microsoft Excel (which is included with Microsoft Office), you might need to translate a few steps here and there because Excel does some things somewhat differently than Works.

# Entering Data

Entering text or numbers into a spreadsheet is easy. Just remember that data is entered into each cell individually—then you can fill up a spreadsheet with hundreds or thousands of cells filled with their own individual data!

To enter data into a specific cell, follow these steps:

1. Select the cell you want to enter data into.

2. Type your text or numbers into the cell; what you type will be echoed in the Entry bar at the top of the screen.

3. When you're done typing data into the cell, press **Enter**.

# Formatting Your Spreadsheet

You don't have to settle for boring-looking spreadsheets. You can format how the data appears in your spreadsheet—including the format of any numbers you enter.

## Applying Number Formats

When you enter a number into a cell, Works applies what it calls a "general" format to the number—it just displays the number, right-aligned, with no commas or dollar signs. You can, however, select a specific number format to apply to any cells in your spreadsheet that contain numbers. Follow these steps:

1. Select the cell (or cells) you want to format.

2. Select **Format**, **Number** to display the Format Cells dialog box.

3. Select the **Number** tab.

4. Check one of the options in the Format list.

5. If the format has additional options (such as decimal points or various date or time formats), configure these as desired.

6. Click **OK**.

## Formatting Cell Contents

You can apply a variety of formatting options to the contents of your cells. You can make your text bold or italic, change the font type or size, or even add shading or borders to selected cells.

To format a cell (or range of cells), follow these steps:

1. Select the cell (or range).

2. Apply the formatting from either the toolbar or the **Format** menu.

# Inserting and Deleting Rows and Columns

Sometimes you need to go back to an existing spreadsheet and insert some new information.

## Insert a Row or Column

To insert a new row or column in the middle of your spreadsheet, follow these steps:

1. Click the row or column header *after* where you want to make the insertion.

2. Pull down the **Insert** menu and select either **Insert Row** or **Insert Column**.

Works now inserts a new row or column either above or to the left of the row or column you selected.

## Delete a Row or Column

To delete an existing row or column, follow these steps:

1. Click the header for the row or column you want to delete.

2. Pull down the **Insert** menu and select either **Delete Row** or **Delete Column**.

The row or column you selected is deleted, and all other rows or columns move up or over to fill the space.

## Adjusting Column Width

If the data you enter into a cell is too long, you'll only see the first part of that data—there'll be a bit to the right that looks cut off. It's not cut off, of course; it just can't be seen, since it's longer than the current column is wide.

You can fix this problem by adjusting the column width. Wider columns allow more data to be shown; narrow columns let you display more columns per page.

To change the column width, move your cursor to the column header, and position it on the dividing line to the right of the column you want to adjust. When the cursor changes shape, click the left button on your mouse and drag the column divider to the right (to make a wider column) or to the left (to make a smaller column). Release the mouse button when the column is the desired width.

# Using Formulas and Functions

Works Spreadsheet lets you enter just about any type of algebraic formula into any cell. You can use these formulas to add, subtract, multiply, divide, and perform any nested combination of those operations.

**tip**

To make a column the exact right width for the longest amount of data entered, position your cursor over the dividing line to the right of the column header and double-click your mouse. This makes the column width automatically "fit" your current data.

## Creating a Formula

Works knows that you're entering a formula when you type an equal sign (=) into any cell. You start your formula with the equal sign and enter your operations *after* the equal sign.

For example, if you wanted to add 1 plus 2, you'd enter this formula in a cell: **=1+2**. When you press **Enter**, the formula disappears from the cell—and the result, or *value*, is displayed.

## Basic Operators

Table 10.1 shows the algebraic operators you can use in Works Spreadsheet formulas.

**TABLE 10.1** Works Spreadsheet Operators

| Operation | Operator |
|---|---|
| Add | + |
| Subtract | - |
| Multiply | * |
| Divide | / |

So if you wanted to multiply 10 by 5, you'd enter =10*5. If you wanted to divide 10 by 5, you'd enter =10/5.

## Working with Other Cells

If all you're doing is adding and subtracting numbers, you might as well use a calculator. Where a spreadsheet becomes truly useful is when you use it to perform operations based on the contents of specific cells.

To perform calculations using values from cells in your spreadsheet, you enter the cell location into the formula. For example, if you wanted to add cells A1 and A2, you'd enter this formula: =A1+A2.

**tip**

If you're unsure about using these operators, click the **Easy Calc** button on the Works Spreadsheet toolbar (see Figure 10.2). You can use the Easy Calc dialog box to walk step-by-step through the creation of most simple formulae.

An even easier way to perform operations involving spreadsheet cells is to select them with your mouse while you're entering the formula. To do this, follow these steps:

1. Select the cell that will contain the formula.
2. Type =.
3. Click the first cell you want to include in your formula; that cell location is automatically entered in your formula.
4. Type an algebraic operator, such as +, -, *, or /.
5. Click the second cell you want to include in your formula.
6. Repeat steps 4 and 5 to include other cells in your formula.
7. Press **Enter** when your formula is complete.

## Quick Addition with AutoSum

The most common operation in any spreadsheet is the addition of a group of numbers. Works Spreadsheet makes summing up a row or column of numbers easy via the AutoSum function.

All you have to do is follow these steps:

1. Select the cell at the end of a row or column of numbers, where you want the total to appear.

2. Click the **AutoSum** button on the Works toolbar, shown in Figure 10.2.

Works automatically sums all the preceding numbers and places the total in the selected cell.

AutoSum

**FIGURE 10.2**

Use AutoSum to automatically add up a row or column of numbers.

EasyCalc

## Using Functions

In addition to the basic algebraic operators previously discussed, Works Spreadsheet also includes a variety of *functions* that replace the complex steps present in many formulas. For example, if you wanted to total all the cells in column A, you could enter the formula =A1+A2+A3+A4. Or, you could use the *SUM* function, which lets you sum a column or row of numbers without having to type every cell into the formula.

In short, a function is a type of prebuilt formula.

You enter a function in the following format: =function(argument), where function is the name of the function and argument is the range of cells or other data you want to calculate. Using the last example, to sum cells A1 through A4, you'd use the following function-based formula: =sum(A1,A2,A3,A4).

> **tip**
>
> When you're referencing consecutive cells in a formula, you can just enter the first and last number or the series separated by a colon. For example, cells A1 through A4 can be entered as A1:A4.

Works Spreadsheet includes more than 100 separate functions. You can access and insert any of Works' functions by following these steps:

1. Select the cell where you want to insert the function.

2. Select **Insert**, **Function** to display the Function dialog box (shown in Figure 10.3).

3. Select a function category, then select a function.

4. Click the **Insert** button.

5 The function you selected is now inserted into the current cell. You can now manually enter the cells or numbers into the function's argument.

**FIGURE 10.3**

Choose from more than 100 separate functions in the Insert Function dialog box.

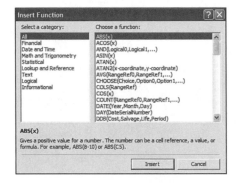

# Sorting a Range of Cells

If you have a list of either text or numbers, you might want to reorder the list for a different purpose. Works lets you sort your data by any column, in either ascending or descending order.

To sort a range of cells, follow these steps:

1. Select all the cells you want to sort.

2. Select **Tools**, **Sort** to display the Sort dialog box, shown in Figure 10.4.

3. Select whether your list does or doesn't have a header row.

4. Pull down the first **Select the Column You Want to Sort By** list, and select which column you want to sort by.

5. Choose to sort in either **Ascending** or **Descending** order.

**note**

If Works asks whether you want to sort the highlighted information or whether you want to sort *all* the information in your spreadsheet, choose to sort only the highlighted information.

6. Repeat steps 4 and 5 to sub-sort on additional columns.

7. Click the **Sort** button to sort the data.

**FIGURE 10.4**

Sort your list by any column, in any order.

## Creating a Chart

Numbers are fine, but sometimes the story behind the numbers can be better told through a picture. The way you take a picture of numbers is with a *chart*, such as the one shown in Figure 10.5.

**FIGURE 10.5**

Some numbers are better represented via a chart.

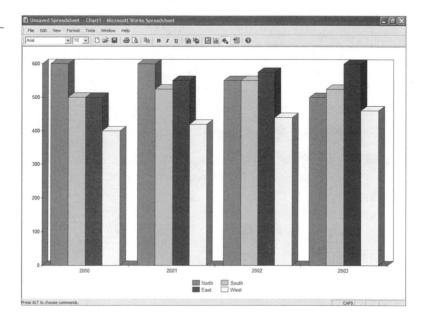

You create a chart based on numbers you've previously entered into your Works spreadsheet, like this:

1. Select the range of cells you want to include in your chart. (If the range has a header row or column, include that row or column when selecting the cells.)

2. Click the **New Chart** button to display the New Chart dialog box, shown in Figure 10.6.

**FIGURE 10.6**

Create one of a dozen types of charts to visually represent your data.

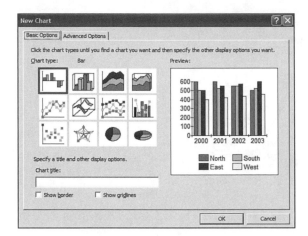

3. Select the **Basic Options** tab.

4. Select a chart type; a preview of the chart of your data appears in the Preview section.

5. Select any desired formatting options. For example, if you want your chart to have a title, enter the title in the Chart Title box. To display a border around your chart, check the **Show Border** option. If you want to show gridlines within your chart, check the **Show Gridlines** option.

6. When you're done, click **OK**.

Your chart now appears in a new, separate, unnamed, and unsaved spreadsheet. To save this new file, select **File**, **Save As**, give the file a name, and click the **Save** button.

# The Absolute Minimum

Here are the key points to remember from this chapter:

- The two most popular spreadsheet programs are Works Spreadsheet (included with Microsoft Works Suite) and Excel (included with Microsoft Office).

- A spreadsheet is composed of rows and columns; the intersection of a specific row and column is called a cell.

- Each cell can contain text, numbers, or formulas.

- You start a Works Spreadsheet formula with an = sign, and follow it up with specific numbers (or cell locations) and operators—such as +, -, *, and /.

- To graphically display your spreadsheet data, select the appropriate cells and then click the **New Chart** button.

## In This Chapter

- Creating a New Database
- Changing Views
- Editing Your Database
- Sorting and Filtering
- Creating a Report

**11**

# Working with a Database

If a spreadsheet is a giant list, a database is a giant file cabinet. Each "file cabinet" is actually a separate database file, and contains individual index cards (called *records*) filled with specific information (arranged in *fields*).

You can use Works Database, included with Microsoft Works Suite, to create and store anything that includes a large amount of data. For example, you can create a database that contains all your favorite recipes or the contents of your CD or video collection.

# Creating a New Database

You launch Works Database the same way you launch most other Works Suite applications, from either the Windows Start menu (select **Start**, **All Programs**, **Microsoft Works**, **Microsoft Works Database**) or the Works Task Launcher.

## Creating a Preformatted Database

Works Database includes several preformatted database applications. These include home inventory worksheets, home lists, and a recipe book. All these databases include ready-made forms and reports specific to that application.

To base your new database on one of these applications follow these steps:

1. Open the **Works Task Launcher**.
2. Select the **Programs** page.
3. Select **Works Database**.
4. Select the application you want.

note

Works Database is a very simple, easy-to-use database program. If you need to create more sophisticated databases, check out Microsoft Access, which is available as a freestanding application and as part of some versions of the Microsoft Office suite.

## Creating a Blank Database

You also can use Works Database to create your own customized applications. This means, of course, that you have to design your own fields, forms, and reports.

When you launch Works Database, you're presented with the Create Database dialog box, shown in Figure 11.1. Now you're faced with some immediate choices. (Don't worry—if you don't like the choices you make, you can always go back and change them later.)

**FIGURE 11.1**

Use the Create Database dialog box to design your database.

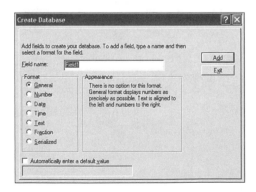

First, you need to decide how many fields to include in your database. In general, you should create one field for each type of information you want to store. If you're creating a database for your movie collection, for example, you might create fields for Title, Lead Actor, Lead Actress, Director, Running Time, and Year.

Each field you add is assigned a specific *format*. You can select from the following formats: **General**, **Number**, **Date**, **Time**, **Text**, **Fraction**, and **Serialized** (for automatic consecutive numbers). Select the format that best fits the type of data you'll enter into that field. Click **Add** to add another field.

After you've finished adding fields to your database, click the **Exit** button. Works now creates a database, based on your specifications.

## Changing Views

You can view your new database in two distinct ways.

The default view, called the *List view*, makes your database look a little like a spreadsheet. As you can see in Figure 11.2, the rows are your records, and the columns are your fields.

**FIGURE 11.2**

Viewing a database in List view.

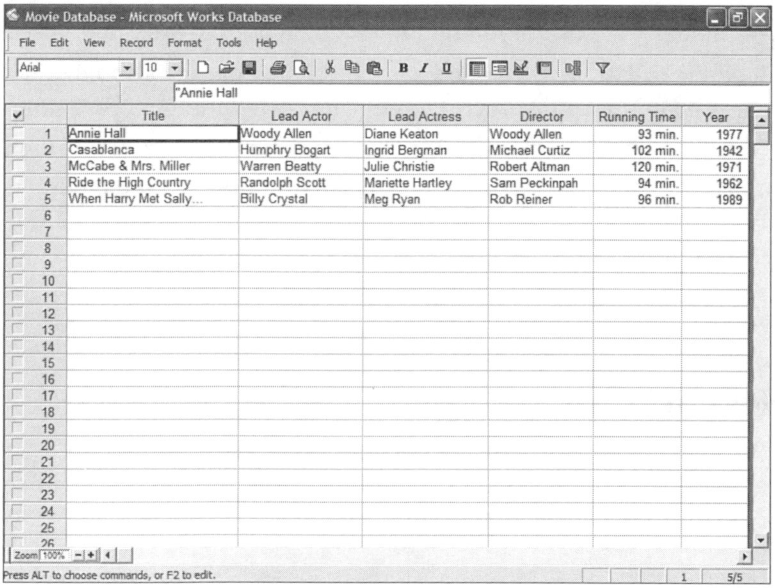

The *Form view*, shown in Figure 11.3 lets you look at one record at a time. You can flip from one record to another by using the arrow keys at the bottom of the screen.

**FIGURE 11.3**

Viewing an individual record in your database, AKA Form view.

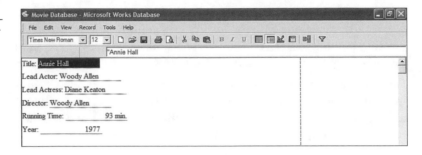

You switch views by using the view buttons on the Works Database toolbar or by pulling down the **View** menu and selecting either **List** or **Form**.

# Editing Your Database

Once you've designed your database, it's time to fill it up. That means entering data into the individual records—and adding as many records as necessary.

## Adding Data

No matter which view you're using, adding data to your database is easy.

If you're in List view, you add data to your database as you'd add data to a spreadsheet. Move your cursor to any particular field, and type your data. Use the **Tab** key to move to the next field in a record; use the **Enter** key to move to the next record.

You might prefer to add data one record at a time, as you'd enter data on an individual card in a file cabinet. Switch to Form view, and enter all the data for the fields in the current record. Use the **Tab** key to move from field to field; when you reach the end of one record, pressing **Tab** moves you to the first field of the next record.

## Adding New Records

If you're in List view, adding a new record is as simple as starting to type in the first empty record row. If you're in Form view, just click the **Insert Record** button; a new blank record appears in the workspace.

## Adding New Fields

After you get going in a database, you might discover that you want to include more information for each record. Going back to our movie database example, you might decide that you want to add a field for Category/Genre.

Fortunately, adding new fields to existing databases is easy. All you have to do is follow these steps:

1. Switch to List view.
2. Position your cursor anywhere in the field before where you want to insert the new field.
3. Select **Record**, **Insert Field**, **After** to display the Insert Field dialog box.
4. Enter a name and format for the new field.
5. Click **Add**.

Works now adds the new field(s) to every record in your database. This field will be blank, of course, so you'll have to go back through your existing records and fill it in, as appropriate.

# Sorting and Filtering

You can add records to your database in any order. You don't have to insert new records alphabetically because you can have the program itself re-sort all the records for you; you can filter your information to display only selected records.

## Sorting Data

You use List view to display all the records in your database. By default, these records are listed in the order in which they're entered. However, you can sort these records by any field—in either ascending or descending order. Follow these steps:

1. From List view, select **Records**, **Sort Records** to display the Sort Records dialog box.
2. Pull down the **Sort By** list and select the first field by which you want to sort.
3. Select whether you want to sort in **Ascending** or **Descending** order.
4. If you want, repeat steps 2 and 3 to sort on a second or third field.
5. Click **OK**.

Works now re-sorts your database as directed.

## Filtering Data

Another option you have in Works Database is to display only those records that match a specific criteria. This is sometimes necessary if your database contains a lot of records and you want to view only a subset of them. This process is called *filtering* the database, and it's easy to do.

For example, in your movie database you might want to display only Humphrey Bogart movies. You would create a filter that looks for all records containing Humphrey Bogart as an actor and displays only those records.

To create a filter, follow these steps:

1. From within List view, select **Tools**, **Filters** to display the Filter Name dialog box.

2. Enter a name for the filter, and then click **OK**.

3. When the Filter dialog box appears, pull down the first **Field Name** box and select the first field you want to filter.

4. Pull down the first **Comparison** list and select a criteria (is equal to, does not contain, and so on) for the filter.

5. In the first Compare To box, enter the value for the selected criteria.

6. Repeat steps 4-6 to apply additional parameters for this filter.

7. Click the **Apply Filter** button.

Using the movie database example, if you wanted to display only Humphrey Bogart movies, you'd select Lead Actor as the Field Name, pull down the Comparison list and select Contains, and then enter `Humphrey Bogart` in the Compare To box. Works Database looks for those records where the Lead Actor field contains Humphrey Bogart and displays only those records.

# Creating a Report

Once you have all your data entered, sorted, and filtered, you can print out a report of key database information. You can then store this hard copy someplace safe, in case you need it at a future date.

**tip**

Don't forget to sort your records before you print!

## Printing a List

If you want to view all the fields in all the records in your database, all you have to do is print the list of records as they appear in List view. You do this by switching to **List** view and then clicking the **Print** button on the toolbar.

If you prefer, you can print only selected records by filtering your database, as explained earlier. Apply the filter, and then print the resulting list of records.

If you just want to print a single record, you don't have to apply some draconian filter. Instead, switch to **Forms** view, navigate to the record you want to print, and then click the **Print** button. Works will print only the current form.

## Using ReportCreator to Create a Report

Even more useful than printing a list is Works' capability to analyze and summarize the contents of a database in a customized *report*. Works Database includes a special ReportCreator tool that makes creating custom reports a snap.

To create a report, follow these steps:

1. Select **Tools**, **ReportCreator** to display the Report Name dialog box.

2. Enter a name for your report and click **OK**; this displays the ReportCreator dialog box.

3. Select the **Title** tab, enter or edit the report title, then select an orientation and a font.

4. Select the **Fields** tab, select those fields you want to include in your report, in the order that you want them to appear, and then click **Add**. If you want to display the field names at the top of your page, check the **Show Field Names at Top of Each Page** option; if you want to summarize the data in your fields, check the **Show Summary Information Only** option.

5. Select the **Sorting** tab, then select which fields you want to sort by, in either **Ascending** or **Descending** order.

6. Select the **Grouping** tab, then select any fields you want to group or subtotal and how you want them grouped.

7. Select the **Filter** tab, then select any previously created filter from the **Select a Filter** list—or click the **Create New Filter** button to create and apply a new filter.

8. Select the **Summary** tab, then select any fields you want to summarize, how you want to summarize them (sum, average, count, and so on), and where you want to display the summaries (under each column, at the end of the report, and so on).

9. Click the **Done** button.

Only sorted fields are available for grouping.

10. You're now asked whether you want to preview or modify the report; click **Preview**.

11. Your report is now displayed onscreen in Preview mode, as shown in Figure 11.4. If you like what you see, click **Print**. If you don't, click **Cancel** and edit your report using the report commands on the **Tools** menu.

**FIGURE 11.4**

Summarize and analyze your database with custom-created reports.

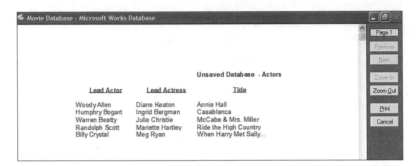

# THE ABSOLUTE MINIMUM

Here are the key points to remember from this chapter:

- A database is like a big electronic filing cabinet.

- Individual items (files) within the database are called records.

- Each record can contain a number of fields; all records within a database have the same fields.

- If all you need is a simple database, use Works Database (included with Microsoft Works Suite); if you need a more sophisticated database, use Microsoft Access (included with some versions of Microsoft Office).

- Works Database lets you view your data in two different views—List view, which looks a little like a spreadsheet (with rows and columns), and Form view, which displays your data one record at a time.

- Use ReportCreator to create printed reports of your database data.

## IN THIS CHAPTER

- Track Your Budget
- Doing Your Banking—Electronically
- Paying Recurring Bills

# 12

# MANAGING YOUR FINANCES

Most new computers come with at least one personal finance program installed. That program might be Microsoft Money, or it might be some variation of Intuit's Quicken. Both programs work similarly, but for purposes of this book we're going to look at Money because it's fully integrated into the Microsoft Works Suite program.

Microsoft Money is a full-featured personal finance program. You can use it to manage your household budgets, track your bank accounts and investments, write checks, and even pay your bills online.

# Configuring Microsoft Money

You can start Money from either the Windows **Start** menu (select **Start**, **All Programs**, **Microsoft Money**) or the Works Task Launcher. But before you use the program, you have to configure it with information about your specific banking and financial accounts.

## First-Time Setup with the Setup Assistant

The first time you start Money you're presented with the Setup Assistant. This assistant walks you step-by-step through setting up your Money accounts; just make sure you've gathered all you personal financial records beforehand, as you'll need all the account numbers and such to set up the program.

Here's what you'll need to know to complete the Setup Assistant:

**note**

The Setup Assistant runs any time you create a new Money file—by selecting **File**, **New**, **New file**.

- **Your Internet connection.** These questions help configure Money's online features.

- **Your sign-in information.** You can choose to secure your Money account with a password, as well as sign up for a Microsoft .NET Passport to access various online features.

- **Your personal information.** This is where you enter your name, and your spouse's name, as well as which currency you intend to use.

- **Your priorities.** This is a short questionnaire concerning your investment, banking, and planning priorities; your answers to these questions help Money determine how best to set up your accounts.

- **Your account details.** Money will track the following types of accounts: checking, savings, credit card, retirement, brokerage/investment, and money market/cash management. For each account you have, you'll need to enter the bank or broker name, the account number, and your current or starting balance.

- **Your paycheck details.** Money can be configured to enter your paycheck on a recurring basis. You'll need to know your employer, your take-home pay, and how often you're paid.

- **Your bills.** You'll need to enter all the different types of bills that you pay regularly—and, for each bill, the payee, estimated amount, and frequency.

After you're finished with the Setup Assistant you can start using Money normally—or you can go back and edit your account information.

## Setting Up Your Accounts

If you need to add a new account, delete an unused account, or just edit any specific account information, follow these steps:

1. From the **Money Home Page**, click the **Account List** button to display the Pick an Account to Use page.

2. Go to the **Common Tasks** list and click **Set Up Accounts**; this displays the Set Up Your Accounts in Money page.

3. To create a new account, click **Add a New Account**.

4. To close an existing account, click **Close or Reopen Accounts**.

5. To delete an account from your system, click **Delete an Account Permanently**.

6. To edit an existing account, click any account listed in the **Change an Account You've Already Created** list.

After you've made your selection, follow the onscreen instructions to complete your action.

## Setting Up Your Categories

You can assign specific expense or income categories to each of your transactions. Money comes with its own built-in categories; you can also add, delete, and modify categories. Just follow these steps:

1. Click the **Categories** button to display the Set Up Your Categories page.

2. To add a category, click the **New** button and complete the New Category Wizard.

3. To delete an existing category, select the category and click **Delete**.

4. To edit an existing category, select the category and click **Modify**; when the Modify Category dialog box appears, make your changes and click **OK**.

**tip**

Money offers a large number of program configuration options—too many to cover in this small space. To access all these options, select **Tools**, **Options** to display the Options dialog box; select a tab to configure specific options.

# Navigating Money

Before you start working with your accounts, it's a good idea to get familiar with the way Money works—starting from the Home page.

## Home Sweet Home

The Money Home page, shown in Figure 12.1, is your "home base" for all your Money-related transactions. From the home page are various links to different activities; you click a link to access that activity.

**FIGURE 12.1**
Start with the Money Home page, and then click to access different activities and transactions.

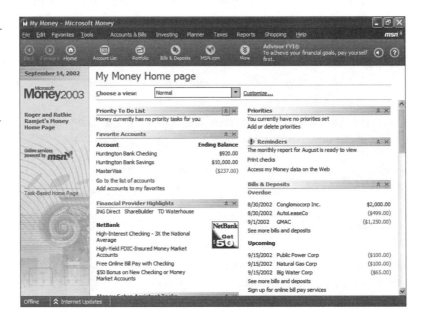

These links are organized into several sections; which sections you see depend on which view of your Home page you select. You select different views from the **Choose a View** list.

For example, the Basic view displays the tasks shown in Figure 12.1. The Investing view displays only those sections related to your investments; the Normal view displays all available sections.

## Money's Financial Centers

Across the top of the Money Home Page are buttons that link to Money's other financial centers. These pages organize tasks and information by specific types of activity.

The buttons across the top of the Money Home page take you directly to these financial centers. Here's what each of these buttons does:

- **Home.** Takes you back to Money's Home page, from anywhere in the program.
- **Account List.** View account balances, add new accounts, manage existing accounts, and link directly to each account's register.
- **Portfolio.** View and edit your investment portfolio, record new investment transactions, and go online to get current stock quotes.
- **Bills and deposits.** Set up new payees, pay bills, and register deposits to your banking accounts.
- **MSN.com.** Connect to the Internet-based financial resources on the MSN.com Web site.
- **Reports.** Create a variety of reports and charts.
- **Cash Flow.** Display a cash flow forecast, based on your current budget.
- **Budget.** Access Money's Budget Planner, which lets you create a budget, create a debt reduction plan, and plan your 401(k).
- **Categories.** Add, delete, and modify the categories used in your accounts.
- **Payees**. Set up and view information about your payees.
- **Money Browser**. Go online to find even more financial information.
- **Customize.** Customize the Money toolbar.

# Track Your Budget

One of the most useful things you can do with Money is to plan a household budget, and track your progress to budget. It's easy to do, using Money's built-in Budget Planner. All you have to do is follow the onscreen instructions—and then stick to the budget you create!

To launch Money's Budget Planner,  click the **Budget** button. When the main Budget Planner page appears, click the **Create a Budget Link**.

The Budget Planner now leads you step-by-step through nine screens of information. Each screen in the Budget Planner focuses on a particular budgeting task; complete all the screens to finish your budget, in this order:

1. Use the Enter Your Income screen to enter all your scheduled deposits, by category. You add new income categories by clicking the **Add** button and following the step-by-step onscreen instructions.

2. Use the Enter Your Expenses screen to enter all your scheduled expenses, by category. To add a new scheduled transaction, double-click the expense category and make a new entry in the Edit dialog box.

3. Use the Savings Goals screen to answer the question, "What do you want to put into long-term savings?" You can select either to **Spend All Excess Income** or to **Save Some or All Excess Income Towards Goals**. If you select the second option, you can then enter specific savings goals.

Money now displays the Budget Summary page, which provides a visual overview of your income, expenses, and savings goals. When you click the **Finish** button, Money displays the Review Your Current Budget Status page, which tracks how your actual income and spending compare to your budget. You can choose to view the status of your budget for the current month, current year, or a forecast for future weeks, months, and years. The information is displayed in a table that compares your actual income and expenses with your budgeted numbers; the difference between actual and budget is also displayed.

**tip**

You can create monthly and yearly budget reports by clicking **View Reports** (on the Common Tasks sidebar) and selecting either **Monthly Budget** or **Annual Budget**.

# Doing Your Banking—Electronically

Many people use Microsoft Money to track their banking transactions. You can enter transactions manually—or, if you're connected to the Internet, download transactions electronically from your banking institution.

## Entering Transactions

Money makes it easy to manually enter transactions into your checking and savings accounts registers. Just follow these steps:

1. From Money's Home page, click the **Account List** button; this displays the Pick an Account to Use page.

2. Click the name for your bank account; this displays the account register for that account, as shown in Figure 12.2.

**FIGURE 12.2**

Enter banking
transactions into
your account
register.

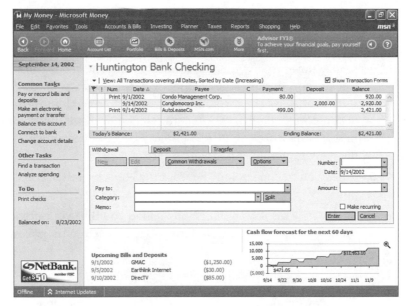

3. To register a withdrawal, click the **Withdrawal** tab, select the payee from the Pay To list, select a transaction category from the **Category** list, select a numbering option from the **Number** list, enter the **Date** of the transaction, and then enter the **Amount** of the withdrawal.

4. To register a deposit, select the **Deposit** tab, select the payer from the **From** list, select a transaction category from the **Category** list, select a numbering option from the **Number** list, enter the **Date** of the transaction, and then enter the **Amount** of the deposit.

5. To register a transfer between accounts, select the **Transfer** tab, select the appropriate accounts from the **From** and **To** lists, select a numbering option from the **Number** list, enter the **Date** of the transaction, and then enter the **Amount** of the transfer.

# Balancing Your Checkbook

When you receive your monthly statement from your bank, you can have Money automatically reconcile your accounts to your statement—which is a lot easier than trying to do it by hand! It's all done via a wizard, like this:

1. Open the account register you want to balance.

2. Click **Balance This Account** from the Common Tasks sidebar; this launches Money's Balance Wizard.

3. When prompted, enter the following information from your monthly statement: statement date, starting balance, ending balance, service charges (if any), and interest earned (if any). Click **Next** to proceed.

4. Money now displays a Balance page for the selected account. Compare the transactions in the Money register with the transactions on your monthly statement. Click the **C** column to clear each matching transaction. If a transaction doesn't match, click the transaction and edit it accordingly. If you're missing any transactions (the primary cause of accounts not balancing), click the **New** button to enter them as new.

5. When you're done balancing, click the **Next** button in the Common Tasks pane.

6. Money now displays a dialog box telling you that your account is balanced. (Congratulations!) Click the **Finish** button to close the wizard.

## Online Banking

An even easier way to handle your banking needs is to let Money do it automatically, by downloading all your transactions from your bank, using the Internet. This way you don't have to enter much of anything—Money interfaces with your bank to track all your transactions.

Before you set up Money to work with your bank's online banking services, you'll need to confirm that your bank offers Money-compatible services. You also might need to sign up for those services (they're not always free) and obtain any necessary account numbers and passwords.

Once you're sure that your banking institution is ready to go, follow these steps:

1. From within Money, select **Accounts & Bills**, **Online Services Manager** to open the Online Services Manager page.

2. Find the account you want to connect to, then click **Setup Online Services**.

3. Money now displays the Online Setup screen. Confirm that your bank is listed here, then click the **Next** button and follow the onscreen instructions.

If your bank is not listed, it does not offer Money-compatible online banking services.

> **caution**
>
> Not all banks offer online banking, and not all online banking services are compatible with Microsoft Money. Some banks let you perform online transactions only from their own Web pages; these banks are not compatible with Money's online banking feature.

# Paying Recurring Bills

Another nice feature of Microsoft Money is being able to schedule recurring payments—so that you don't have to enter the same transaction, month after month after month.

Money lets you set up a list of your recurring transactions. After you've entered a recurring payee, all you have to do is click a few buttons to pay that bill each month, every month.

## Scheduling the Payment

The first thing you need to do is to tell Money who you pay your bills to. You do this by adding payees to your scheduled bills list, like this:

1. Click the **Bills & Deposits** button to display the Manage Scheduled Bills and Deposits page.

2. Click the **New** button and select **Bill**; this displays the Create a Recurring Bill page, shown in Figure 12.3.

3. Enter the name and other payment information for this bill—including the next payment date and frequency.

4. Click **OK** when done.

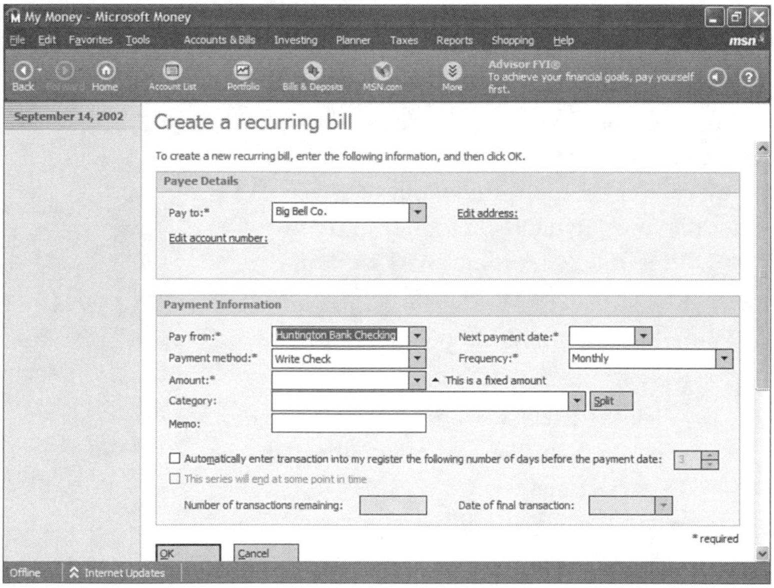

**FIGURE 12.3**

Set up Money for all your recurring bills.

## Paying the Bill

After you've set up a recurring payment, you can manually write a check and enter that transaction in the Money register. All you have to do is follow these steps:

1. Click the **Bills & Deposits** button to display the Manage Scheduled Bills and Deposits page.

2. Double-click the bill you want to pay; this displays the Record Payment dialog box, shown in Figure 12.4.

3. Enter the correct payment amount for the bill into the **Amount** field.

4. Enter the check number into the **Number** field.

5. Click the **Record Payment** button.

**FIGURE 12.4**

Entering a payment.

## Printing Checks in Money

You can also use the Record Payment dialog box to instruct Money to print a check for this payment. You'll need to purchase Money-compatible blank checks for your printer, but then you can enter all your payments in Money and print them out in a batch, or one check at a time.

To instruct Money to print a check (instead of just entering a manual bill payment), follow these steps:

1. Click the **Bills & Deposits** button to display the Manage Scheduled Bills and Deposits page.

2. Double-click the bill you want to pay; this displays the Record Payment dialog box.

**tip**

You can't print checks on plain white laser paper; you have to purchase special check forms to use with your specific banking accounts. You should be able to find Money-compatible check forms at your local office supply store, or you can order them directly from Microsoft at 800-432-1285 or on the Web at www.microsoft.com/money/checks.htm.

3. Enter the correct payment amount for the bill into the **Amount** field.

4. Pull down the **Number** list and select **Print This Transaction**.

5. Click the **Record Payment** button.

This transaction is now entered in your account register, and the check is sent to Money's "to-do" list for printing at a later time.

Once you've entered all the transactions for which you want to print checks, it's time to print. (You can print one check at a time, too.) Follow these steps:

1. From anywhere in Money, select **File**, **Print Checks** to display the Print Checks dialog box.

2. Select which checks you want to print (all or selected), what type of check forms you're using, the number of the first check form in your printer, and how many checks are on the first page.

3. Make sure you have blank checks loaded into your printer, then click **Print** to print the selected check(s) .

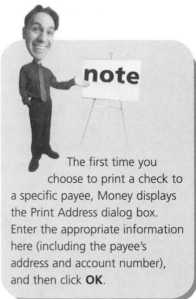

The first time you choose to print a check to a specific payee, Money displays the Print Address dialog box. Enter the appropriate information here (including the payee's address and account number), and then click **OK**.

## Paying Bills Online

If you're tired of dealing with paper checks—even those that Money itself prints—then you need to start paying your bills electronically. Money enables you to sign up with an electronic bill paying service to handle all your bills online, via the Internet.

Most bill payment services charge either a monthly or per-payment fee.

Money's bill paying service of choice is MSN Bill Pay. (It's also owned by Microsoft.) You can set up a new MSN Bill Pay account from within Money, by following these steps:

1. From anywhere in Money, select **Accounts & Bills**, **Online Services Manager**; this displays the Online Services Manager screen.

2. Click **Set Up Electronic Bill Pay Service**, to display the Set Up Online Payment Provider page.

3. Pull down the **Select an Online Payment Provider** list and select a provider, then click the **Next** button.

4. Money now downloads information specific to the bill pay provider you selected; follow the balance of the onscreen instructions to setup your new account.

Once you're signed up with your bill pay service, paying a bill electronically is as easy as following these steps:

1. Click the **Account List** button to display the Pick an Account to Use page.

2. Select the account you want to use to pay your bills; this displays the account register.

3. From the Common Tasks pane, select **Make an Electronic Payment** or **Transfer**, **Make an Electronic Payment**; this displays the Record Payment dialog box.

4. Enter the payment information.

5. Make sure you're connected to the Internet, then click **Submit Payment**.

> **tip**
>
> The first time you enter an electronic payment for a payee, Money prompts you for certain details, such as the payee's name, address, and account number. Be sure you enter the correct information (typically available on your most recent bill from that payee), and then click **OK**.

# THE ABSOLUTE MINIMUM

Here are the key points to remember from this chapter:

- You can use any financial management program—including Microsoft Money and Quicken—to manage your banking and investment transactions.

- When you first start Microsoft Money, you need to enter key personal and financial information—including the names and numbers of your banking and investment accounts.

- You can use Money's Budget Planner to set up your household budget, and then track your progress to budget.

- Money lets you track your bills three ways: by manually entering checks you write into Money's account register, by printing those checks for you, and by sending payment information over the Internet via an electronic bill pay service.

**13**

# CREATING GREETING CARDS AND OTHER COOL PROJECTS

There are many things you can create with your new computer. Sure, you can use Word to write letters and Works Spreadsheet to crunch numbers, but you can also use other software to create other, more fun, types of projects.

For example, did you know you can use your computer to make your own Christmas cards? Or to create invitations and banners for your children's birthday parties? Or even to send electronic greeting cards to friends and family, via the Internet?

That's right, your new personal computer can be your main workstation for all sorts of cool home projects. Read on to learn more—and to get creative!

# Using Home Publishing Software

Microsoft Word is a very versatile word processing program, and even includes some very simple home projects. For example, you can use Word to create very basic greeting cards. But if you want to really get fancy, you'll want a software program specifically designed for graphic projects—what we call home publishing software. Most home publishing programs come with templates for a variety of different home-related projects, as well as a large number of clip art pictures, which you can use to add visual diversity to your projects.

Here's a quick overview of some of the most popular home publishing programs:

- **Greeting Card Factory Deluxe**. This program does nothing but greeting cards—but it's great at what it does. The software include more than 7,500 greeting card templates, and more than 50,000 pieces of clip art. (Go to www.novadevcorp.com/mainus/products/gdw/ for more information.)

- **CorelDRAW Essentials**. A fully-featured desktop publishing suite, comlete with clip art, fonts, and other utilities. (Go to www.corel.com for more information.)

- **Hallmark Card Studio.** Hallmark produces several versions of this low-priced program, each geared around a specific theme: Holiday, Comedy, Christian, Scrapbook, and so on. (Go to www.hallmarksoftware.com for more information.)

- **Microsoft Greetings**. This program includes thousands of templates and images for making professional-looking greeting cards. (Go to www.microsoft.com for more information.)

- **Microsoft Picture It! Photo**. This program is included as part of Microsoft Works Suite. While it's mainly used for editing digital photos, it also includes quite a few built-in photo-related projects, such as photo albums, picture postcards, and photo greeting cards. (Go to www.microsoft.com for more information.)

- **Microsoft Picture It! Publishing.** This is a full-featured home publishing program that lets you create everything from greeting cards to banners to newsletters. (Go to www.microsoft.com for more information.)

- **Microsoft Publisher**. Even more fully featured than Picture It! Publishing (but a little harder to use), Publisher is included with some versions of Microsoft Office. (Go to www.microsoft.com/publisher/ for more information.)

- **Print Shop**. Print Shop is, without a doubt, the most popular home publishing program. It's affordable (under $50), it's easy to use, and it lets you create all manner of fun projects. (Go to www.broderbund.com for more information.)

- **PrintMaster.** Another popular home publishing suite (lower-priced than Print Shop), complete with all manner of home-related projects. (Go to www.broderbund.com for more information. )

note

Don't confuse relatively simple home publishing programs with more sophisticated (and more expensive) desktop publishing programs, such as Adobe Pagemaker and QuarkXPress, or graphics editing programs, such as Adobe Photoshop and Paint Shop Pro.

Figure 13.1 shows the home screen (called "the Hub") for PrintMaster, a very popular (and affordable) home publishing program. You can use PrintMaster to create banners, brochures, business cards, calendars, crafts, envelopes, forms, greeting cards, invitations, labels, letterheads, newsletters, postcards, and posters.

**FIGURE 13.1**

Use PrintMaster (and other home publishing programs) to create greeting cards, banners, photo albums, and other fun projects.

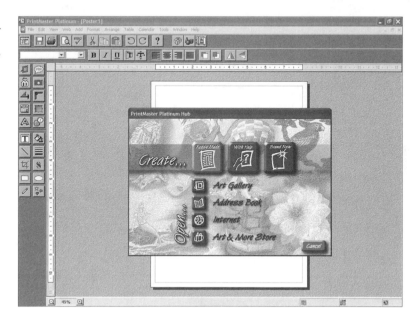

# Sending Electronic Greeting Cards

You don't have to buy a software program to make your own greeting cards—if you want to send them over the Internet, that is. There are many Web sites that offer free electronic cards that you can personalize and send to friends and family, as easily as you send email messages.

## Popular Greeting Card Sites

Most online greeting card sites offer their services for free; they make their money by selling advertising. Other sites charge a small fee, or offer basic cards for free and more deluxe cards for a price. In any case, check the terms and requirements before you start clicking!

Here are some of the most popular online greeting cards sites on the Web:

- Beat Greets (www.beatgreets.com)
- Birthday Cards.com (www.birthdaycards.com)
- Blue Mountain (www.bluemountain.com)
- Disney's D-Cards (disney.go.com/dcards/)
- eFun.com (www.efun.com)
- Hallmark E-Cards (www.hallmark.com)
- Lollipop Cards (www.lollipopcards.com)
- Museum of Modern Art E-Cards (moma.e-cards.org)
- Ohmygoodness (www.ohmygoodness.com)
- Yahoo! Greetings (greetings.yahoo.com)

## Sending a Card at Yahoo! Greetings

The two biggest online greeting card sites are Blue Mountain and Yahoo! Greetings. Let's take a quick look at how to send an online card, using Yahoo! Greetings as an example.

1. Launch Internet Explorer and connect to the Yahoo! Greetings Web site (greetings.yahoo.com). Figure 13.2 shows the Yahoo! Greetings home page.

**note**

Learn how to connect to the Internet and use Internet Explorer in Chapters 17 and 18.

**FIGURE 13.2**

The many different types of online greeting cards available at Yahoo! Greetings.

2. Click the type of card you want to send; this displays a selection of available cards.
3. Click the specific card you want to send; this displays the Personalize This Greeting page, shown in Figure 13.3.

**FIGURE 13.3**

Personalizing your online greeting card.

4. Scroll down to the Personalize Your Greeting Form and enter the required information (your name and email address, the recipient's name and email address, and an optional personal message).

5. Click the **Preview Your Greeting** button to preview your card.

6. Click the **Send This Greeting** button to send the card.

Your recipient now receives an email message from Yahoo! Greetings. This message doesn't include the card itself, but rather informs the recipient that they have a card waiting for them on the Yahoo! Greetings site. When the recipient clicks the link included in the email message, he or she is taken to the Yahoo! Greetings site, where your personalized greeting card is displayed.

# The Absolute Minimum

Here are the key points to remember from this chapter:

- When you want to create your own greeting cards, banners, albums, and so forth, you need home publishing software.

- Popular home publishing programs include Microsoft Picture It! Publishing, Print Shop, and PrintMaster.

- You can also send greeting cards electronically, over the Internet, from a variety of greeting card Web sites—including Blue Mountain and Yahoo! Greetings.

**14**

# LEARNING WITH EDUCATIONAL SOFTWARE

Personal computers aren't just for adults. Your PC can be a valuable learning tool for your children, especially if you get them started with the right educational software.

When you stroll the aisles of your local computer or electronics store, you'll find all manner of children's software. Not all of this software is educational; there are a lot of games (and game-like) software out there. (Don't take my word for it; turn to Chapter 15, "Playing Games," to learn more.)

Better to sit your kids down in front of your PC with a good educational program up and running. There are educational programs for all ages of kids, from preschool to high school, and beyond. Read on to learn about some of the best educational programs—including some really terrific encyclopedia software!

# Finding the Best Educational Software

The following list presents some of the best educational software on the market today, organized by age group. The publishers' Web site addresses are included, so you can log onto the Internet to find out more about each program.

**tip**

For reviews of the very latest educational software, turn to the SuperKids Web site (www.superkids.com).

## Early Learning

Early learning software is designed for your very youngest children—infant (or as soon as they can use a mouse) to preschool age. Most of this software is as fun as it is educational, with lots of brightly colored characters and fun music.

- Adventure Workshop: Preschool-1st Grade (www.broderbund.com)
- Curious George Downtown Adventure (www.vugames.com)
- Mickey Mouse Toddler/Mickey Mouse Preschool (disney.go.com/DisneyInteractive/learning/software.html)
- Pencil Pal Preschool (www.schoolzone.com)
- Reader Rabbit (www.broderbund.com)
- Sesame Street Toddler/Sesame Street Preschool (www.encoresoftware.com)

## Elementary

Educational software for elementary age children (K-6) introduces solid instructional technique, while still keeping things fun and lively.

- Adventure Workshop (www.broderbund.com)
- Discover Intensive Phonics for Yourself (www.intensivephonics.com)
- Earth's Dynamic Surface (www.tasagraphicarts.com/progeds.html)
- Flying Colors (www.magicmouse.com)
- JumpStart Series (www.vugames.com)
- Kid Performer (www.el2100.com)
- Kidspiration (www.kidspiration.com)
- Math Blaster (www.vugames.com)
- Reading Blaster (www.vugames.com)

Figure 14.1 shows one of the fun lessons in Math Blaster. Story problems were never this fun when I was a kid!

**FIGURE 14.1**

The fun way to learn mathematics skills— Math Blaster!

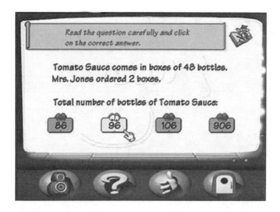

## High School

Educational software for junior high and high school kids is typically heavier on the education and lighter on the fun and games. This software is particularly helpful if your child is having trouble in a particular subject; it's like having a dedicated tutor on your PC!

- Cyber Ed Chemistry (www.cybered.net)
- Inspiration (www.kidspiration.com)
- Kaplan SAT, PSAT & ACT (www.kaplan.com)
- Math Advantage (www.encoresoftware.com)
- StudyWorks! Mathematics Deluxe (www.studyworksonline.com)

## Continuing Education

Continuing education software is for students of all ages—equally valuable for a 40 year-old adult as for an ambitious high schooler. Particularly popular are language education programs, as well as typing tutors.

- ChineseNow! (www.transparent.com)
- Easy Language Deluxe (www.bmsoftware.com/easylanguageds.htm)
- FrenchNow! (www.transparent.com)
- Learn to Speak Spanish (www.broderbund.com)
- Mavis Beacon Teaches Typing (www.broderbund.com)
- SpanishNow! (www.transparent.com)

# Using Encyclopedia Programs

One of the most popular types of educational software is the electronic encyclopedia. These encyclopedia programs are typically offshoots of respected print encyclopedias, supplemented with all manner of multimedia effects—including relevant audio and video clips.

## The Best Encyclopedia Software

The top-selling encyclopedia programs on the market today include:

- Encyclopedia Britannica (www.britannica.com)
- Grolier Multimedia Encyclopedia (gi.grolier.com)
- Microsoft Encarta (encarta.msn.com/reference/)
- World Book Encyclopedia (www.worldbook.com)

Encarta is particularly popular, as it's included as part of Microsoft Works Suite—which means that if you just purchased a new PC, you already have Encarta pre-installed.

## Using Microsoft Encarta

Since Encarta is so widely available, we'll use it as an example for our tour of encyclopedia programs. You can launch Encarta from either the Windows Start menu or the Works Task Launcher. When you launch Encarta, you'll be asked to insert the Encarta Encyclopedia disc. This is because Encarta is so large, so comprehensive, it can only be stored on CD-ROM. So insert the CD and get started!

When Encarta launches, it displays the Encarta Home screen, shown in Figure 14.2. From this screen you can:

- Use the Find box to search for specific information
- Choose from a master list of articles (called the *Pinpointer*)
- Go to the Article Center to view both Encarta articles and related articles on the Web
- View the Dynamic World Atlas for information on specific countries
- Go to the Maps Center to view more current and historical maps
- Go to the Multimedia Center to view articles that incorporate special audio and video features

**FIGURE 14.2**

Encarta's home page—you can find virtually anything from here!

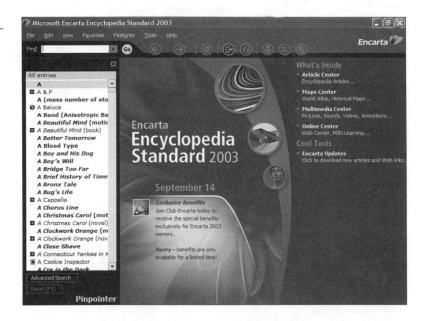

To navigate within Encarta, you use the buttons on the Encarta toolbar, located at the top of the screen. This toolbar is similar to Internet Explorer's toolbar, with navigation buttons to take you back and forward through individual pages. You can also use the pull-down menus to access specific features and tools—and return to Encarta Home at any time by clicking the **Home** button.

Encarta includes traditional text-based articles (like the one shown in Figure 14.3), as well as animations, sounds, images, videos, maps, and what Encarta calls *InterActivities*, which are hands-on interactive activities. (Select **Features**, **Games** to view a list of InterActivities.) Some Encarta entries are linked to the Encarta Web site, so you can go online to get additional or updated information. All in all, using Encarta is a rich and rewarding experience—and a fun way to find all sorts of information!

**FIGURE 14.3**

A typical Encarta article— all about big band jazz.

# THE ABSOLUTE MINIMUM

Here are the key points to remember from this chapter:

- There are all sorts of educational programs available for your children— including software targeted at specific skills and age groups.

- One of the most popular educational programs is the Microsoft Encarta encyclopedia, which is included as part of Microsoft Works Suite.

- Encarta includes traditional text-based articles, multimedia-enhanced articles, and links to additional information on the Web.

## In This Chapter

- Building a State-of-the-Art Gaming System
- Installing and Playing PC Games
- Playing Games Online
- Playing Games—Against Other Players

15

# Playing Games

One of the most popular uses of a personal computer has nothing to do with work—and everything to do with play. That's right, most people use their PCs, even just a little, for playing games.

There are all sorts of games you can play on your new PC. You can play traditional PC games, that you buy at your local computer store and install on your PC's hard disk. You can play simple games over the Internet, where you pit your skills against a competing computer. And you can also use the Internet to link to other gamers and play sophisticated multi-player online games, which can be a real trip.

Read on to learn how to get your computer system in tip-top shape for all this game playing—and then discover the best places to play these exciting games.

# Building a State-of-the-Art Gaming System

Believe it or not, the most demanding application for your new computer system is probably a game. With all those fancy graphics, gee-whiz sound effects, and high-speed action, computer games definitely put your computer system through its paces.

In fact, to get the *best* game play possible, you need a truly state-of-the-art computer system. If you purchased a low-end computer, you might find that it doesn't play the latest games quite as fast or as smoothly as you might have expected.

What can you do to beef up your system for better game play? Here are some things to keep in mind:

- If you're using an older PC, you might think about buying a new system with a fairly powerful processor. Think Pentium 4 or AMD Athlon, running at 1GHz or more.

- Whether you have a newer or an older PC, you'll want to increase its memory to at least 256MB, and probably to 512MB.

- You'll also need a lot of hard disk storage because the newer games take up a lot of disk space. Go for at least a 40GB hard disk—bigger if you can afford it.

- You should also consider upgrading to a DVD drive because many new games come on single DVDs rather than multiple CDs.

- You might need to upgrade your sound card. Consider going with a high-quality 3D sound card, and be sure you have a quality speaker system, complete with subwoofer.

- The capability to handle rapidly moving graphics is essential. If your PC's original video card isn't quite up to snuff, upgrade to either a 32MB or 64MB 3D video card with graphics accelerator.

- Big games look better on a big screen, so think about a 17" or even a 19" video monitor, if you have the desktop space.

- Finally, you need something other than your mouse to control your games. You'll want to invest in a good-quality joystick or similar game controller.

Learn more about installing new hardware in Chapter 33, "Adding New Hardware to Your System."

# Installing and Playing PC Games

Before you play a new PC game, you'll have to install the game software according to instructions. You might also, in some instances, need to keep the game CD in your PC's CD-ROM drive. (This is because many games access the CD to load images and sounds during the course of the game.)

You'll also need to have your game controller installed and connected, and then you're ready to play. You launch the new game from the Windows **Start** menu.

Every game operates a little bit differently. You typically are presented with some type of opening screen, sometimes in the form of an animated movie. Most games let you skip this animation by clicking somewhere (or anywhere) within the movie window.

After you get past the opening, you might need to configure various parameters for the game. For example, you might have to choose a user level (try starting with "beginner"), enter your player name, and so on. You should also take this opportunity to read the game's instructions, either onscreen (sometimes via the Help menu) or in an accompanying booklet.

Many games let you pause or save games in progress, so if you have to stop for the day, you can start up again tomorrow in the same spot. To save a game, follow the game's specific instructions to save your particular game file—typically by accessing some sort of "save" or "file" menu or function.

When you're ready to start playing again, all you have to do is load the previously saved game. This is typically accomplished as the game is loading, or via some type of "resume" or "file" menu. After the game is reloaded, you can resume play exactly where you stopped the day before.

## caution

Don't be *too* quick about bypassing the opening animation. Sometimes information essential to the game is presented in this movie.

## tip

There are several sites on the Internet that offer PC games you can download to your computer's hard disk—and a lot of them are free! Check out Free Games Net (www.free-games-net.com), GameSpot (www.gamespot.com), Gigex (www.gigex.com), and Tucows Games (games.tucows.com).

# Playing Games Online

Some of the most fun PC games don't have to be installed on your hard disk. Many sites on the Web offer all sorts of games to play online—often for free. Whether you're looking for a quick game of checkers or an evening-long session of Quake II, you can find dozens of sites to satisfy your craving for action and strategy.

You can play most online games by going to a gaming site and clicking the appropriate links. Everything you need to play the game is automatically loaded into your Web browser.

You'll need to read the instructions first, of course, especially if you need to find an online partner to play a particular game. Don't get too nervous about this; most sites make it extremely easy to play their most popular games.

What will you find when you log onto one of these online gaming emporiums? As you can see in Figure 15.1, most games sites include all sorts of games, including arcade games, board games, card games, casino games, puzzle games, trivia games, and word games. Most of these online games can be played free of charge—and some sites even hand out prizes to winning players! You can log on to these sites with a minimal amount of pre-play registration and then start playing with a few clicks of your mouse.

**FIGURE 15.1**

Play online games at MSN Gaming Zone.

If you're interested in playing some simple single-player online games, check out these Web sites:

- All Games Free (www.allgamesfree.com)
- ArcadeTown.com (www.arcadetown.com)
- BoxerJam.com (www.boxerjam.com)
- Flipside.com (www.flipside.com)
- Games Arena (www.thegamesarena.com)
- Games.com (play.games.com)
- Internet Chess (www.chessclub.com)
- Internet Park (www.internet-park.com)
- Lycos Gamesville (www.gamesville.lycos.com)
- MSN Gaming Zone (zone.msn.com)
- Playsite (www.playsite.com)
- Pogo.com (www.pogo.com)
- Yahoo! Games (games.yahoo.com)

# Playing Games—Against Other Players

Most PC games sold at retail today include a multiplayer option. This option lets you play the game against a human opponent. You can play another player on your local area network or find and play an opponent over the Internet.

Setting up a multiplayer game is relatively straightforward. You start by launching the game on your computer, then you connect to the Internet and log on to a specific Web site. This site can be hosted by the game manufacturer, or it can be a general gaming site that has licensing access to a particular game. In many cases, the site you need to log in to is hard-wired into the game software itself. All you have to do is pull down the menu and select the multiplayer option; then the game automatically connects itself to the proper Web site, using your normal Internet connection.

**tip**

The faster your Internet connection, the smoother the game play you'll experience. Broadband is better than dial-up.

After you're logged on to the site, you access the area of the site dedicated to your particular game. You can then choose to host a game (and look for other players) or join a game already in progress. You're then connected to the other player(s), and the game begins.

Most sites offering multiplayer gaming operate on a subscription basis—in other words, you have to pay to play. Subscription fees vary per site but are typically assessed on an hourly, a monthly, or a yearly basis. (Fees can run as low as $20 for lifetime access or as high as $2 per hour of play.) For this fee, you get the privilege of connecting to other users, as well as using the site's services to organize and coordinate both individual match-ups and tourneys.

The most popular of these multiplayer sites include:

- Battle.net (www.battle.net)
- EA.com (www.ea.com)
- GameSpy Arcade (www.gamespyarcade.com)
- Kahn (www.kahncentral.net)
- Kali (www.kali.net)
- MSN Gaming Zone (zone.msn.com)
- Ultimate Gamers (www.ultimategamers.com)

> **tip**
>
> There are also numerous sites on the Web that offer tips and reviews for the latest videogames. These sites include CheatStation (www.cheatstation.com), Extreme Gamers Network (www.extreme-gamers.net), Future Games Network (www.fgn.com), and IGN Guides (guides.ign.com).

# The Absolute Minimum

Here are the key points to remember from this chapter:

- To play games on your PC, you'll probably want to install a joystick or other type of game controller.
- You may also need to upgrade parts of your computer system to play some of the more audio and visually demanding PC games.
- There are many sites on the Internet that let you play simple single-player games.
- Many computer games feature multi-player options; you can play against other players over a home network, or on the Internet.

# Using the Internet

16 Understanding the Internet . . . . . . . . 179

17 Getting Connected to the Internet . . . . 183

18 Surfing the Web . . . . . . . . . . . . . . . 191

19 Finding Stuff Online . . . . . . . . . . . . 199

20 Buying and Selling Online . . . . . . . . . 209

21 Sending and Receiving Email . . . . . . . 221

22 Using Instant Messaging and Chat . . . . 231

23 Using Newsgroups, Message Boards,
   and Mailing Lists . . . . . . . . . . . . . . 237

24 Downloading Files . . . . . . . . . . . . . 243

25 Creating Your Own Web Page . . . . . . . 247

## IN THIS CHAPTER

- What the Internet Is—and What It Isn't
- How an Internet Connection Works
- The Most Important Parts of the Internet

# 16

# UNDERSTANDING THE INTERNET

It used to be that most people bought personal computers to do work—word processing, spreadsheets, databases, the types of programs that still make up the core of Microsoft Works Suite and Microsoft Office. But today, a large number of people also buy PCs to access the Internet—to send and receive email, surf the Web, and chat with other users.

# What the Internet Is—and What It Isn't

If you're new to the Internet, keep one thing in mind: The Internet isn't a thing. You can't touch it or see it or smell it; you can't put it in a box and buy it. The Internet is like the huge power grid that provides electricity to homes across the country—it exists between the points of usage.

So, if the Internet isn't a physical thing, what is it? It's really more simple than you might think; the Internet is nothing more than a really big computer network. In fact, it's a computer network that connects other computer networks—what some would call a "network of networks."

Just being connected to the Internet, however, really doesn't accomplish anything. It's much the same as having electricity run to your home—that wall outlet doesn't do anything until you plug something into it. The same thing is true with the Internet; the Internet itself just kind of sits there until you plug something into it that takes advantage of it.

# How an Internet Connection Works

A dial-up Internet connection, such as the one shown in Figure 16.1, is actually fairly simple. It works like this:

**FIGURE 16.1**

Your computer connects to the Internet via your ISP's network.

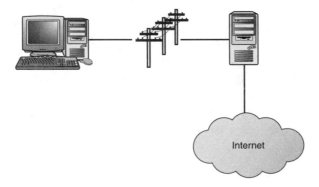

1. Your personal computer connects to a normal phone line, using a piece of hardware called a *modem*.

2. Your modem dials into your *Internet service provider (ISP)* and logs in to your personal account. (Your ISP has a modem on its end that converts the analog signals from your modem into digital signals that its computers can understand.)

3. Your ISP plugs the signal from your computer into the Internet.

Your computer is now connected to the Internet, through your ISP. After you're connected, you can access any site or service on the Internet, as well as any mail or news servers run by your ISP. When you disconnect from your ISP (hang up your phone line), you're no longer connected to the Internet, and you can't access any Internet-based sites or services—until you connect again, that is.

Now, the only problem with connecting to the Internet via a dial-up connection is that it's relatively slow.  Connection speed is measured in kilobits per second (Kbps), and a typical dial-up connection runs at 56.6Kbps—and can take a long time to download big files and graphically intense Web pages.

You can connect faster through what is called a *broadband* connection. Broadband uses special DSL phone lines or cable lines to connect anywhere from 400Kbps to 2000Kbps. If you're interested in a broadband connection, contact your local phone company (for DSL service) or cable company (for cable broadband) about availability.

# The Most Important Parts of the Internet

When you're connected to the Internet, there are a variety of services you can use. These include messaging services (email and chat), community services (Usenet newsgroups), and interactive/informational services (the World Wide Web). The Internet itself doesn't actually perform any of these activities, but it does *enable* these activities to occur. And when you connect to the Internet through your personal computer, you have access to all these activities and more.

What follows is a little background on each of these popular services.

- **World Wide Web.** The World Wide Web is the showiest part of the Internet, the place where information of all types is presented in a highly visual, often multimedia, format. You view a Web page with a Web *browser*, such as Microsoft's Internet Explorer and Netscape Navigator. Chances are you have one or both of these browsers. (Learn more in Chapter 18, "Surfing the Web.")

- **Email.** Electronic mail *(email)* is a means of communicating with other Internet users via letters, written and delivered electronically over the Internet. Although email messages look a lot like traditional letters, email itself is very different from the so-called "snail mail" delivered by the United States Postal Service—delivery is almost instantaneous, and it's free. (Learn more in Chapter 21, "Sending and Receiving Email.")

- **Instant messaging (IM).** This is a method for real-time, one-on-one text-based conversations between two Internet users. (Learn more in Chapter 22, "Using Instant Messaging and Chat.")

- **Internet Relay Chat (IRC)**. IRC is a series of servers and chat channels where groups of Internet users "talk" to each other (via text messages), in real-time. (Learn more in Chapter 22, "Using Instant Messaging and Chat.")

- **Usenet newsgroups**. Usenet is a collection of online bulletin boards you can use to communicate with users interested in a particular topic. ("Learn more in Chapter 23, "Using Newsgroups, Mailing Lists, and Message Boards.")

- **File Transfer Protocol (FTP)**. This is a method for downloading computer files from dedicated servers. (Learn more in Chapter 24, "Downloading Files.")

- **Internet radio**. This is the part of the Internet where Web-based radio stations "broadcast" in real-time. (Learn more in Chapter 28, "Playing Internet Audio and Video.")

- **MP3**. This is a file format for digitally storing songs and other audio, used by many to download and record near-CD quality music from the Internet. (Learn more in Chapter 29, "Downloading and Playing Digital Music.")

# THE ABSOLUTE MINIMUM

Here are the key things to remember about the Internet:

- The Internet is nothing more than a giant computer network.

- You connect to the Internet through an Internet service provider, which you reach through normal phone lines.

- The typical dial-up connection is a relatively slow 56.6Kbps; faster broadband connections (via cable or DSL) transfer data up to 35 times faster.

- After you're connected to the Internet, you can perform a variety of activities, including sending and receiving email and surfing the World Wide Web.

## IN THIS CHAPTER

- Different Types of Connections
- Choosing an ISP
- Before You Connect
- Setting Up a Completely New Account
- Setting Up an Existing Account
- Sharing an Internet Connection
- Connecting

17

# GETTING CONNECTED TO THE INTERNET

Before you can go online, you have to subscribe to Internet service through an Internet service provider (ISP) and then configure your computer for the new connection.

With Windows XP, setting up your computer for your particular Internet connection is fairly easy. After you have your ISP account established, all you have to do is tell Windows about your account and plug in a few cables, and then you're ready to start surfing!

# Different Types of Connections

The first step in going online is establishing a connection between your computer and the Internet. Depending on what's available in your area, you can choose from two primary types of connections:

- **A dial-up connection**—A dial-up connection means that you connect to the Internet over normal phone lines. The fastest dial-up connections transmit data at 56.6Kbps (kilobits per second). Most ISPs charge $20–$30 for normal dial-up service.

- **A broadband connection**—Broadband offers ultra-fast speeds, using DSL, digital cable, or satellite technology. With a broadband connection, data is transmitted at anywhere from 400Kbps to 2000Kbps. (Cable is typically the fastest connection, and satellite is the slowest; DSL is somewhere in between.) This means that a broadband connection is anywhere from 7 to 35 times faster than a typical dial-up connection. Most ISPs charge $40–$50 for broadband service.

# Choosing an ISP

A pure ISP does nothing but connect you to the Internet and provide you with an email address and mailbox—and, in some cases, storage space for your own personal Web page. You can probably find a few local ISPs operating in your city or town, or you can turn to one of a handful of national ISPs. These national ISPs offer dial-up numbers all across the U.S. (great for when you're traveling).

Commercial online services, such as America Online (AOL) and the Microsoft Network (MSN), function like ISPs but also provide their own unique content and interfaces. If you sign up for AOL, for example, you use AOL's software to connect to the Internet and can also access AOL-specific content and services not available anywhere else.

> **tip**
>
> The two largest national ISPs are AT&T WorldNet (www.att.net) and EarthLink (www.earthlink.net). You can find a list of more than 10,000 national and local ISPs at The List (thelist.internet.com).

Many new computer users prefer to connect to AOL because it's so easy to use. (You can see what the main AOL screen looks like in Figure 17.1.) On the other hand, many experienced computer users don't like being forced to use AOL's software and prefer to go with a normal ISP.

**FIGURE 17.1**
Connecting to
the Internet via
America Online.

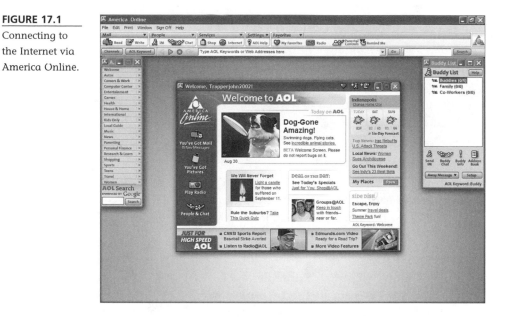

Whichever type of service you choose, you'll pay about the same amount each
month.

# Before You Connect

When you sign up with an ISP, both you and the
ISP have to provide certain information to each
other. You provide your name, address, and
credit card number; your ISP provides a variety
of semi-technical information, including:

- The phone number to dial into
- Your username and password
- Your email address
- The names of the ISP's incoming and out-
  going mail servers
- Your email account name and password
- The name of your ISP's Usenet news server

> **tip**
>
> For most ISPs, your user-
> name, email account name,
> and the first half of your
> email address will all be the
> same. It's also likely that you
> will be assigned a single
> password for both your ini-
> tial login and email access.

You'll need this information for when you configure Windows for your new Internet
connection—which we'll discuss next.

# Setting Up a Completely New Account

If you don't yet have an account with an ISP, you can use Windows XP's New Connection Wizard to find and subscribe to an ISP. All you have to do is connect your telephone line to your PC's modem and follow these steps:

1. Click the **Start** button to display the **Start** menu.

2. Select **Connect to**, **Show All Connections**; this displays the Network Connections window.

3. Select **Create a New Connection** (from the Network Tasks panel) to launch the New Connection Wizard.

4. Click the **Next** button to display the Network Connection Type screen.

5. Check the **Connect to the Internet** option and then click the **Next** button to display the Getting Ready screen.

6. Check the **Choose from a List of Internet Providers** option and then click the **Next** button.

**note**

If the Show All Connections option doesn't appear on your Start menu, open My Computer, select Network Places, and then select View Network Connections.

7. Check the **Select from a List of Other ISPs** option and then click the **Finish** button. (Alternatively, if you want to set up an account with MSN, you can click the **Get Online with MSN** option.)

8. Windows now opens the Online Services window. You can choose from one of the providers listed here or click the **Refer Me to More Internet Service Providers** icon.

9. If you choose to look for more ISPs, the wizard now dials into the Microsoft Internet

**caution**

The Microsoft Internet Referral Service isn't always accurate or complete and might not always find all the ISPs available in your area.

Referral Service and downloads a list of available ISPs. Select an ISP from this list, and follow the onscreen instructions to sign up for a new account.

After you've selected an ISP, the wizard does everything else for you—including setting up a new connection within Windows.

# Setting Up an Existing Account

If you already have an account set up with an ISP, you can create a new connection for that ISP by entering its settings manually. Just follow these steps:

1. Click the **Start** button to display the **Start** menu.

2. Select **Connect to**, **Show All Connections** to open the Network Connections window.

3. Select **Create a New Connection** (from the Network Tasks panel) to launch the New Connection Wizard.

4. Click the **Next** button to display the Network Connection Type screen.

5. Check the **Connect to the Internet** option and then click the **Next** button to display the Getting Ready screen.

6. Check the **Set Up My Connection Manually** option, then click **Next** to display the Internet Connection screen.

7. Select how you want to connect to the Internet. If you're connecting through a dial-up connection, check the **Connect Using a Dial-Up Modem** option. If you're connecting via a DSL or cable modem connection that requires manual login, check the **Connect Using a Broadband Connection That Requires a Username and Password** option. If you're connecting through an always-on LAN, cable modem, or DSL connection, check the **Connect Using a Broadband Connection That Is Always On** option. Click **Next** when you've made your selection.

> **tip**
>
> If your ISP provided you with an installation CD, check the **Use the CD I Got from an ISP** option and follow the onscreen instructions from there.

8. Follow the onscreen instructions for your specific type of installation. You'll probably need to enter your username, password, and specific information about your ISP. The wizard now completes your connection.

# Sharing an Internet Connection

If you have more than one PC in your home, you can connect them to share a single Internet connection. This is particularly useful if you have a high-speed broadband connection.

To do this, you must have your computers networked together, as shown in Figure 17.2. The main computer—the one connected to the Internet—is designated as the *host*, and all the others are called *clients*. Each of the client computers must have a network card installed, and the host must have *two* network cards installed—one to connect to your broadband modem and the other to connect to your other computers.

**FIGURE 17.2**

Connecting all your computers in a network to share an Internet connection.

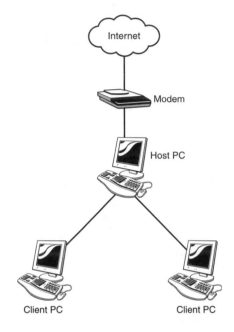

## Configuring the Host PC

Assuming that you already have your computers connected in a network, setting up the network to share an Internet connection is relatively easy. Just follow these steps:

1. On the host computer, click the **Start** button to display the **Start** menu.

2. Select **Connect to**, **Show All Connections** to open the Network Connections window.

3. Right-click the icon for the Internet connection you want to share, and then select **Properties** from the pop-up menu; this opens the Properties dialog box for that connection.

**note**

To learn how to connect your computers in a home network, see Chapter 34, "Setting Up a Home Network."

4. Select the **Advanced** tab.

5. Check the **Allow Other Network Users to Connect Through This Computer's Internet Connection** option.

6. Click **OK**.

## Configuring the Client PCs

Now you need to configure each of the other PCs on your network—the *client* PCs—to share this connection. If the computers are all running Windows XP, the process is fairly straightforward. Just follow these steps for each client PC:

1. Click the **Start** button to display the **Start** menu.

2. Select **Connect to**, **Show All Connections** to open the Network Connections window.

3. Select **Create a New Connection** (from the Network Tasks panel) to launch the New Connection Wizard.

4. Click the **Next** button to display the Network Connection Type screen.

5. Check the **Connect to the Internet** option and then click the **Next** button to display the Getting Ready screen.

6. Check the **Set Up My Connection Manually** option, then click **Next** to display the Internet Connection screen.

7. Check the **Connect Using a Broadband Connection That Is Always On** option, then click **Next**.

8. Click the **Finish** button.

note

When you configure Windows XP to share an Internet connection, it automatically activates the Internet Connection Firewall to protect your system from hackers and other outside attacks. To learn more about protecting your system, see Chapter 32, "Protecting Your PC Online."

## Configuring Non-Windows XP PCs

If any of your client computers are running older (pre-Windows XP) versions of Windows, you must run the Network Setup Wizard directly from your Windows XP installation CD.

To run the Network Setup Wizard on a pre-XP machine, follow these steps:

1. Insert the Windows XP installation CD in the PC's CD-ROM drive.

2. When the setup program launches, click the **Perform Additional Tasks** option.

3. When the next screen appears, select **Set Up a Home or Small Office Network**.

4. Follow the onscreen instructions to activate Internet Connection Sharing.

## Connecting

After you've configured your PC for your ISP account, you're ready to get connected and start surfing.

How you initiate a connection differs a bit from ISP to ISP. Depending on how your ISP sets things up, you can use one or more of the following methods:

■ If your ISP or online service installed its own connection software, you must launch that connection program and follow its instructions to make a connection. For example, America Online installs its own AOL software; launch this software, and then use it to connect to the Internet.

■ You can probably connect to your ISP directly from Windows. Click the **Start** button to display the **Start** menu; then select **Connect to** and select your ISP from the list of available connections.

■ If you have an always-on broadband connection, you don't need to do anything—you're already connected! Just launch Internet Explorer, Outlook Express, or any other Internet program, and you're ready to surf.

# THE ABSOLUTE MINIMUM

When you're configuring your new PC system to connect to the Internet, remember these important points:

■ You connect to the Internet through an Internet service provider; you need to set up an account with an ISP before you can connect.

■ Most ISPs offer either dial-up or broadband connections. Broadband is faster but costs about twice as much per month.

■ After you have an account with an ISP, you need to run the New Connection Wizard to configure Windows for your new account.

■ If you have more than one computer at home, you can connect them in a network and share a single Internet connection.

## In This Chapter

- Understanding the Web
- Using Internet Explorer
- Basic Web Surfing
- Advanced Operations
- Let's Go Surfin'!

**18**

# Surfing the Web

After you're signed up with an ISP and connected to the Internet, it's time to get surfing! The World Wide Web is a particular part of the Internet with all sorts of cool content and useful services, and you surf the Web with a piece of software called a *Web browser*.

The most popular Web browser today is Microsoft's Internet Explorer, and you probably have a copy of it already installed on your new PC. This chapter shows you how to use Internet Explorer and then takes you on a quick trip around the Web—just enough to get your online feet wet!

# Understanding the Web

Before you can surf the Web, you need to understand a little bit about how it works.

Information on the World Wide Web is presented in *pages*. A Web page is similar to a page in a book, made up of text and pictures (also called *graphics*). A Web page differs from a book page, however, in that it can include other elements, such as audio and video, and links to other Web pages.

It's this linking to other Web pages that makes the Web such a dynamic way to present information. A *link* on a Web page can point to another Web page on the same site or to another site. Most links are included as part of a Web page's text and are called *hypertext links*. (If a link is part of a graphic, it's called a *graphic link*.) Links are usually in a different color from the rest of the text and often are underlined; when you click a link, you're taken directly to the linked page.

Web pages reside at a Web *site*. A Web site is nothing more than a collection of Web pages (each in its own individual computer file) residing on a host computer. The host computer is connected full-time to the Internet so you can access the site—and its Web pages—anytime you access the Internet. The main page at a Web site usually is called a *home page*, and it often serves as an opening screen that provides a brief overview and menu of everything you can find at that site. The address of a Web page is called a *URL*, which stands for uniform resource locator. Most URLs start with `http://`, add a `www.`, continue with the name of the site, and end with a `.com`.

**note**

Of course, you can use any Web browser to surf the Web—the instructions here work equally as well with Netscape or MSN Explorer, or the browser built into America Online.

**tip**

You can normally leave off the `http://` when you enter an address into your Web browser.

# Using Internet Explorer

Internet Explorer (IE) is a very easy program to use. To launch IE, follow these steps:

1. Click the **Start** button to display the **Start** menu.
2. Select **Internet** (at the very upper-left part of the menu).

Figure 18.1 shows the various parts of the IE program, and Table 18.1 tells you what each of the buttons on the toolbar does.

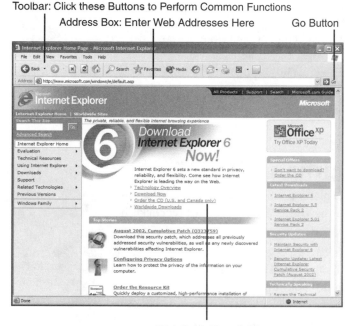

Toolbar: Click these Buttons to Perform Common Functions

Address Box: Enter Web Addresses Here        Go Button

**FIGURE 18.1**
Microsoft's
Internet Explorer
Web browser.

Web Page Hyperlink

## TABLE 18.1.   Internet Explorer Toolbar Buttons

| | Button | Operation |
|---|---|---|
| Back ▾ | Back | Return to the previously viewed page |
| → ▾ | Forward | View the next page |
| ✕ | Stop | Stop loading the current page |
| ↻ | Refresh | Reload the current page |
| ⌂ | Home | Return to your designated start page |
| Search | Search | Display the Search pane and initiate a Web search |
| Favorites | Favorites | Display the Favorites pane |
| Media | Media | Display the Media pane—for listening to Internet audio and watching online videos |

**TABLE 18.1.** Internet Explorer Toolbar Buttons

| Button | Operation |
|--------|--------|------|
| ⊘ | History | Display the History pane to see a list of recently viewed pages |
| ✉ ▾ | Mail | Launch your email program |
| 🖨 | Print | Print the current page |
| W ▾ | Edit | Launch your HTML Web page editor |

# Basic Web Surfing

Internet Explorer enables you to quickly and easily browse the World Wide Web—just by clicking your mouse. Here's a step-by-step tour of IE's basic functions:

**tip**

To change Internet Explorer's home page, drag a page's icon from Internet Explorer's Address box onto the Home button on the toolbar.

1. When you first launch Internet Explorer, it loads your predefined home page.

2. Enter a new Web address in the Address box, and press **Enter** (or click the **Go** button). Internet Explorer loads the new page.

3. Click any link on the current Web page. Internet Explorer loads the new page.

4. To return to the previous page, click the **Back** button (or press the **Backspace** key on your keyboard). If you've backed up several pages and want to return to the page you were on last, click the **Forward** button.

5. To return to your start page, click the **Home** button.

# Advanced Operations

Before we take our first cruise on the Web, let's examine a few advanced operations in Internet Explorer that can make your online life a lot easier.

## Saving Your Favorite Pages

When you find a Web page you like, you can add it to a list of Favorites within Internet Explorer. This way you can easily access any of your favorite sites just by selecting them from the list.

To add a page to your Favorites list

1. Go to the Web page you want to add to your Favorites list.
2. Pull down the **Favorites** menu, and select **Add to Favorites**.
3. When the Add Favorite dialog box appears, confirm the page's Name and then click the **Create In** button to extend the dialog box.
4. Select the folder where you want to place this link, and then click **OK**.

To view a page in your Favorites list

1. Click the **Favorites** button.  The browser window will automatically split into two panes, with your favorites displayed in the left pane (see Figure 18.2).

**FIGURE 18.2**

Click the **Favorites** button to display the Favorites pane.

2. Click any folder in the Favorites pane to display the contents of that folder.
3. Click a favorite page, and that page is displayed in the right pane.
4. Click the **Favorites** button again to hide the Favorites pane.

## Revisiting History

Internet Explorer has two ways of keeping track of Web pages you've visited, so you can easily revisit them without having to re-enter the Web page address.

To revisit one of the last half-dozen or so pages viewed in your current session, click the down-arrow on the **Back** button. This drops down a menu containing the last nine pages you've visited. Highlight any page on this menu to jump directly to that page.

To revisit pages you've viewed in the past several days, you use IE's History pane. Just follow these steps:

1. Click the **History** button. The browser window automatically splits into two panes, with your history for the past several days displayed in the left pane.

2. Your history is organized into folders for each of the past several days. Click any folder in the History pane to display the sites you visited that day.

3. Each site you visited on a particular day has its own subfolder. Click a subfolder to display the pages you visited within that particular site.

**tip**

To sort the sites in the History pane by site, by most visited, or by most visited today, pull down the **View** menu within the pane and make a new selection.

4. Click a specific page to display that page in the right pane.

5. Click the **History** button again to hide the History pane.

## Printing

Printing a Web page is easy— just click the **Print** button. If you want to see a preview of the page before it prints, pull down the **File** menu and select **Print Preview**.

# Let's Go Surfin'!

Okay, now you're ready to launch Internet Explorer and head out to the World Wide Web. Follow these step-by-step instructions for a quick cruise around the Web—just to see what's out there:

1. Connect to your ISP, and then launch Internet Explorer. IE appears on your desk top and displays its default home page. (Typically, this is some page on Microsoft's Web site.)

2. Let's find out what's happening out in the real world by heading over to one of the most popular news sites. Enter www.cnn.com into the Address box, and

then click the Go button. This takes you to the CNN.com site, shown in Figure 18.3. Click any headline to read the complete story.

**FIGURE 18.3**

Get informed at CNN.com.

**FIGURE 18.3**

Get informed at CNN.com.

3. Now, let's do a little searching at Google, one of the Web's premier search sites. (You can learn more about searching in Chapter 19, "Finding Stuff Online.") Enter www.google.com in the Address box, and then click the **Go** button. (Figure 18.5 shows Google's home page.) Ready to search? Enter molehill group in the Google search box, and then click the **Google Search** button.

**FIGURE 18.4**

Search for other Web sites at Google.

4. When the search results page appears, find the listing for The Molehill Group and click the link. You're now taken to *my* Web site, The Molehill Group (shown in Figure 18.6). Click the Michael Miller button (at the top of the page) to learn more about me.

**FIGURE 18.5**

Learn more about the author at the Molehill Group Web site.

That's your quick surfing tour. You can keep surfing from here, or close Internet Explorer and disconnect from the Internet. As you can see, surfing the Web is as easy as clicking your mouse!

# THE ABSOLUTE MINIMUM

Here are the key things to remember about surfing the Web:

■ You surf the Web with a program called a Web browser; Internet Explorer is probably the browser installed on your new PC.

■ You can go to a particular Web page by entering the page's address in the Address box and then clicking the **Go** button.

■ Click a hyperlink on a Web page to jump to the linked page.

■ Use IE's Favorites list to store your favorite Web pages for easy retrieval.

■ Use the **Back** button or the History pane to revisit recently viewed Web pages.

## In This Chapter

- How to Search
- Where to Search
- Searching for People
- Searching for News, Sports, and Weather
- Searching for Financial Information
- Searching for Medical Information
- Searching—For Seniors

**19**

# Finding Stuff Online

Now that you know how to surf the Web, how do you find the precise information you're looking for? If you're lucky, someone has given you a URL for a specific site, and it's easy to enter that URL into Internet Explorer's Address box. If you're *not* lucky, you'll have to search for that site yourself.

Fortunately, there are numerous sites that help you search the Web for the specific information you want. These sites—called *search engines* and *directories*—all work in pretty much the same fashion.

This chapter is all about searching the Web. You'll learn the best places to search, and the best ways to search. I'll even help you cheat a little by listing some of the most popular sites for different types of information.

So pull up a chair, launch your Web browser, and loosen up those fingers—it's time to start searching!

# How to Search

Almost every search site on the Web contains two basic components—a *search box* and a *search button*. You enter your query—one or more *keywords* that describe what you're looking for—into the search box, and then click the Search button (or press the Enter key) to start the search. The search site then returns a list of Web pages that match your query; click any link to go directly to the page in question.

## Constructing a Query

How you construct your query determines how relevant the results will be that you receive. It's important to focus on the keywords you use, because the search sites look for these words when they process your query. Your keywords are compared to the Web pages the search site knows about; the more keywords found on a Web page, the better the match.

You should choose keywords that best describe the information you're looking for—using as many keywords as you need. Don't be afraid of using too many keywords; in fact, using too *few* keywords is a common fault of many novice searchers. The more words you use, the better idea the search engine has of what you're looking for.

## Using Wildcards

But what if you're not quite sure which word to use? For example, would the best results come from looking for *auto*, *automobile*, or *automotive*? Many search sites let you use *wildcards* to "stand in" for parts of a word that you're not quite sure about.

**tip**

If you're searching for a specific phrase, enclose that phrase in quotation marks. For example, to search for Monty Python, enter **"Monty Python"** and *not* **Monty Python**; the first query returns pages about the comedy troupe, while the second returns pages about snakes and guys named Monty.

In most instances, the asterisk character (*) is used as a wildcard to match any character or group of characters, from its particular position in the word to the end of that word. So, in the previous example, entering `auto*` would return all three words—auto, automobile, *and* automotive (as well as automatic, autocratic, and any other word that starts with "auto").

# Where to Search

Now that you know how to search, *where* should you search?

There are two ways to organize the information on the Web. One way is to physically look at each Web page and stick it into a hand-picked category. After you get enough Web pages collected, you have something called a *directory*.

The other way to organize the information on the Web is to use a *search engine*. Unlike a directory, which is organized by people, a search engine isn't powered by human hands. Instead, a search engine uses a special type of software program (called a *spider* or *crawler*) to roam the Web automatically, feeding what it finds back to a massive bank of computers. These computers hold *indexes* of the Web, hundreds of millions of pages strong—many more pages than are found in the typical Web directory.

# Directory Searching with Yahoo!

A directory doesn't actually search the Web—in fact, a directory catalogs only a very small part of the Web. But a directory is very organized, and very easy to use, and lots and lots of people use Web directories every day.

The most popular Web directory is Yahoo! (www.yahoo.com), shown in Figure 19.1. When you access Yahoo!'s main page, you can choose to search the Yahoo! directory or to browse through the directory's main categories. Since Yahoo! is so well-organized, clicking through the categories is a good way for less-experienced users to find what they want.

**FIGURE 19.1**

The most popular directory on the Web: Yahoo!

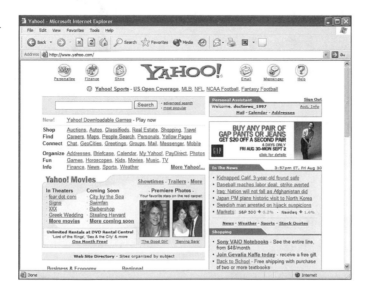

## Index Searching with Google

When you enter a query at a search engine site, your query is sent to the search engine's index. (You never actually search the Web itself, you only search the index that was created by the spiders crawling the Web.) The search engine then creates a list of pages in its index that match, to one degree or another, the query you entered.

The best (and most popular) search engine today is Google (www.google.com), which you first saw back in Chapter 18, "Surfing the Web." Google is easy to use, is extremely fast, and returns highly relevant results. That's because it indexes more pages than any other site. While Google's results aren't as well-organized as Yahoo!'s, you'll receive a lot more pages that match your query.

**note**

Some search directories supplement their listings with results from search engines. For example, Yahoo! supplements its directory listings with results from the Google search engine.

## Other Good Search Sites

While Yahoo! and Google are the best directory and search engines, respectively, there are lots of other search sites that also provide more (or just different) results. These search sites include:

- About.com (www.about.com)
- AllTheWeb (www.alltheweb.com)
- AltaVista (www.altavista.com)
- Ask Jeeves! (www.askjeeves.com)
- Excite (www.excite.com)
- HotBot (www.hotbot.com)
- LookSmart (www.looksmart.com)
- Lycos (www.lycos.com)
- Open Directory (www.dmoz.org)

**tip**

There are also a number of search engines that let you search multiple search engines and directories from a single page—which is called a *metasearch*. The top metasearchers include Dogpile (www.dogpile.com), GoGettem (www.gogettem.com), Mamma (www.mamma.com), MetaCrawler (www.metacrawler.com), OneSeek (www.oneseek.com), WebCrawler (www.webcrawler.com), and WebTaxi(www.webtaxi.com) .

# Searching for People

As good as Google and other search sites are for finding specific Web pages, they're not that great for finding people. When there's a person (or an address or a phone number) you want to find, you need to use a site that specializes in people searches.

People listings on the Web go by the common name of *white pages directories*, the same as traditional white pages phone books. These directories typically enable you to enter all or part of a person's name and then search for his address and phone number. Many of these sites also let you search for personal email addresses and business addresses and phone numbers.

The best of these directories include

- AnyWho (www.anywho.com)
- InfoSpace (www.infospace.com)
- Switchboard (www.switchboard.com)
- WhitePages.com (www.whitepages.com)
- WhoWhere (www.whowhere.lycos.com)

# Searching for News, Sports, and Weather

The Internet is a great place to find both news headlines and in-depth analysis. Most news-related Web sites are updated in real-time, so you're always getting the latest news—on your computer screen, when you want it.

## Searching for the Latest News

Some of the biggest, most popular news sites on the Web are run by the major broadcast and cable news networks, or by the major national newspapers. You can turn to these sites to get the latest headlines, and—in many cases—live audio and video feeds.

The major news sites on the Web include

- ABC News (www.abcnews.com)
- CBS News (www.cbsnews.com)
- CNN (www.cnn.com)
- Fox News (www.foxnews.com)
- MSNBC (www.msnbc.com)
- *New York Times* (www.nytimes.com)
- *USA Today* (www.usatoday.com)

## Searching for Sports Headlines and Scores

The Web is a great resource for sports fans of all shapes and sizes. Whether you're a fan or a participant, there's at least one site somewhere on the Web that focuses on your particular sport.

The best sports sites on the Web resemble the best news sites—they're actually portals to all sorts of content and services, including up-to-the-minute scores, post-game recaps, in-depth reporting, and much more. If you're looking for sports information online, one of these portals is the place to start:

> **tip**
>
> If you follow a particular sports team, check out that team's local newspaper on the Web. Chances are you'll find a lot of in-depth coverage there that you won't find at these other sites.

- CBS SportsLine (www.sportsline.com)
- CNN/Sports Illustrated (sportsillustrated.cnn.com)
- ESPN.com (espn.go.com)
- FOXSports (foxsports.lycos.com)
- NBC Sports (www.nbcsports.com)
- The Sporting News (www.sportingnews.com)

## Searching for Weather Reports

Weather reports and forecasts are readily available on the Web; most of the major news portals and local Web sites offer some variety of weather-related services. There are also a number of dedicated weather sites on the Web, all of which offer local and national forecasts, weather radar, satellite maps, and more.

Here are the most popular weather sites on the Web:

- AccuWeather (www.accuweather.com)
- Intellicast (www.intellicast.com)
- National Weather Service (www.nws.noaa.gov)
- Weather Underground (www.wunderground.com)
- Weather.com (www.weather.com)

Figure 19.2 shows the Weather.com site, from the folks at the Weather Channel.

**FIGURE 19.2**

Getting the latest weather reports at Weather.com.

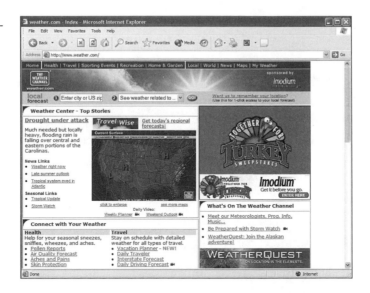

## Searching for Financial Information

The Internet is a great place to find up-to-the-minute information about stocks and other securities. Several sites and services specialize in providing real-time (or slightly delayed) stock quotes—for free!

Here's a short list of the best financial sites on the Web—both free and for-a-fee:

- CBS Marketwatch (cbs.marketwatch.com)
- CNN/Money (money.cnn.com)
- Hoovers Online (www.hoovers.com)
- Motley Fool (www.fool.com)
- MSN MoneyCentral (moneycentral.msn.com)
- Yahoo! Finance (finance.yahoo.com)

## Searching for Medical Information

The Internet is a fount of information of all different types. It's a particularly good research tool for health-related information.

A number of Web sites offer detailed information about illnesses, diseases, and medicines. Many of these sites focus on preventive medicine and wellness, and almost all help you match symptoms with likely illnesses and treatments. Indeed, some of these sites provide access to the same medical databases used by most physicians—without waiting for an appointment!

The top medical sites on the Web include

- healthAtoZ.com (www.healthatoz.com)
- kidsDoctor (www.kidsdoctor.com)
- MedExplorer (www.medexplorer.com)
- MedicineNet (www.medicinenet.com)
- National Library of Medicine (www.nlm.nih.gov)
- Planet Wellness (www.planetwellness.com)
- WebMD Health (my.webmd.com)

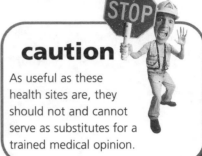

**caution**

As useful as these health sites are, they should not and cannot serve as substitutes for a trained medical opinion.

Figure 19.3 shows the WebMD Health Web site.

**FIGURE 19.3**

Search for medical information at WebMD Health.

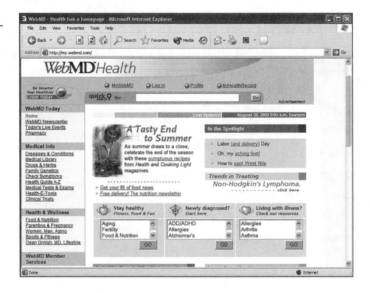

## Searching—For Seniors

Older users are making up a larger and larger percentage of the Internet population. Because of this, there are now several sites that specialize in information of interest to seniors. The best of these sites include

- AARP Webplace (www.aarp.org)
- Senior Information Network (www.senior-inet.com)
- Senior Surfers (www.seniorsurfers.org)
- Senior Women Web (www.seniorwomen.com)
- ThirdAge (www.thirdage.com)

**tip**

You can also use the Web to search for a new or specialist physician in your area. Some of the best physician search sites include AMA Physician Select (www.ama-assn.org/aps/), Best Doctors (www.bestdoctors.com), DoctorDirectory.com (www.doctordirectory.com), and mydoctor.com (www.mydoctor.com).

# THE ABSOLUTE MINIMUM

Here are the key points to remember from this chapter:

- When you need to search for specific information on the Internet, you can use one of the Web's many search engines and directories.
- A directory includes a smaller number of hand-picked Web sites, typically organized by category; a search engine includes a larger number of Web sites discovered by automated software "spiders."
- The most popular Web directory is Yahoo!; the most popular search engine is Google.
- It's better to search for people (and their phone numbers and addresses) at specific people-search sites, such as InfoSpace and Switchboard.
- The most popular news sites on the Web are those run by traditional news organizations, such as CNN and Fox News.

## IN THIS CHAPTER

- Shopping Online
- Buying a Car—Online
- Buying a Home—Online
- Making Online Reservations
- Buying and Selling at Online Auctions

**20**

# BUYING AND SELLING ONLINE

Many users have discovered that the Internet is a great place to buy things—and to sell them! All manner of online merchants (sometimes called *e-tailers*) make it easy to buy books, CDs, and other merchandise with the click of a mouse. And online auction sites—led by the extremely successful eBay—serve as online marketplaces for users wanting to buy and sell all manner of merchandise.

In spite of the popularity of online retailing, many users are still a little hesitant to do their shopping online. While there certainly is some amount of online credit card theft, in general the Internet is a fairly safe place to shop—if you follow the rules, and take a few simple precautions.

Read on, then, to find out the best places to shop online—and how to shop safely!

# Shopping Online

For many users, shopping online is easier than shopping at traditional "bricks-and-mortar" retailers. You can sit down in front of your computer screen at any time of the day or night, dressed or undressed, and use your PC to search the Web for just the right item you want to buy—you don't have to get dressed or start your car or bother with boisterous crowds.

## How to Shop—Safely

To purchase an item online, all you have to do is enter your name, address, and credit card number, and the online merchant will arrange to have the item delivered directly to your house within a matter of days. It's that easy!

The big online retailers are just as reputable as traditional retailers, offering safe payment, fast shipping, and responsive service. Just to be safe, look for the following features before you shop at a given site:

- Payment by major credit card. (Not being able to accept credit cards is the sign of either a very small or fly-by-night merchant.)

- A *secure server* that encrypts your credit card information. (This keeps online thieves from stealing your credit card numbers.)

- Good contact information—email address, street address, phone number, fax number, and so on. (You want to be able to physically contact the retailer if something goes wrong.)

- A stated returns policy and satisfaction guarantee. (You want to be assured that you'll be taken care of if you don't like whatever you ordered.)

- A stated privacy policy that protects your personal information. (You don't want the online retailer sharing your email address and purchasing information with other merchants—and potential spammers.)

- Information *before you finalize your order* that tells you whether the item is in stock and how long it will take to ship. (More feedback is better.)

> **tip**
>
> All major credit card companies limit your liability if your card gets stolen, whether that's on the Web or in the so-called real world. So, go ahead and use your credit card online—there's nothing to worry about! (But don't use your debit card—the same safety programs don't always apply.)

# The Biggest—and the Best—Online Retailers

Even though there are thousands and thousands of merchants on the Web, a handful of online retailers garner the most user traffic—and sales. When you're looking for the best of the best, these are the online merchants to turn to:

- **Amazon.com** (www.amazon.com). The world's largest online shopping site (shown in Figure 20.1), offering books, CDs, videotapes, DVDs, video games, computer hardware, electronics, toys, and other types of consumer merchandise

**FIGURE 20.1**

Online shopping at the world's largest e-tailer, Amazon.com.

- **Barnes and Noble.com** (www.bn.com). The online branch of the largest bricks-and-mortar bookstore, selling books, CDs, DVDs, videotapes, and video games

- **Buy.com** (www.buy.com). Offering computers, wireless phones, video games, office products, consumer electronics products, sporting gear, and more

- **CDNow** (www.cdnow.com). Offering CDs, DVDs, and videotapes

- **Crutchfield** (www.crutchfield.com). Offering a wide selection of audio, video, home theater, and other consumer electronics products

- **Eddie Bauer** (www.eddiebauer.com). The online branch of the popular catalog merchant, offering clothing and other merchandise

- **J.Jill** (www.jjill.com). The online site of the popular catalog merchant, offering women's apparel

- **L.L. Bean** (www.llbean.com). The online branch of the popular catalog merchant, offering clothing and other merchandise
- **Land's End** (www.landsend.com). The online branch of the popular catalog merchant, offering clothing and other merchandise
- **Nordstrom** (store.nordstrom.com). The online branch of the popular department store, offering shoes, clothing, and other merchandise

> **tip**
>
> There are several Web sites that act as "virtual malls" or shopping comparison services; you can use these sites to search for the best or lowest-priced online merchants. These sites include Active Buyer's Guide (www.active-buyersguide.com), mySimon (www.mysimon.com), PriceGrabber.com (www.price-grabber.com), StoreScanner (www.storescanner.com), and Yahoo! Shopping (shopping.yahoo.com).

# Buying a Car—Online

There are a number of Web sites that offer all sorts of information about new and used cars—including dealer cost information that can help you negotiate a better purchase price. Most of these sites offer some combination of new-car buying guides, reviews, dealer pricing information, and used-car classifieds; some even direct your inquiry to local car dealers, who offer special Internet-only pricing to online shoppers.

When you visit one of these sites, you'll be prompted to search for a particular car by manufacturer and model. You can read reviews and specifications for particular cars and then compare prices and specs between different models.

Here are the best of the Web's auto-research sites:

- Auto-By-Tel (www.autobytel.com)
- AutoNation.com (www.autonation.com)
- AutoSite (www.autosite.com)
- Autoweb (www.autoweb.com)
- Cars.com (www.cars.com)
- Edmunds.com (www.edmunds.com)
- MSN CarPoint (carpoint.msn.com)

Figure 20.2 shows one of the top online auto sites, Cars.com.

**FIGURE 20.2**

Shopping for
new and used
cars at
Cars.com—the
online home of
NPR's *Car Talk*
radio show.

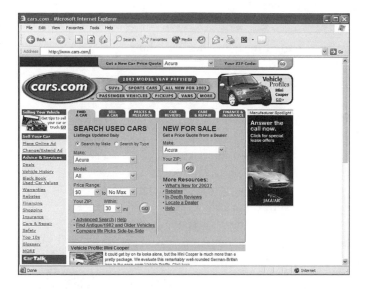

**FIGURE 20.2**

Shopping for new and used cars at Cars.com—the online home of NPR's *Car Talk* radio show.

# Buying a Home—Online

The biggest single purchase most people make in their entire lives is their home.
Numerous home-buying resources are available on the Internet, offering everything
from real estate listings to mortgage information. You can use these sites to research
what kind of home you want (and can afford), and then search for a new or resale
home in a particular region and price range.

Some of the more popular home-buying sites include

- eRealty.com (www.erealty.com)
- FSBO.com (www.fsbo.com)
- Homes.com (www.homes.com)
- HomeScape.com (www.homescape.com)
- iHomeowner.com (www.ihomeowner.com)
- iOwn (www.iown.com)
- MSN HomeAdvisor (homeadvisor.msn.com)
- NewHomeNetwork.com (www.newhomenetwork.com)
- Realtor.com (www.realtor.com)

# Making Online Reservations

Savvy travelers use the Internet to book all their travel reservations—plane tickets, hotel rooms, rental cars, and more. To book reservations, all you need to know is where you're going and when—and all the numbers from your favorite charge card.

The Web's general travel sites all offer similar content and services, including the ability to book airline tickets, hotel rooms, and rental cars all in one place. Most of these sites let you search for the lowest rates, or for flights and lodging that match your specific requirements.

Here are the best of these "online travel agents":

- Expedia (www.expedia.com)
- Hotwire (www.hotwire.com)
- Orbitz (www.orbitz.com)
- Priceline (www.priceline.com)
- TravelNow.com (www.travelnow.com)
- Travelocity (www.travelocity.com)
- Trip.com (www.trip.com)

> **tip**
>
> When you make reservations online, look for a site that employs real people behind the scenes—and offers a 24/7 800-number to contact those people if something goes wrong. Talking to a real person over the phone can be a real lifeline if you're stranded somewhere without a reservation.

Figure 20.3 shows Travelocity, one of the top full-service online travel sites.

**FIGURE 20.3**

Shopping for airline and hotel reservations at Travelocity.

# Buying and Selling at Online Auctions

An *online auction* is, quite simply, a Web-based version of a traditional auction. You find an item you'd like to own and then place a bid on the item. Other users also place bids, and at the end of the auction—typically a seven-day period—the highest bidder wins.

An online auction is a great place to find things you just can't find anyplace else—especially rare collectables. It's also a great place to get rid of things that you don't want anymore—there's a good chance that somebody, somewhere, will want to buy what you want to sell.

Far and away the largest online auction site is eBay (www.ebay.com), shown in Figure 20.4. eBay has more items listed and more bidders than all the other auction sites combined, with more than five million individual listings on any given day. Do a search from eBay's main page, and you can find everything from rare collectibles and vintage sports memorabilia to the latest electronics equipment.

**FIGURE 20.4**

The world's largest online marketplace—eBay!

# How Online Auctions Work

All online auctions work in a similar fashion:

1. The seller places an ad.
2. The buyer searches for an item.
3. The buyer makes a bid.
4. The bidding continues....

5. The high bidder wins.

6. The seller contacts the high bidder with a final price (including shipping and handling).

7. The high bidder sends payment to the seller.

8. The seller ships the item to the high bidder.

That's it. If everything works right, it's a pretty painless process—and a potentially profitable one, for the seller.

## Bidding—and Buying—on eBay

We'll start our tour of eBay by looking at what you need to do as a potential bidder. (And remember—just because you bid on an item doesn't mean you'll win the auction!)

### Making a Bid

After you've browsed through eBay's many categories (or used the search feature) to find an item you want, it's time to bid. To make a bid, you have to enter your eBay user ID and password and the *maximum bid* you are willing to make.

It's important that you enter the maximum amount you'd be willing to pay, even if the current bid is much lower than that theoretical maximum—and even though you hope the bidding doesn't go up that high. That's because eBay uses automated bidding software. The software won't bid your maximum unless it absolutely has to; it actually enters the current bid amount as your bid, and holds your higher number in reserve for future bids, if necessary.

As the auction continues and other users place their bids, it's possible that your maximum bid will be outbid. When this happens, you'll receive an email from eBay; you can then choose to make a higher bid or to bow out of the bidding.

**caution**

To bid on an eBay auction, you first have to sign up for eBay membership. Membership is free, and eBay will provide you with a user ID and password—which you must enter when you want to bid on an item.

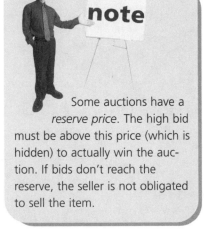

**note**

Some auctions have a *reserve price*. The high bid must be above this price (which is hidden) to actually win the auction. If bids don't reach the reserve, the seller is not obligated to sell the item.

## Winning—and Paying

If you're the high bidder at the end of the auction, you win! You should receive a confirmation email from eBay, as well as a message from the item's seller. The seller should provide you with the total price (your high bid plus shipping and handling charges), as well as information on where to send payment.

How should you pay?

The least safe method of payment is to send cash; there's nothing to track, and it's very easy for someone to steal an envelope full of cash.

Also considered less safe (but better than cash) are cashier's checks and money orders—although these methods are preferred by many sellers. Like cash, they provide no money trail to trace if you want to track down the seller.

Paying by check gives you a minor trail to trace, but once the check is cashed, it's still pretty much a done deal. In addition, most sellers hold your merchandise for ten days or more for your check to clear your bank.

A safer way to pay is by credit card. When you pay by credit card, you can always go to the credit card company and dispute your charges if the item you bought never arrived or was misrepresented. The same safety measures typically apply to credit card payments made through PayPal and other electronic payment services that let you use your credit card for payment.

**tip**

To increase your chances of winning an auction, use a technique called *sniping*. When you snipe, you hold your bid until the very last seconds of the auction. If you bid high enough and late enough, other bidders won't have time to respond to your bid—and your high bid will win!

**tip**

Check the seller's feedback rating before you bid. Avoid sellers with low feedback numbers or negative comments; if other buyers had trouble with that seller, you might, too.

## Receiving the Item—and Leaving Feedback

After you've received the auction item—and you're satisfied with your purchase—you need to leave feedback about the seller. Feedback can be either positive, neutral, or negative. Just go to the auction page for the item you just received, click the Leave Feedback link, and fill in the resulting form.

# Selling on eBay

To sell an item on eBay, you first have to register with the service and provide a credit card number. This is so eBay can charge you the appropriate fees for your item listing.

## Placing Your Ad

You create an item listing by going to eBay's home page and clicking the Sell button. eBay displays a series of forms for you to complete; the information you enter into these forms is used to create your item listing.

You'll need to enter the following information:

eBay makes its money by charging sellers two types of fees. (Buyers don't pay any fees to eBay.) *Insertion fees* are based on the minimum bid or reserve price of the item listed. *Final value fees* are charged when you sell an item, based on the item's final selling price. Fees are typically charged directly to the seller's credit card account.

- Category for your item listing
- A title and detailed description for the item
- The URL for an accompanying picture (optional)
- Your city and state
- The amount of your minimum (starting) bid
- The duration of your auction (3, 5, 7, or 10 days)
- What types of payments you'll accept
- Acceptable locations to ship to (you can opt not to ship outside the U.S., or only to specific regions)
- Who pays shipping (typically the buyer)

After you enter all the information, eBay creates and displays a preliminary version of your auction listing. If you like what you see, click OK and let your auction get started!

## Handling Payment

When you're listing an item for auction at eBay, you can choose what types of payment you'll accept from the winning bidder. This might seem like an easy decision, but each type of payment needs to be handled differently on your end:

■ **Cash**—While it might be nice to receive cash in the mail, it's not very safe for your buyers; cash is too easy to rip off and virtually untraceable. Don't expect buyers to pay by cash—but if they do, it's okay to ship the item immediately on payment.

■ **Personal checks**—This is the most common form of payment—it's very convenient for buyers. If you accept checks, make sure you wait for the check to clear (typically 10 business days) before you ship the item.

■ **Money orders and cashier's checks**—To a seller, these are almost as good as cash. You can cash a money order immediately, without waiting for funds to clear, which means you can ship on payment.

■ **Credit cards**—Because most individuals aren't set up to receive credit card payments, you can use an electronic payment service to receive credit card payments on your behalf. These services, such as PayPal, accept the credit card payments for you and then deposit the money in your checking account. (They typically charge a slight fee for this service.) When you accept credit card payments in this fashion, you can ship items immediately on payment.

## After the Auction

As soon as an auction ends, eBay emails both the seller and the winning bidder. As soon as you receive this confirmation, you should send your own email to the winning bidder. Your message should include the total cost of the item, including shipping and handling; the payment methods you accept (and prefer); and details on where to send the payment.

The winning bidder should then respond to your email and arrange payment. If the buyer *doesn't* respond to you within three business days, that high bidder forfeits her position as the winning bidder. You should then contact eBay about refunding your selling fees and relisting the item for sale.

## Shipping the Item—and Leaving Feedback

When you receive payment,  you need to pack it up and ship it out. Be sure you pack the item in an efficient yet sturdy manner, so the item doesn't get damaged in shipment. Then, take the item to the post office or one of the major shipping services and arrange shipment.

After you've shipped the item, email the buyer that the item is on its way, log back onto eBay to leave feedback for the winning bidder, and congratulate yourself for a successful online auction!

# THE ABSOLUTE MINIMUM

Here are the key points to remember from this chapter:

- You can find just about any type of item you want to buy for sale somewhere on the Internet.

- Internet shopping is very safe, especially if you buy from a major merchant that offers a secure server and a good returns policy.

- Online shopping isn't limited to small items; you can also purchase airline tickets, new cars, and houses over the Web!

- If you have an item you want to sell, use an online auction site, such as eBay. (eBay is also a great place to buy merchandise—especially rare collectables!)

## IN THIS CHAPTER

- Setting Up Your Email Accounts
- Understanding the Outlook Express Window
- Composing a Message
- Reading New Messages
- Replying to a Message
- Sending Files via Email
- Listing Your Friends in an Address Book

# 21

# SENDING AND RECEIVING EMAIL

Email is the modern way to communicate with friends, family, and colleagues. An email message is like a regular letter, except that it's composed electronically and delivered almost immediately via the Internet.

There are several programs you can use to send and receive email messages. If you're in a corporate environment, or running Microsoft Office, you can use Microsoft Outlook for your email. (Outlook is also a scheduler and personal information manager.) If you're connecting from home, the simpler Outlook Express is probably a better choice; it's easier to learn and use than its bigger brother, Outlook. Plus, Outlook Express is pre-installed on all Windows PCs, free of charge.

Using Outlook Express to send and receive email is a snap. Once you get it configured for your particular Internet service provider and email account, checking your messages is as easy as clicking a button.

# Setting Up Your Email Accounts

Back in Chapter 17, "Getting Connected to the Internet," you learned how to config-ure your computer for your particular Internet service provider. When you did your main configuration, you should have entered information about your email account.

If you later change email providers, or add a new email account, you'll have to access your email settings separately. To configure Outlook Express for a new email account, you'll need to know the following information:

■ The email address assigned by your ISP, in the format ***name@domain.com***.

■ The type of email server you'll be using; it's probably a POP3 server. (It could also be an HTTP, IMAP, or SMTP server, but POP3 is more common.)

■ The address of the incoming email server, and the outgoing mail server.

■ The account name and password you use to connect to the email servers.

Once you have this information (which should be supplied by your ISP), you can enter it manually into Outlook Express by following these steps:

1. From within Outlook Express, select **Tools**, **Accounts** to display the Internet Accounts dialog box.

2. Select the **Mail** tab.

3. To change the settings for an existing account, select the account and click **Properties**.

4. To enter a new account, click the **Add** button and select **Mail**.

5. When the Properties dialog box appears, select the **General** tab, then enter a name for this account, your name (first and last), and the email address assigned by your ISP.

6. Select the **Servers** tab and enter the fol-lowing information: type of server, incoming email server address, outgoing email server address, your assigned account name, and your password.

7. Click **OK**.

**tip**

To avoid entering your password every time you check your email, select the Remember Password option in the Properties dialog box.

You're now ready to send and receive email.

# Understanding the Outlook Express Window

Before we start working with email, let's take a look at the Outlook Express window. As you can see in Figure 21.1, the basic Outlook Express window is divided into three panes. The pane on the left is called the Folder list, and it's where you access your Inbox and other message folders. The top pane is the Message pane, and it lists all the messages stored in the selected folder. The bottom pane is the Preview pane, and it displays the contents of the selected message.

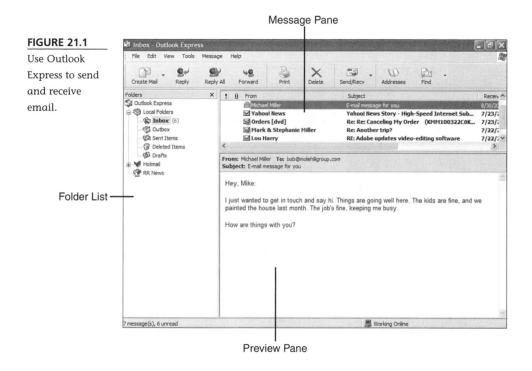

Message Pane

**FIGURE 21.1**

Use Outlook Express to send and receive email.

Folder List —

Preview Pane

The way it all works is that you select a location in the Folder List (typically your inbox), select a message header in the Message pane, and view the contents of that message in the Preview pane.

# Composing a Message

It's easy to create a new email message. Just follow these steps:

1. Click the **Create Mail** button on the Outlook Express toolbar; this launches a New Message window, similar to the one shown in Figure 21.2.

**FIGURE 21.2**

Use the New Message window to compose a new email message.

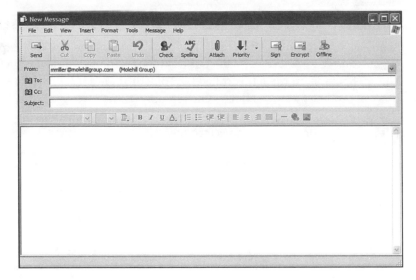

2. Enter the email address of the recipient(s) in the **To** field, then enter the address of anyone you want to receive a carbon copy in the **Cc** box. You can enter multiple addresses, as long as you separate multiple addresses with a semicolon (;), like this: `mmiller@molehillgroup.com;gjet-son@sprockets.com`.

3. Move your cursor to the main message area and type your message.

4. When your message is complete, send it to the Outbox by clicking the **Send** button.

**tip**

You can test your email account by sending a message to yourself; just enter your own email address in the **To** field.

Now you need to send the message from your Outbox over the Internet to the intended recipient (you!). You do this by clicking the **Send/Recv** button on the Outlook Express toolbar. Assuming your computer is connected to the Internet, your message will now be sent.

# Reading New Messages

When you receive new email messages, they're stored in the Outlook Express Inbox. To display all new messages, select the **Inbox** icon from the **Folders** list. All waiting messages now appear in the Message pane.

To read a specific message, select its header in the Message pane. The contents of that message are displayed in the Preview pane.

# Replying to a Message

To reply to an email message, follow these steps:

1. Select the message header in the Message pane.

2. Click the **Reply** button on the Outlook Express toolbar; this opens a Re: window, which is just like a New Message window except with the text from the original message "quoted" in the text area and the email address of the recipient (the person who sent the original message) pre-entered in the To field.

3. Enter your reply text in the message window.

4. Click the **Send** button to send your reply back to the original sender.

> **tip**
>
> You also can double-click a message header to display the message in a separate window.

# Sending Files via Email

From time to time you'll want to share one of your files with another computer user. What kinds of files might you want to share? How about these:

- Graphics files, such as pictures of your kids and family.
- Audio files, such as MP3 song files or audio clips from your favorite television programs.
- Video clips, such as files captured from your videotaped home movies.
- Documents, such as Microsoft Word documents or Excel spreadsheets.

There are several different ways to share files. You can copy a file to a floppy disk or writable CD and send the disk or CD to the other user. If you're both connected to the same computer network, you can use the Windows Copy command to copy the file from one computer to another. Or, if you're both connected to the Internet, you can send the file via email, as an *attachment*.

## Attaching a File to an Email Message

If two users are both connected to the Internet, the easiest way to send a file is via email. To send a file via email, you attach that file to a standard email message.

When the message is sent, the file travels along with it; when the message is received, the file is right there, waiting to be opened.

To attach a file to an outgoing email message, follow these steps:

1. Start with a new message and then click the **Attach** button in the message's toolbar; this displays the Insert Attachment dialog box.

2. Click the **Browse** button to locate and select the file you want to send.

3. Click **Attach**.

The attached file is now listed in a new **Attach**: field below the **Subject**: field in the message window. When you click the **Send** button, the email message and its attached file are sent together to your Outbox.

## Opening an Email Attachment

When you receive a message that contains a file attachment, you'll see a paper clip icon in the message header and a paper clip button in the preview pane header, as shown in Figure 21.3.

**FIGURE 21.3**

Receiving an email message with an attachment in Outlook Express.

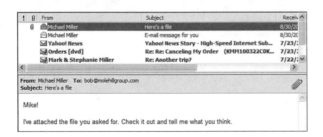

When you receive a message with an attachment, you can choose to view (open) the attached file or save it to your hard disk.

To view or open an attachment, click the **paper clip** button in the **Preview** pane header, and then click the attachment's filename. This opens the attachment in its associated application. (If you're asked whether you want to save or view the attachment, select view.)

To save an attachment to your hard disk, click the **paper clip** button in the **Preview** pane header, and then select **Save Attachments**. When the Save Attachments dialog box appears, select a location for the file and click the **Save** button.

## Watching Out for Email Viruses

Computer viruses are files that can attack your system and damage your programs and documents. One of the more popular ways of spreading viruses is through attachments to email messages.

Most email viruses are spread when someone sends you an unexpected file attachment—and then you open the file. It's just too easy to receive an email message with a file attached, click the file to open it, and then launch the virus file. Boom! Your computer is infected.

Viruses can be found in many types of files. The most common file types for viruses are .EXE, .VBS, .PIF, and .COM. Viruses can also be embedded in Word (.DOC) or Excel (.XLS) files. You *can't* catch a virus from a picture file, so viewing a .JPG, .GIF, .TIF, and .BMP file is completely safe.

Learn more about computer viruses in Chapter 32, "Protecting Your PC Online."

The best way to avoid catching a virus via email is to *not* open any .EXE, .VBS, .PIF, or .COM files attached to incoming email messages—even if you know the sender. That's because some viruses are capable of taking over an email program and sending copies of themselves to all the contacts in a user's address book. (Pretty tricky, eh?)

You can also configure Outlook Express to automatically reject files that might contain viruses. You do this by following these steps:

1. Select **Tools**, **Options** to display the Options dialog box.
2. Select the **Security** tab.
3. Check both the **Warn Me When Other Applications Try to Send Email As Me** and **Do Not Allow Attachments to Be Saved or Opened That Could Potentially Be a Virus** options.
4. Click **OK** when done.

# Listing Your Friends in an Address Book

Windows includes a contact manager application, called *Address Book*, that you can use to store information about your friends, family, and business associates. As you can see in Figure 21.4, you can store individual names, addresses, phone numbers, email addresses, birthdays, and other important information and then import your contacts into Outlook Express (to send email), Microsoft Works Calendar (to remind you of birthdays), and Microsoft Word (to personalize letters and address envelopes and labels).

**FIGURE 21.4**

Store all your email contacts in the Address Book.

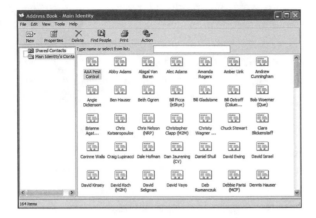

Address Book is incorporated into both Outlook Express and Microsoft Works Suite. You can launch Address Book from the Windows Start menu, from the Works Task Launcher, or from within Outlook Express (click the Addresses button on the toolbar).

## Adding New Contacts

To add a new contact to your Address Book, follow these steps:

1. From within Address Book, click the **New** button on the toolbar and then select **New Contact**; this opens the Properties dialog box, shown in Figure 21.5.

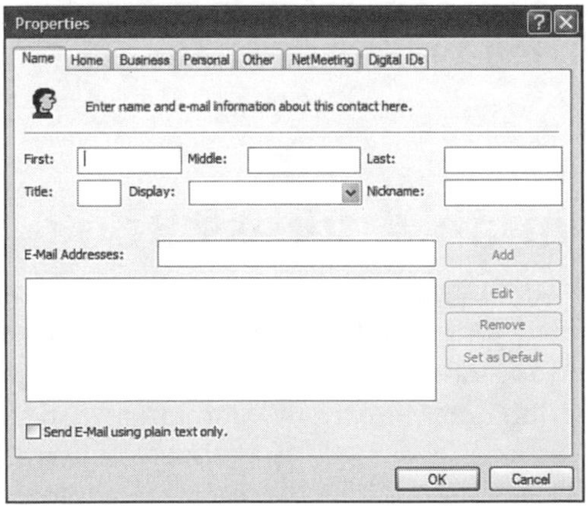

**FIGURE 21.5**

Entering information for a new Address Book contact.

2. Select the **Name** tab and enter the contact's name (first, middle, and last), title, display name (how you want to list the name in the Address Book), nickname, and email address.

3. Select the other tabs in the Properties dialog box to enter other types of information, including Home, Business, Personal, and Other types of info.

4. When you're done entering information, click **OK**.

> **tip**
>
> You don't have to enter all the information that can be entered into the Address Book. If all you know is a last name and email address, you can still create a contact for that person. Just enter as much information as you know, and work from that.

You can also add contacts from any email messages you receive. Just right-click the sender's name in the email message and select Add Sender to Address Book. This creates a new contact for that person; you can then go to the Address Book and add more detailed information later—as described next.

## Editing Contacts

If you want to edit information for an existing contact, follow these steps:

1. From the main Address Book contact list, select the contact name you wish to edit and then click the **Properties** button; this opens the Properties dialog box for that contact.

2. Change whatever information you want.

3. Click **OK**.

## Sorting and Searching

By default, your Address Book list is sorted by contact name. You can sort your list by any of the other columns by clicking that column head. Click the head twice to sort in the reverse order.

You also can change the way your Address Book displays the contact list. Pull down the **View** menu, and select from **Large Icon**, **Small Icon**, **List**, or **Details** (the default view).

If you have a *lot* of people in your Address Book, you might have trouble finding any single person. To search your Address Book, click the **Find People** button on the toolbar. When the Find People dialog box appears, enter either the name, email address, street address, or phone number of the person you're looking for, and then click **Find Now**. Address Book will return a list of contacts matching your query.

## Sending Email to a Contact

To send an email to one of your contacts, follow these steps:

1. From within your Address book, select the contact.

2. Click the **Action** button, and then select **Send Mail**; this opens an Outlook Express New Message window.

3. Enter the subject and text of your message.

4. Click **Send** when done.

You can also add names from your Address Book while you're composing a new email message. Just click the To button in your new message to display the Select Recipients dialog box; select the contact(s) you want, then click either the To, Cc, or Bcc buttons. Click OK when you're done adding names.

**note**

A Cc (carbon copy) message is one that is sent to someone other than the main recipient. A Bcc (blind carbon copy) is just like a Cc, except the Bcc recipient is hidden from the other recipients.

# THE ABSOLUTE MINIMUM

Here are the key points to remember from this chapter:

- Email is a fast and easy way to send electronic letters over the Internet.

- You can send and receive email messages using the Outlook Express program, pre-installed on most new PCs.

- You have to configure Outlook Express with information about your email account; you should be able to get this information from your ISP.

- Sending a new message is as easy as clicking the **Create Mail** button; reading a message is as easy as selecting it in the Message pane (and viewing it in the Preview pane).

- You can store frequently used email addresses in the Address Book utility.

## IN THIS CHAPTER

- Sending and Receiving Instant Messages
- Chat with Friends Online

**22**

# USING INSTANT MESSAGING AND CHAT

People like to talk—even when they're online.

There are two primary means of "talking" to other users via the Internet, both of which let you carry on text-based conversations in real time. When you want to hold a private one-on-one talk, you use an application called *instant messaging*. When you want to talk publicly, with a large group of people, you use *Internet chat*.

Instant messaging is the ideal medium for very short, very immediate messages. Online chat is better for longer discussions, and for group discussions. (And neither one is great for longer, more formal communications; email is best for those sort of messages.)

If you want to compare each method of online communication with their offline equivalents, think of email as the online version of written letters, online chat as the online version of phone conferences, and instant messaging as the online version of paging. Read on to learn more about both instant messaging and chat—and then get ready to start talking!

# Sending and Receiving Instant Messages

Instant messaging lets you communicate one on one, in real-time, with your friends, family, and colleagues. It's faster than email and less chaotic than chat rooms (discussed later in this chapter). It's just you and another user—and your instant messaging software.

There are several big players in the instant messaging market today, including:

- AOL Instant Messenger (www.aim.com)
- ICQ (web.icq.com)
- MSN Messenger (messenger.msn.com)
- Windows Messenger (pre-installed with Windows XP)
- Yahoo! Messenger (messenger.yahoo.com)

Unfortunately, most of these products don't work well (or at all) with each other; if you're using MSN Messenger, for example, you won't be able to communicate with someone running AOL Instant Messenger.

Depending on your computer configuration, you probably have either MSN Messenger or Windows Messenger installed on your new PC; Windows Messenger is really just an updated version of MSN Messenger. We'll use Windows Messenger for our examples in this chapter, although all instant messaging programs work pretty much the same way.

> **caution**
>
> Instant messaging only works if both parties are online at the same time; you can't send an instant message to someone who isn't available.

## Getting Connected

You launch MSN/Windows Messenger from the Windows **Start** menu. The first time you use the program, you need to sign up for Microsoft's .NET Messenger service. The sign-up is free and lets you choose your own unique sign-in name that other users will know you by. Click the **Click Here to Sign In** link to register; then follow the onscreen instructions.

## Adding New Contacts

To send an instant message to another user, that person has to be on your Messenger contact list.

To add a contact to your list, follow these steps:

1. From within Messenger, click the **Add** button to launch the Add a Contact Wizard.

2. To add a contact manually, select **By Email Address or Sign-In Name** and click **Next**; when the next page appears, enter the user's email address, then click **Next**. If the user you specified has a Microsoft Passport, that contact will be added to your contact list; if not, you'll be notified.

3. To search for a contact, select the **Search for a Contact** option and click **Next**; when the next page appears, enter their first name, last name, and country, then select to search from either the Hotmail Member Directory or the address book on your hard disk, and click **Next**. Any users matching your search will now be listed; select the name you want to add and click Next to add them to your contact list.

After you add contacts to your list, they appear in the main Messenger window, as shown in Figure 22.1. Contacts who are currently online are listed in the Online section; those who aren't are listed as Not Online. To remove a contact from your list, right-click the name and then select **Delete Contact**.

**FIGURE 22.1**

Choose a contact to send an instant message to.

## Sending a Message

To send an instant message to another user, follow these steps:

1. Double-click a name in your contact list to open the Conversation window, shown in Figure 22.2.

2. Enter your message in the lower part of the window.

3. Click the **Send** button (or press **Enter**).

Your message now appears in the top part of the window, as will your contact's reply. Continue talking like this, one message after another. Your entire conversation is displayed in the top part of the window, and you can scroll up to reread earlier messages.

## Receiving a Message

When someone else sends you an instant message, Windows lets out a little bleeping sound and then displays an alert in the lower-right corner of your screen. To open and reply to the message, click the alert. (Naturally, you have to be connected to the Internet to receive these messages.)

If you happen to miss the alert, Windows displays a flashing message button in the taskbar. You can click this button to read your message.

# Chat with Friends Online

An online chat is different from an instant message. Whereas instant messaging describes a one-to-one conversation between two users, online chat involves real-time discussions between large groups of users. These chats take place in public *chat rooms* (sometimes called *chat channels*).

You can find chat rooms at any number of Web sites, accessible via Internet Explorer or any other Web browser. There's also a form of Internet chat, called IRC, that operates on its own network of Internet servers; we'll discuss this later in the chapter.

## Chatting at Yahoo!

One of the most popular chat sites is Yahoo! Chat, which is part of the giant Yahoo! portal. You access Yahoo! Chat by clicking the Chat link on the Yahoo! home page or by going directly to chat.yahoo.com.

The main Yahoo! Chat page is your home page for all of Yahoo!'s chat activities. From here you can access featured chat rooms and chat events or click the Complete Room List link for a list of all available Yahoo! Chat rooms.

After you select a chat room, Yahoo! has to load special chat software into your Web browser. This is done automatically, using Java technology.

**tip**

The first time you visit Yahoo! Chat, you'll be prompted for your Yahoo! ID and password; if you don't yet have a Yahoo! ID, take this opportunity to register. (It's free.)

When you enter a chat room, you see the screen shown in Figure 22.3. All messages are displayed in the Chat pane; everyone chatting in the room is listed in the Chatters pane.

**FIGURE 22.3**

A typical Yahoo! chat room— enter a message in the **Send** box, and then chat away!

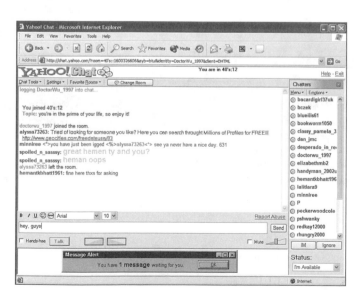

You enter your messages in the Send box and then click the Send button or press Enter to send the message to the room. After you send a message, it appears in the Chat pane, listed in-line with all the other messages.

Everybody else in your chat room is listed in the Chatters list. In addition, you can display a list of all the participants in every Yahoo! Chat room by clicking the Who's Chatting button in the Tools section.

If you want to change chat rooms, click the Change Room button in the Tools section. When you click this button, Yahoo! displays the chat room list; click a room name to change to that room.

## Other Chat Sites

If you're serious about online chat, you might want to check out some of the other major chat communities on the Web. These sites include:

- Excite Super Chat (chat.excite.com)
- Internet TeleCafe (www.telecafe.com)
- Lycos Chat (chat.lycos.com)
- MSN Chat (chat.msn.com)

If you're a subscriber to America Online, you can also access AOL's proprietary chat rooms. These are some of the busiest chat rooms on the Internet, and they're reserved exclusively for AOL members.

> **tip**
>
> There's another form of Internet chat, called Internet Relay Chat (IRC), that operates in a subset of the Internet and requires its own chat software. IRC isn't for beginners; if you want to learn more (or download the popular mIRC software), check out the mIRC Web site, at www.mirc.com.

# THE ABSOLUTE MINIMUM

Here are the key points to remember from this chapter:

- Where email is great for longer, more formal messages, instant messaging is better for short one-on-one conversations—and Internet chat is good for more public discussions.
- There are many different incompatible instant messaging networks, including AOL Instant Messenger, ICQ, MSN/Windows Messenger, and Yahoo! Messenger.
- To message another user, you both must be online at the same time, using the same instant messaging software.
- Internet chat rooms can be found on many different Web sites, such as Yahoo! Chat—as well as part of the America Online service.

## IN THIS CHAPTER

- Sending and Receiving Instant Messages
- Chat with Friends Online
- Using Good "Netiquette"
- Read and Post to Usenet Newsgroups
- Message Boards
- Email Mailing Lists

**23**

# USING NEWSGROUPS, MESSAGE BOARDS, AND MAILING LISTS

The Internet is a great way for people with special interests to gather and exchange ideas. Whether you're into model trains, European soccer, or soap operas, you can find a legion of similar fans online.

There are three distinct types of *online communities*: newsgroups, message boards, and mailing lists. The best way to think of these forums is that they're like old-fashioned bulletin boards. A user begins by posting a message regarding a specific topic. That first message serves the important function of conversation starter. Some members of the community decide to respond to it, and post replies. Other users read the first replies, and then reply to those replies. Others read the replies to the replies, and add even more replies of their own. Before long you have a intricate *thread* of messages, all branching out from that initial posting.

So go online and learn how to interact with others who share your specific interests. Chances are, there's an online community waiting just for you—and it's no further away than your computer keyboard.

## Using Good "Netiquette"

When you're communicating in one of these online forums, you need to follow a set of unstated rules, or you risk offending other users—and possibly setting off a so-called *flame war* of diatribes and personal attacks. Acceptable online behavior is sometimes called *netiquette*, and adheres to the following advice:

- Don't write in all capital letters—it looks like you're SHOUTING!
- Be specific when creating a message header; this helps readers determine which messages to read and which to avoid.
- Don't post off-topic messages. Postings that veer off topic just add unnecessarily to the clutter and noise level.
- Don't make your messages longer than they need to be. Brevity is a prized trait when communicating online.
- Don't *cross-post* a message in more than one section in an online forum, or in more than one newsgroup.
- Don't advertise. It isn't seemly, and it's sure to inspire a rash of vitriolic replies.
- Be polite. Don't use offensive language, don't be unnecessarily insulting, and treat other users as you would like to be treated yourself.

By the way, it's okay to read a message and not reply. You're not required to respond to every message you see online!

## Read and Post to Usenet Newsgroups

Usenet is a subset of the overall Internet, and its host to more than 30,000 topic-specific *newsgroups*. A newsgroup is kind of like an online bulletin board where users post messages (called *articles*) about a variety of topics; other users read and respond to these articles. The result is a kind of ongoing, freeform discussion, in which hundreds of users can participate.

You use a *newsreader* program to access Usenet newsgroups. Outlook Express, the email program we discussed back in Chapter 21, "Sending and Receiving Email," doubles as a newsreader.

## Understanding Newsgroup Names

A newsgroup name looks a little like a Web site address, with single words or phrases separated by periods. Newsgroup names are more logical, however, in that each break in the name signifies a different subset of the major topic.

So, as you read a newsgroup name, your focus moves from left to right, until you zero in on a very specific topic. For example, the `rec.arts.cinema` group tells you that the newsgroup is in the *recreational* section of Usenet and that it discusses the *art* of the *cinema*.

## Searching for Newsgroups and Articles

To find a specific newsgroup, follow these steps:

1. Click the icon in the Outlook Express folder list for your particular news server. (This should have been set up when you first configured your computer for your particular Internet service provider.)

2. If this is the first time you've used Outlook Express's newsgroup function, you'll be prompted to view a list of all newsgroups. If not, you'll need to click the **Newsgroups** button on the toolbar to view a list of all available newsgroups.

3. When the Newsgroups dialog box appears (shown in Figure 23.1), click the **All** tab (at the bottom of the dialog box).

**FIGURE 23.1**

Search through more than 30,000 newsgroups for the topic you're interested in.

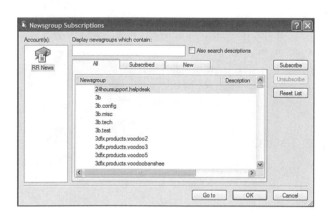

4. Select a newsgroup from the main list. You can scroll through the list or search for a specific group by entering key words in the **Display Newsgroups Which Contain** box.

5. When you find a newsgroup you want to read, click the **Go To** button; all the articles from that newsgroup will now appear in Outlook Express's Message pane.

6. Click a message header to read the contents of that article in the **Preview** pane.

## Creating and Posting Newsgroup Articles

To reply to an existing article, select the message in the **Message** pane and then click the **Reply** button. To create a new article, click the **New Post** button. Enter your message in the New Message window, and then click the **Send** button to post the message to the current newsgroup.

**tip**

If you're interested in viewing older Usenet articles, you can search the newsgroup archives housed at the Google Groups Web site (`groups.google.com`).

# Message Boards

Message boards are similar to Usenet newsgroups in that they let you post and read messages related to a specific topic. Message boards differ from newsgroups in that they're not part of an Internet-wide network; message boards are tied to specific Web sites.

There are hundreds, if not thousands, of Web sites that offer topic-specific message boards. Most message boards work in a similar fashion, so we'll look at the largest message host—Yahoo! Message Boards—to learn how message boards work.

## Using Yahoo! Message Boards

To access Yahoo! Message Boards, click the Message Boards link on the Yahoo! home page, or go directly to `messages.yahoo.com`. When the Yahoo! Message Boards page appears, you can choose to browse for boards by category, or search for a specific board.

After you've selected a specific message board, you'll see the message board's main page, like the one shown in Figure 23.2. The theme of the board (in the form of a

**note**

Message boards also differ from newsgroups in that you can read them with any Web browser—no special software program is necessary.

"starter" message) is sometimes displayed at the top of the page; all the message threads are listed (by topic) below the Topic heading. Click a topic to read the first message in a thread.

**FIGURE 23.2**

Reading the messages at Yahoo! Message Boards.

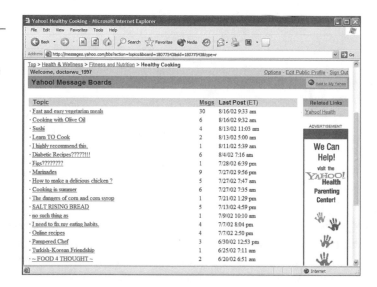

Each message in the thread appears in its own page. Click the **Next** link to read the next message in the thread; click the **Previous** link to back up and read the previous message. To reply publicly to a message, click the **Reply** link; to send a private email to the author of the message, click the author's name.

To post a new message in a new thread, click the **Create a Topic** link on the main message board page. When the next page appears, enter a subject for your message in the **Type Message Subject** box, and then enter the text of your message in the **Type Message** box. When you're ready to send your message, click the **Post Message** button; remember, any message you post will be visible to anyone visiting this message board!

## Other Web Message Boards

There tend to be two types of sites that host Web message boards. The first type consists of portals, like Yahoo!, that offer a collection of different boards. The second type is a topic-specific site that offers a message board in conjunction with other content and services on the site.

If you're looking for a portal-type collection of message boards, here's a short list of sites to check out:

■ Excite Message Boards (boards.excite.com)

■ ezboard (www.ezboard.com)

■ iVillage (www.ivillage.com/boards/)

■ Lycos (boards.lycos.com)

■ MSN Web Communities (communities.msn.com)

# Email Mailing Lists

If you're searching for a slightly more private online discussion venue, you should take a look at an email *mailing list.* There are tens of thousands of these special-interest lists, which are run by *list managers* who encourage discussion and debate on selected topics. For example, if you're interested in Marilyn Monroe, you can subscribe to a Marilyn Monroe mailing list; if you're interested in parish nursing, subscribe to one of the parish nursing mailing lists.

When you subscribe to a mailing list, you'll receive periodic email messages from other mailing list members. In most cases you can opt to receive individual messages as they're posted, or a *digest* of all messages sent within a specified time period. When you want to post a message, you send it via email to the list moderator; your message is then distributed to other members of the list, either on its own or as part of a digest.

The two best listings of mailing lists are Liszt (www.liszt.com) and Yahoo! Groups (groups.yahoo.com). Both of these sties let you browse through a hierarchical directory of topics, or search for mailing lists by keyword. Yahoo! Groups also serves as a hosting service for tens of thousands of topic-based communities (called *groups*) .

# THE ABSOLUTE MINIMUM

Here are the key points to remember from this chapter:

■ Usenet is a collection of more than 30,000 topic-specific newsgroups.

■ You access Usenet newsgroups via a newsreader software program; Outlook Express is a good choice for a newsreader.

■ Web-based message boards are similar to physical bulletin boards, in that they enable users to exchange messages about a common topic.

■ Email mailing lists are probably the most orderly of these online forums; membership and postings are controlled by list moderators.

■ You can find lists of mailing lists at both the Liszt and Yahoo! Groups sites.

## IN THIS CHAPTER

- Finding Files Online
- Downloading from a File Archive
- Downloading Files from Any Web Page

# 24

# DOWNLOADING FILES

The Internet is a huge repository for computer files of all shapes and sizes, from utilities that help you better manage your disk drive to full-featured email and newsgroup programs. There are hundreds of thousands of these programs available *somewhere* on the Internet; if you can find them, you can download them to your computer.

Interestingly, many of the program files you find online are available free of charge; these programs are called *freeware*. Other programs can be downloaded for no charge, but they require you to pay a token amount to receive full functionality or documentation; these programs are called *shareware*. (Both types of programs are in contrast to the software you buy in boxes at your local computer retailer, which is *commercial software*.)

# Finding Files Online

Before you can use any of the programs available online, you first have to find them and then download them from their current locations to your PC. Fortunately, downloading files is a fairly easy process.

There are some variations to the procedure, but overall, it's pretty straightforward. In a nutshell, all you have to do is the following:

1. Create a special download folder on your computer's hard drive—typically in the My Documents folder.

2. Find and download the file you want.

3. If the file was compressed (with a ZIP extension), decompress the file using Windows XP Extraction Wizard.

4. If the file you downloaded was a software program, you'll need to install the software. Installation instructions are usually included somewhere on the download information page or in a readme file included with the file download. In most cases, installation involves running a file named `setup.exe` or `install.exe`; after the setup program launches, follow the onscreen instructions to complete the installation.

5. Delete the compressed file you originally downloaded.

> **caution**
>
> If you download files from less-recognized Web sites, you might be at risk of downloading a file infected with a computer virus. To learn more about viruses, see Chapter 32, "Protecting Your PC Online."

# Downloading from a File Archive

Where do you find all these wonderful files to download? The best places to look are Web sites dedicated to file downloading. These sites are called *file archives*, and they typically store a huge variety of freeware and shareware programs and utilities.

Downloading a file from any of these archives is typically fairly easy. Once you locate the file you want, you're prompted to click a specific link to begin the download. Some sites will begin the download automatically; other sites will prompt Windows to display a dialog box asking if you want to save or open the file (you want to save it), and where you want to save it. Follow the onscreen instructions to begin the download.

When you're looking for files to download, here are some of the best download repositories on the Internet:

- Download.com (`download.cnet.com`)
- IT Pro Downloads (`www.itprodownloads.com`)
- Jumbo (`www.jumbo.com`)
- Tucows (`www.tucows.com`)
- ZDNet Downloads (`www.zdnet.com/downloads/`)

Figure 24.1 shows the main page at Tucows—just look at all the different types of software you can download!

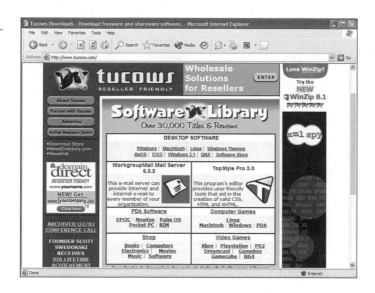

There are several good reasons to download from one of these well-established sites. First, they all have really big collections; the more files available, the more likely it is you'll find what you're looking for. Second, they all make the download process relatively easy. And, third, they all check their files for viruses before offering them to the public.

In other words, these sites make downloading safe and easy!

# Downloading Files from Any Web Page

You don't necessarily have to go to a software archive to find files to download. You can actually download files you find on any Web page—especially graphics files.

That's because if you see a pretty picture on a page, that picture is actually a graphics file; any background on a Web page is also a file. And any graphics file on a Web page can be downloaded to your PC.

To download a picture file from a Web page, follow these steps:

1. Right-click the picture to display the pop-up menu shown in Figure 24.2.

2. Select **Save Picture As**.

3. When prompted, select a location for the file; then, click **Save**.

The graphics file will now be downloaded to the location you specified.

**tip**

If a Web page contains a link to a file, you can download that file (of any type) without actually jumping to the file. Just right-click the link to the file and select **Save Target** as from the pop-up menu. When prompted, select a location for the file, and then click **Save** to start the download.

**FIGURE 24.2**

How to download a graphics file from a normal Web page.

Open Link
Open Link in New Window
Save Target As...
Print Target

Show Picture
Save Picture As...
E-mail Picture...
Print Picture...
Go to My Pictures
Set as Background
Set as Desktop Item...

Cut
Copy
Copy Shortcut
Paste

Add to Favorites...

Properties

# The Absolute Minimum

Here are the key points to remember from this chapter:

- The Internet is a great place to find computer software and utilities of all different types—many of which are available free of charge.

- The best places to find files to download are the major software download archives, such as Tucows and Download.com.

- You can download any graphic you find on any Web page, by right-clicking the picture and selecting **Save Picture As** from the pop-up menu.

## IN THIS CHAPTER

- Creating a Home Page at Yahoo! GeoCities
- Using Page Building Software
- Uploading Your Pages

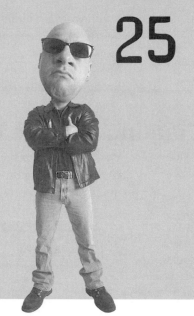

**25**

# CREATING YOUR OWN WEB PAGE

It seems like everybody and their brother has their own personal Web pages these days. If you want to keep up with the Joneses (and the Smiths and the Berkowitzes), you need to create a personal Web page of your own.

All Web pages are based on a special programming code, called Hypertext Markup Language (HTML). Fortunately, you don't need to learn HTML to create a simple Web page. That's because there are a number of software programs and Web sites that make it easy to generate good-looking pages without you having to learn any fancy programming.

If you want an all-in-one solution, turn to one of the major *home page communities* on the Web. These sites—such as Yahoo! GeoCities (geocities.yahoo.com), Angelfire (angelfire.lycos.com), and Tripod (tripod.lycos.com)—not only help you create your own Web pages, they even host your pages on the Web. And, best of all, this basic hosting service is free!

# Creating a Home Page at Yahoo! GeoCities

When it comes to home page communities, the biggest (and the best) is Yahoo! GeoCities, shown in Figure 25.1. GeoCities makes it easy to create your own page and post it to the Web—at no charge to you.

**FIGURE 25.1**

Yahoo! GeoCities: The largest home page community on the Internet.

Yahoo! GeoCities offers several different ways to build a page:

- **Yahoo! PageWizards.** The easiest way to build a simple Web page; just answer a few questions and the form-based engine will generate your page automatically.

- **Yahoo! PageBuilder.** PageBuilder is a Java-based application than runs on your desktop while you're online, and provides a step-by-step page-building environment. You pick a category and a template for your page, and then modify the template for your own personal needs.

■ **HTML Editor.** If you want to create more sophisticated Web pages, you have to get down and dirty with the underlying HTML code. Yahoo! GeoCities provides the Advanced Editor, just for this purpose. You can enter HTML code directly into the Advanced Editor window; GeoCities converts that code into a finished Web page.

The easiest way to create a simple Web page is to use the PageWizard feature. Just follow these steps:

1. Click the **Yahoo! PageWizards** link on the Yahoo! GeoCities home page.

2. When the Yahoo! PageWizards page appears, as shown in Figure 25.2, click the page design you want to use.

> **tip**
>
> Many Internet service providers also offer free personal home pages to their subscribers; check with your ISP to see what services are available. In addition, if you're an American Online member, you can avail yourself of the AOL Hometown home page community. (AOL Hometown is accessible from within the AOL service, or on the Web at home-town.aol.com.)

**FIGURE 25.2**

As simple as filling in a form: Yahoo! PageWizards.

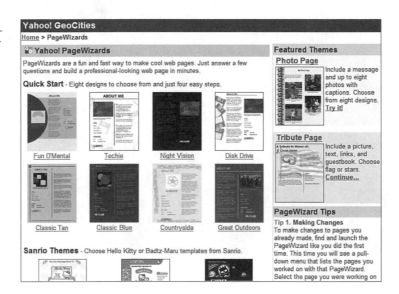

3. A new Quick Start Web Page Wizard window will now appear on your desktop. Press the **Begin** button to proceed.

4. When the Choose a Look for Your Page page appears, select a style for your page. (The style you originally selected should be checked; you can continue with this style, or change to another style.) Click the **Next** button to proceed.

5. When the Enter Your Page Title and Text page appears, enter a title to appear at the top of your page, and then enter the text to appear in the body of your page. Click the **Next** button to proceed.

6. When the Pick Your Picture page appears, click the **Browse** button to select a picture file from your hard disk, then enter a caption for the picture. (If you want to use the stock picture for this page style, skip this step without selecting a picture.) Click the **Next** button to proceed.

7. When the Enter Your Favorite Links page appears, enter up to four other Web sites (both the name and the address). Click the **Next** button to proceed.

8. When the Enter Your Information page appears, enter your name and email address. If you use Yahoo! Instant Messenger and want your Web page to display a graphic when you're online, click the **Put This On My Page** option. Click the **Next** button to proceed.

9. When the Name Your Page page appears, enter a name for your page. (This will appear as part of the page's URL.) Click the **Next** button to complete the process.

The wizard will now display a Congratulations page. The URL for your new page will be displayed here; write it down for future reference, or click the link to view your page. Figure 25.3 shows the kind of page you can create with the PageWizard.

> **tip**
>
> You can edit any pages you created with PageWizard with Yahoo! PageBuilder. Just relaunch PageBuilder, click the **Open** button, and select the page you want to edit.

**FIGURE 25.3**

A personal Web page created with the Yahoo! PageWizard.

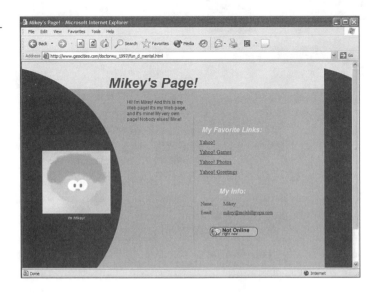

# Using Page Building Software

The Web page you create at Yahoo! GeoCities is a relatively simple one. If you want to create more sophisticated pages—or multiple pages, in a complete Web site—you need a more powerful tool. Fortunately, there are numerous software programs available you can use to build really fancy Web pages.

Here's a short list of some of the most popular page-building software available today:

- Adobe GoLive (www.adobe.com)
- Dreamweaver (www.macromedia.com)
- HomeSite (www.macromedia.com)
- Microsoft FrontPage (www.microsoft.com/frontpage/)

Figure 25.4 shows Microsoft FrontPage, one of the most popular page builder programs. FrontPage lets you build everything from simple personal pages to sophisticated e-commerce Web sites—and it's easy to use, thanks to its Office-like interface.

**FIGURE 25.4**

Build sophisticated Web pages and sites with Microsoft FrontPage.

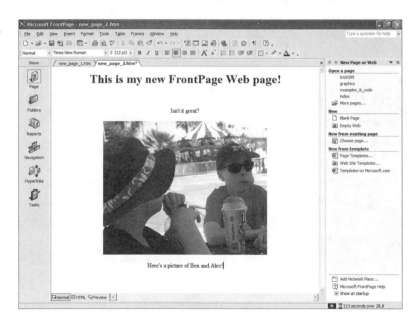

# Uploading Your Pages

Web pages with one of these software programs, you still have to find a site on the Web to host your pages. Yahoo! GeoCities and the other home page communities offer separate page hosting services (usually for a fee), geared towards personal Web pages. If you need a host for a complete Web site (or for small business purposes), you should probably examine a service that specializes in more sophisticated Web site hosting.

A Web site hosting service will manage all aspects of your Web site. For a monthly fee, you'll receive a fixed amount of space on their servers, your own Web site address (and your own personal domain, if you want to pay for it), and a variety of site management tools. Pricing for these services typically start at $10 or so a month, and goes up from there.

Perhaps the best way to look for a Web site host is to access a directory of hosting services. Most of these directories let you search for hosts by various parameters, including monthly cost, disk space provided, programming and platforms supported, and extra features offered. Among the best of these host search sites are the following:

- CNET Internet Services (www.cnet.com/internet/)
- HostIndex.com (www.hostindex.com)
- HostSearch (www.hostsearch.com)
- TopHosts.com (www.tophosts.com)
- WebHosters.com (www.webhosters.com)

# THE ABSOLUTE MINIMUM

Here are the key points to remember from this chapter:

- Web pages are built using the HTML programming language—although you don't have to know how to program to create a simple Web page.
- To create a personal Web page, check out one of the large page building communities, such as Yahoo! GeoCities.
- To create a more sophisticated Web page or Web site, use a dedicated page building program, such as Microsoft Frontpage.

# PART V

# Working with Music and Pictures

26  Working with Pictures . . . . . . . . . . . . 255

27  Playing CDs and DVDs . . . . . . . . . . . . 269

28  Playing Internet Audio and Video . . . . . 277

29  Downloading and Playing Digital Music . 283

30  Burning Your Own CDs . . . . . . . . . . . 295

31  Editing Your Own Home Movies . . . . . . 299

## ĬN THIS CHAPTER

- Working with a Digital Camera
- Scanning Your Photos
- Managing Your Photos
- Editing Your Photos—with Microsoft Picture It! Photo
- Printing Your Photos
- Emailing a Picture
- Printing Photos Online

# WORKING WITH PICTURES

One of the hottest pieces of gear today is the digital camera. Digital cameras work like normal film cameras, except they capture images electronically, instead of on film. These digital images are stored within the camera, on special memory cards. You can then transfer the digital photos to your personal computer—or to a photo processing service.

Once you've transferred a digital photo from your camera to your PC, you have lots of options available to you. A digital picture file is just like any computer file, which means you can store it, copy it, delete it, or whatever. You can also use special graphics editing software to manip-ulate your photos—to touch up bad spots and red eye, crop the edges, and apply all sorts of special effects. (And, if you don't have a camera, you use a computer scanner to scan in all your old photo prints—and do all the same touch up you can with digital photos.)

Once your photos are all touched up, you can choose to store them on your hard disk, create digital photo albums, use them in all manner of picture-related projects and documents, or print them out—either on your own four-color printer, or at a traditional photo processor. The combination of digital photography and personal computing is definitely the way to go—it's a lot more versatile than traditional film-based photography!

# Working with a Digital Camera

There are actually several different ways you can transfer photos to your computer. If you don't have a digital camera, you can always scan your photo prints (using a scanner, discussed later in this chapter) into electronic files. Of course, there's always the option of obtaining photos from someone else, either on CD or over the Internet. But the best way to go is to take your own pictures using a digital camera—and then connect that camera directly to your PC.

## Connecting Your Digital Camera

Connecting a digital camera to your new PC is extremely easy, especially if you're using Windows XP and you have a relatively new camera. Chances are your camera is Plug and Play–compatible and connects to your PC via a USB connection. Just use the cable that came with your camera to connect the camera to one of your PC's USB ports. When you turn on your camera (and switch it to "PC" or "transfer" mode), Windows automatically recognizes your camera and installs the appropriate software drivers.

If Windows does *not* recognize your camera, you can use the Scanners and Cameras utility to install the camera on your system. Just follow these steps:

1. Click the **Start** button to display the Start menu.
2. Select **Control Panel** to open the Control Panel folder.
3. Select **Scanners and Cameras** to open the Scanners and Cameras folder.
4. In the Imaging Tasks pane, click **Add an Imaging Device** to launch the Scanner and Camera Installation Wizard.
5. Follow the onscreen instructions to identify the make and manufacturer of your camera, and then install the proper drivers.

When you exit the wizard, your new camera appears as a device in the Scanners and Cameras folder, as shown in Figure 26.1.

**FIGURE 26.1**

Use the Scanners and Cameras folder to access your digital camera.

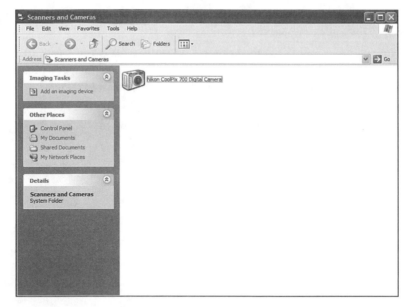

## Transferring Pictures to Your PC

When you connect your digital camera and activate its "transfer" mode, Windows displays the Choose Pictures to Copy dialog box.

At this point you can select from four actions:

**tip**

You can also display this dialog box by opening the My Pictures folder and selecting **Get Pictures from Camera or Scanner**—or by opening the Scanner and Cameras folder and selecting **Get Pictures**.

- **Acquire Photos**—Choose this option to select photos to copy to your hard disk.

- **View a Slideshow of the Images**—Select this option and Windows displays a full-screen slideshow of the images currently stored in your camera. No copying of the images is necessary.

- **Print the Pictures**—Select this option to print individual photos without first copying them to your hard disk.

- **Open Folder to View Files**—Select this option when you want to view, delete, rename, or otherwise manage the  camera.

When you select **Acquire Photos** (and click **OK**), the Scanner and Camera Wizard launches, and you're presented with thumbnails of all the photos currently stored in your camera. You don't have to copy all these photos to your hard drive—although you can, by clicking the **Select All** option. Just select which photos you want to copy, then click the **Next** button.

Now you're presented with the Select a Picture Name and Destination screen. This is where you select the destination folder and filenames for your pictures. By default, Windows XP copies your pictures to the My Pictures folder.

Windows XP names all your photos with a common filename, followed by a unique number. So, for example, if you entered `Vacation` as the picture name, your photos would be named `Vacation 001`, `Vacation 002`, `Vacation 003`, and so on.

After you've entered all this information, click the Next button and the wizard copies your selected pictures to your hard disk.

## Working with Pictures in Your Camera

Interestingly, you don't have to copy photos from your camera to your hard disk to work with them. Windows XP also lets you work directly with the pictures currently stored in your digital camera.

When you connected your camera to your computer, you were presented with four options. (You can also display these options by selecting the **camera** icon in the Scanners and Cameras folder and clicking the **Get Pictures** option in the Imaging Tasks pane.) You select the **Acquire Pictures** option to copy pictures to your hard disk, but you can select one of the other options to work with the pictures while they're still in your camera.

To print selected photos from your camera, choose the **Print the Pictures** option. All the photos in your camera will be displayed, and all you have to do is choose which photos you want to send to your printer.

To delete or rename the pictures in your camera, select the **Open Folder to View Files** option. This displays the contents of your camera in a My Pictures–like folder. You can use the commands in this folder to perform a full range of file-management tasks with your pictures.

If your camera contains any movie files, you can play these movies on your PC by selecting the **Play the Video Files** option. Because many digital still cameras also let you record short MPEG movies, this option is a nice way to view your movies without first copying them to your hard disk.

> **note**
>
> Some digital cameras come with their own image-management software. You can use your camera's software in lieu of Windows's image management functions, if you wish.

# Scanning Your Photos

If you don't have a digital camera—or if you have a lot of old prints lying around that you'd like to work with—there's another way to get your photos into your computer. All you need is a low-cost desktop scanner.

## Connecting and Configuring a Scanner

If you're shopping for a new scanner, choose one that connects via your computer's USB or FireWire port. USB and FireWire scanners require very little setup. When you connect the scanner, Windows recognizes it and begins the driver installation process.

If Windows does not recognize your scanner, you can add the scanner to your system via the Scanners and Cameras utility; just follow the steps described in the "Connecting Your Digital Camera" section, earlier in this chapter.

**note**

Learn more about installing new hardware in Chapter 33, "Adding New Hardware to Your System."

## Making a Scan

Some scanners come with their own scanning software. You can use this software to initiate a scan, or you can use the scanning features built in to Windows XP.

When you press the **Scan** button on your scanner, Windows senses this event and launches the Scanner and Camera Wizard. As you can see in Figure 26.2, the scanner part of this wizard lets you control how your picture is scanned.

**FIGURE 26.2**

Use Windows XP to scan a photograph and preview your scan before you accept it.

Start by selecting one of the Picture Type options—**Color Picture**, **Grayscale Picture**, **Black and White Picture or Text**, or **Custom**. When you make a selection, the wizard displays a preview of what you're scanning.

If you like what you see, you can tell the wizard to finish the scan. If you don't like what you see, you can change the settings and look at another preview.

The wizard then saves your scan in the folder you select. By default, scanned photos are saved in the My Pictures folder.

## Managing Your Photos

By default, Windows XP stores all your picture files in the My Pictures folder, shown in Figure 26.3. This folder includes a number of features specific to the management of picture files, found in the Picture Tasks panel. These features include:

**FIGURE 26.3**

Use the My Pictures folder to store and organize your digital pictures.

- View as a slide show
- Order prints online
- Print this picture
- Set as desktop background

You can also change the way files are displayed in this folder. To display a thumbnail of each file, select **View**, **Thumbnails**. To view the selected file as a large image with all the other files in a scrolling list, select **View**, **Filmstrip**. To view details about each picture (its size, when it was taken, and so on), select **View**, **Dimensions**.

# Editing Your Photos—with Microsoft Picture It! Photo

Not all the pictures you take are perfect. Sometimes the image might be a little out-of-focus or off-center, or maybe your subject caught the glare of a flash for a "red eye" effect. The nice thing about digital pictures is that you can easily edit them to correct for these and other types of flaws.

To fix the flaws in a picture, you use a picture editing program. One of the most popular of these programs is Microsoft Picture It! Photo—and it's included as part of Microsoft Works Suite.

> **tip**
>
> Other popular picture editing programs include Adobe Photoshop Elements (www.adobe.com), CorelDRAW Essentials (www.corel.com), Micrografx Picture Publisher (www.micrografx.com), and PhotoSuite (www.roxio.com).

## Opening a Picture for Editing

You can launch Picture It! Photo from either the Windows Start menu or the Works Task Launcher. To open a specific picture for editing, follow these steps:

1. From the Startup window, click the **Open** icon to display the File Browser window.
2. Navigate to and select the picture you want to edit.
3. Click the **Open** button.

> **tip**
>
> You can display the Startup window at any time by selecting **File**, **Startup Window**. You can also display the File Browser by selecting **File**, **Open**.

The picture now appears in the program's canvas area, as shown in Figure 26.4. All open pictures are shown in the Tray at the bottom of the workspace, and the Common Tasks panel appears on the left side. (This panel changes based on which option you select.) At the right of the workspace is the Stacks area, which displays different layers of the picture currently in the workspace.

Canvas                    Stack (Holds Picture Components)

**FIGURE 26.4**
Edit your pictures with Microsoft Picture It! Photo.

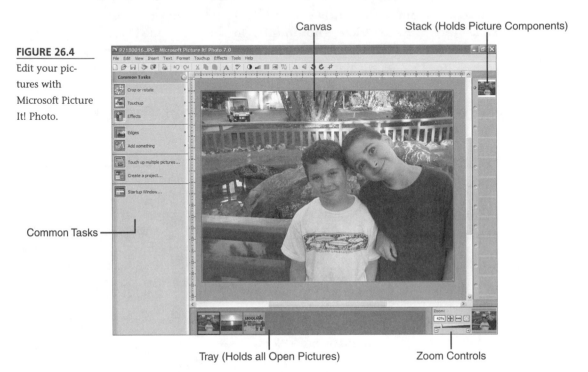

Common Tasks

Tray (Holds all Open Pictures)                    Zoom Controls

## Touching Up a Picture

To perform basic touch-up operations, select Touchup from the Common Tasks panel. You have several types of touch-ups to choose from:

- **Levels autofix**—Automatically adjusts brightness, contrast, and color levels for a more pleasing picture
- **Brightness and contrast**—Lets you lighten or darken your picture
- **Adjust tint**—Lets you change the color level and tint
- **Fix red eye**—Removes the red tint caused by inappropriate flash
- **Sharpen or blue**—Helps you sharpen a dull picture, or soften a picture with a lot of visible defects

When you select one of these options, the Common Tasks pane changes to display the options for that selection. Follow the onscreen directions to make the appropriate changes.

## Cropping a Picture

One of the more common picture flaws comes when the subject of the picture isn't ideally positioned. You can fix this type of flaw by *cropping* the picture to eliminate unwanted areas of the image.

To crop a picture with Picture It! Photo, follow these steps:

1. Select **Crop or Rotate** from the **Common Tasks** panel, and then select **Crop Canvas**.

2. Pick a shape for your final cropped image.

3. Move and resize the final image in the canvas area, as shown in Figure 26.5.

4. Click the **Done** button to complete the crop.

**FIGURE 26.5**

Applying a star-shaped crop to a picture.

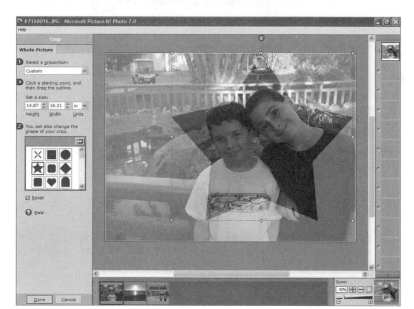

## Adding Special Effects

Picture It! Photo includes lots of other neat special effects you can add to your pictures—more than can be described here. You can find most of these special effects on the Common Tasks panel, under the Effects, Edges, and Add Something options. The best way to discover these effects is to experiment on your own—which can also be a lot of fun!

## Creating Photo Albums and Other Projects

Picture It! Photo lets you create all sorts of projects with your digital photos. For example, you can create a great-looking photo album, or professional looking picture postcards or holiday cards.

When you select Create a Project from the Common Tasks pane, Picture It! Photo displays the Pick a Design screen, shown in Figure 26.6. Click the type of project you want to create, choose a subcategory (if prompted), then select a particular design theme. Continue following the onscreen instructions to add your own photos to the selected project, and you'll be pleasantly pleased by the results!

**FIGURE 26.6**

Use Picture It! Photo to create fun photo projects.

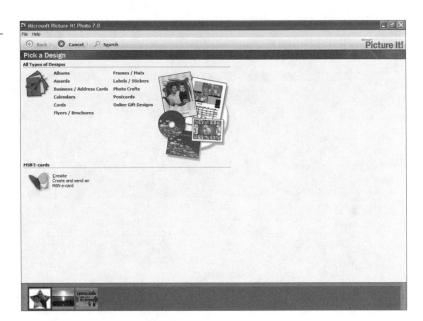

## Printing Your Photos

Once you've touched up (or otherwise manipulated) your photos, it's time to print them out—a task that's really easy in Windows XP.

## Choosing the Right Printer—and Paper

If you have a color printer, you can make good-quality prints of your image files. Even a low-priced color inkjet can make surprisingly good prints, although the better your printer, the better the results.

Some manufacturers sell printers specifically designed for photographic prints. These printers use special photo print paper and output prints that are almost indistinguishable from those you get from a professional photo processor. If you take a lot of digital photos, one of these printers might be a good investment.

The quality of your prints is also affected by the type of paper you use. Printing on standard laser or inkjet paper is okay for making proofs, but you'll want to use a thicker, waxier paper for those prints you want to keep. Check with your printer's manufacturer to see what type of paper it recommends for the best quality photo prints.

## Printing from a Program

Any picture editing program will let you print your pictures from within the program—often with useful options. For example, Microsoft Picture It! Photo lets you select the size of the final print and the orientation of the picture (portrait or landscape). The program even lets you mirror the image, for printing iron-on tee shirt transfers.

To initiate printing from Picture It! Photo, follow these steps:

1. Select **File**, **Print**; the Common Tasks pane changes to a Print pane.
2. Select the printer you want to use in the **Select a Printer** list.
3. Select the number of copies you want to print.
4. Select either portrait or landscape orientation.
5. If you're printing an iron-on transfer, check the **Mirror for T-Shirt Printing** option, otherwise leave this box unchecked.
6. Select a size for your prints from the **Select a Print Size List**; all standard print sizes are listed here, and there's also a custom size option.
7. If you want your picture stretched to fit within your selected dimensions, check the **Fit Within Area** option.
8. Click **Print**.

**tip**

Picture It! Photo can also print labels, sheets with multiple copies of the same photo, and index sheets. Select **File**, **Print Special**, and then make a selection.

## Using the Photo Printing Wizard

Windows XP also includes some useful options for printing pictures, via the Photo Printing Wizard. When you use the Photo Printing Wizard, you don't have to open a separate photo editing program to print your pictures.

You launch this wizard by opening the My Pictures folder, selecting a picture, and then selecting the Print Pictures option in the Picture Tasks panel. The Photo Printing Wizard then appears, and walks you step-by-step through the printing process. Here are some of the options you can select:

- Which pictures to print
- Which printer to use
- Which layout to use—full-page fax print, full-page photo print, 35-print contact sheet, 8×10 prints, 5×7 prints, 4×6 cutout prints, 4×6 album prints, 3.5×5 wallet prints, or nine wallet prints
- How many prints to print

When you complete the wizard, the printing starts, just as you specified.

# Emailing a Picture

Windows XP also gives you the option of emailing your pictures to others. Emailing images can be tricky because you face a compromise between file size and quality. Higher-quality images create larger-sized files, which take longer for your recipients to download. Smaller files make for faster downloads but can also compromise image quality.

When you let Windows XP email your pictures for you, you can choose to send the pictures at their original sizes or to make the pictures smaller for easier emailing. All you have to do is follow these steps:

1. Open the My Pictures folder and select the picture you want to email.

2. Select **Email This File** from the **File and Folder Tasks** panel; this displays the Send Pictures via Email dialog box.

3. Chose one of the two basic options (**Make All My Pictures Smaller** or **Keep the Original Sizes**), or click **Show More Options** to select from **Small**, **Medium**, and **Large** options. Choose the best size for your recipient—in most cases, smaller is better.

4. Windows now launches your email program (Outlook Express, by default), with a new message open. This message already includes your selected picture as an attachment. Just enter the recipient's email address, a subject for the message, and any desired message text. Click the **Send** button to send this message to your Outbox.

note

Learn more about sending email messages in Chapter 21, "Sending and Receiving Email."

# Printing Photos Online

If you don't have your own photo-quality printer, you can use a professional photo-processing service to print your photos. There are a number of ways you can create prints from your digital photos:

- Copy your image files to disk, and deliver the disk by hand to your local photo finisher.
- Go to the Web site of an online photo-finishing service, and transfer your image files over the Internet.
- Use the Order Prints from the Internet option in Windows XP's My Pictures folder.

The first option is kind of old-fashioned, and not always convenient. For many users, it's a lot less hassle to order photo prints from the comfort of their computer keyboards—however you do it.

## Ordering from a Photo-Processing Site

There are dozens and dozens of Web sites offering photo-processing services. They all operate in pretty much the same fashion.

After you register with the site, you upload the pictures you want printed from your hard drive to the Web site. Most sites accomplish this by giving you a few buttons to click and forms to fill out; a handful of sites let you send them your picture files as email attachments. After you upload the photos, you choose what size prints and how many copies you want, along with how fast you want them shipped. Enter your name, address, and credit card number, and your order is complete.

If you're looking for online photo services, here are some of the best and the biggest sites to consider:

- Club Photo (www.clubphoto.com)
- dotPhoto (www.dotphoto.com)
- FotoTime (www.fototime.com)
- MSN Photos (photos.msn.com)
- Ofoto (www.ofoto.com)
- PhotoAccess (www.photoaccess.com)
- PhotoFun.com (www.photofun.com)
- PhotoWorks (www.photoworks.com)
- PrintRoom (www.printroom.com)

■ Shutterfly (www.shutterfly.com)

■ Snapfish (www.snapfish.com)

## Ordering from Within Windows XP

If your new PC is running the Windows XP operating system, you can order prints directly from the My Pictures folder. All you have to do is select the files you want to print and then click the **Order Prints** from the **Internet** option in the **Picture Tasks** panel.

This launches the Internet Print Ordering Wizard. The wizard lets you pick which service you want to use, as well as what type and how many prints to make. You have to fill in all the normal shipping and payment information, of course. You'll receive your prints in a few days, just like you would if you ordered directly from that site via your Web browser.

> **tip**
>
> A lower-priced alternative to making lots of photo prints is to create your own online photo album that your friends and family can view over the Internet. Check with your favorite online photo site to see what kind of online photo album options it offers.

# THE ABSOLUTE MINIMUM

Here are the key points to remember from this chapter:

■ Use the Scanners and Camera utility to configure your PC to connect a digital camera or scanner to your computer.

■ Once you transfer your digital photos to your PC, you can use a picture editing program (such as Picture It! Photo) to touch up or edit the pictures.

■ Some of the most popular "touch ups" include removing red eye, adjusting brightness and contrast, changing color and tint, cropping the edges of the photo, and sharpening or blurring the picture.

■ You can print your photos to any four-color printer, or sent them (via the Internet) to an online photo processor for printing.

■ You can even email photos to friends and family—and let Windows XP automatically resize your pictures for quicker transmittal.

## IN THIS CHAPTER

- Play a CD on Your PC
- Using Windows Media Player
- Playing a CD
- Playing a DVD

**27**

# PLAYING CDs AND DVDs

Your personal computer can do more than just compute. It can also serve as a fully functional audio/video playback center!

That's right, you can use your PC to listen to your favorite audio CDs, and to watch the latest movies on DVD. Of course, the playback quality is limited by your PC's (small) speakers and (also small) screen, but it's a pretty convenient way to entertain yourself when you're working at the old keyboard.

And, best of all, in most cases you don't need to buy a single piece of hardware or software to use your PC for audio/video playback. Just pop a CD or DVD disc into your PC's drive, sit back, and prepare to be entertained!

# Play a CD on Your PC

Most new computer systems come complete with a CD-ROM drive. This drive reads computer CD-ROMs and plays back normal audio CDs.

In most cases this drive is installed and configured at the factory, so you don't have to do anything to use it. That's because almost all new CD drives come configured so that they start automatically when you insert an audio CD. In this scenario, your drive should start spinning, some sort of media player program will launch, and your CD should start playing through your computer's speakers. If this describes how your system works, you don't have to do anything other than sit back and listen to the music.

If, on the other hand, your CD *doesn't* start playing automatically, you have to manually launch a media player program. Fortunately, Windows includes its own media player (which might or might not be the player that launches automatically on some systems), called the Windows Media Player.

# Using Windows Media Player

Windows Media Player (WMP) is a great little program you can use for many purposes—playing CDs, recording CDs, listening to Internet radio broadcasts, watching Webcasts, and playing DVDs. It works similarly to most other media players, so if you know how to use WMP, you should be able to figure out any other media player program.

Whether you're playing a CD, DVD, or digital audio file, you use the controls located at the bottom of the WMP window, shown in Figure 27.1. These are the normal transport buttons you find on a cassette deck or VCR, including **Play/Pause**, **Stop**, **Rewind**, and **Fast Forward**. WMP also includes **Next** and **Previous track** buttons, along with a volume control and **Mute** button.

> **tip**
>
> By default, WMP is launched in its Full mode. If you'd rather display the player without all the extraneous controls, you can switch to the more compact Skin mode by clicking the **Switch to Skin Mode** button—or by pulling down the **View** menu and selecting **Skin Mode**. When you're in Skin mode, a small anchor window appears at the bottom left of your desktop; double-click this window to return to Full mode.

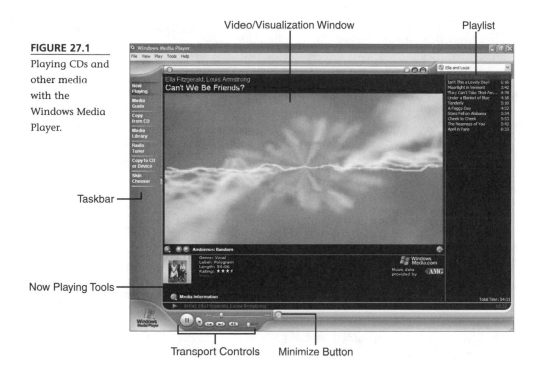

Video/Visualization Window

Playlist

**FIGURE 27.1**
Playing CDs and other media with the Windows Media Player.

Taskbar

Now Playing Tools

Transport Controls

Minimize Button

The biggest part of the WMP window is an area which displays the picture when you're playing back DVDs. When you're listening to music, this area can be used to display what Microsoft calls "visualizations" while you're listening to music. (Think of a visualization as a kind of "live" wallpaper that moves along with your music.) You can choose which visualizations are displayed by pulling down the View menu, selecting Visualizations, and then making a choice.

To the right of the video/visualization window is the Playlist area. Individual tracks of a CD or DVD are listed here. This area also displays the songs in any playlists that you create from the MP3 files stored on your hard drive. (You'll learn more about playlists and MP3 files in Chapter 29, "Downloading and Playing Digital Music.")

**note**

To display this information, your computer must be connected to the Internet. WMP automatically goes out to the Internet to retrieve information about any commercial CD or DVD you're playing.

Between the playback controls and the video/visualization window is an area called the Now Playing Tools area. This area typically displays information about the currently playing CD or audio file.

Finally, the seven buttons along the left of the window (contained in what is called the Taskbar) link to key features of the player. Click a button and the entire player interface changes to reflect the selected feature—**Now Playing**, **Media Guide**, **CD Audio**, **Media Library**, **Radio Tuner**, **Portable Device**, or **Skin Chooser**.

## Playing a CD

If WMP doesn't start automatically when you load a CD into your PC's CD-ROM drive, you can launch it manually from the Windows Start menu. You can then start playback by clicking WMP's Play button.

To pause playback, click the **Pause** button (same as the **Play** button); click **Play** again to resume playback. To skip to the next track, click the **Next** button. To replay the last track, click the Previous button. You stop playback completely by clicking the **Stop** button.

## Playing a DVD

If you have a DVD-ROM drive in your computer and the proper DVD decoder software installed, it's a snap to play DVD movies on your computer monitor.

New PCs with DVD drives installed typically come all set up for movie playback, so no additional configuration is required. If you've just added a DVD drive to an existing computer, you'll need to be sure you install the appropriate DVD decoder software. If your system is running Windows XP, you can add DVD capability with one of the DVD Decoder Pack add-ins from CyberLink, InterVideo, or Ravisent. (These cost around $30 each and are available wherever Windows is sold.) These packs add DVD playback capability to Windows Media Player (WMP)—which is probably the best software to use to play back DVD movies.

**tip**

If the sound is too loud (or not loud enough), you can change the volume by dragging the Volume slider—to the right of the transport controls—to the right (louder) or left (softer). If you need to mute the sound quickly, click the **Mute** button to the left of the Volume slider. Click the **Mute** button again to unmute the sound.

**tip**

To play the songs on a CD in a random order, select **Play**, **Shuffle**—or click the **Turn Shuffle On** button. WMP will now shuffle randomly through the tracks on the CD.

## Using Windows Media Player to Play DVDs

When you insert a DVD in your DVD drive, playback should start automatically. Your system should sense the presence of the DVD, launch Windows Media Player, and start playing the movie. (You can also initiate playback from within WMP by pulling down the Play menu and selecting DVD.)

As you can see in Figure 27.2, the picture from the DVD displays in WMP's video window. The individual tracks on the DVD are displayed in the Playlist area to the right of the screen, and information about the DVD (including the DVD cover) is displayed beneath the video window.

Video Window                    Movie Chapters

**FIGURE 27.2**

Watching a DVD movie with Windows Media Player.

Click to Display the DVD's Menu

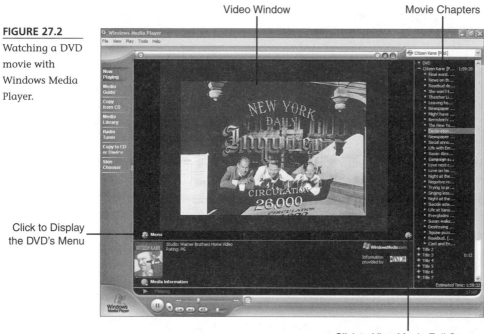

Click to View Movie Full Screen

## Changing Display Size

You can watch your movie in WMP's video window, or you can view the DVD using your entire computer screen. Just click the **Full Screen** button (at the lower-right corner of the video window)—or select **View**, **Full Screen**—and the movie will enlarge to fill your entire screen. Press **Esc** to return to normal viewing mode.

## Navigating DVD Menus

Almost all DVDs come with their own built-in menus. These menus typically lead you to special features on the disc and allow you to select various playback options and jump to specific scenes.

To display the DVD's main menu, select **View**, **DVD Features**, **Title Menu**. To display the DVD's special features menu, pull down the **View** menu and select **DVD Features**, **Top Menu**. When the special features menu is displayed, you can click any of the options onscreen to jump to a particular feature.

**note**

You have to be connected to the Internet for WMP to find and display this DVD information and cover art.

## Changing Audio Options

Many DVDs come with an English-language soundtrack, as well as soundtracks in other languages. Some DVDs come with different types of audio—mono, Dolby Pro Logic surround, Dolby Digital 5.1 surround, and so on. Other DVDs come with commentary from the film's director or stars on a separate audio track.

You can select which audio track you listen to by selecting **View**, **DVD Features**, **Audio and Language Tracks**. This displays a list of available audio options. Select the track you want to listen to, and then settle back to enjoy the movie.

## Playing in Slow Motion—or Fast Motion

WMP provides a variety of special playback features. You can pause a still frame, advance frame-by-frame, or play the movie in slow or fast motion. To access these special playback features, select **View**, **Now Playing Tools**, **DVD Controls**. This displays a set of special controls in the Now Playing Tools area of the WMP window. Use these tools to vary the playback speed or pause the movie on a still frame.

## Displaying Subtitles and Closed Captions

Many DVDs include subtitles in other languages. To turn on subtitles, select **View**, **DVD Features**, **Subtitles and Captions**, and then select which subtitles you want to view.

Other DVDs include closed captioning for the hearing impaired. You can view closed captions by selecting **View**, **DVD Features**, **Subtitles and Captions**, **Closed Captions**.

# THE ABSOLUTE MINIMUM

Here are the key points to remember from this chapter:

- Any PC with a CD-ROM drive can play back audio CDs; if your PC has a DVD drive, it can also play back DVD movies.

- To play CDs and DVDS, you use a media player program—such as Windows Media Player.

- When WMP is connected to the Internet, it will automatically download information about the currently playing CD or DVD.

- When you're playing an audio CD, you can minimize WMP by switching to Skin mode; when you're playing a DVD you can maximize the movie by switching to full-screen mode.

## IN THIS CHAPTER

- Listening to Internet Radio
- Watching Webcasts

**28**

# PLAYING INTERNET AUDIO AND VIDEO

In the last chapter you learned how to listen to audio CDs on your PC. But that's not the only music you can play on your computer; if you're connected to the Internet, you can also listen to *Internet radio*—live audio broadcasts transmitted via the Internet.

Even better, some Web sites broadcast television programs of various sorts. These video broadcasts are called *Webcasts*, and, like Internet radio, are streamed over the Internet direct to your PC.

Read on to find out how to listen to and watch these online broadcasts—and how to find the best programs online!

# Listening to Internet Radio

Many real-world radio stations broadcast over the Internet using a technology called *streaming audio*. Streaming audio is different from downloading an audio file (which you'll learn more about in Chapter 29, "Downloading and Playing Digital Music"). When you download a file, you can't start playing that file until it is completely downloaded to your PC. With streaming audio, however, playback can start before an entire file is downloaded. This also enables live broadcasts—both of traditional radio stations and made-for-the-Web stations—to be sent from the broadcast site to your PC.

**tip**

While you can listen to Internet radio over a traditional dial-up connection, you'll hear better quality sound over a broadband connection.

## Listening with Windows Media Player

In Chapter 27, "Playing CDs and DVDs," you discovered how to use Windows Media Player to listen to audio CDs. You can also use WMP to listen to many Internet radio programs. Just follow these steps:

1. Launch the Windows Media Player, then click the **Radio Tuner** button on the WMP taskbar. This automatically connects WMP to the Internet and displays a list of available Internet radio stations, as shown in Figure 28.1.

**FIGURE 28.1**

Listening to Internet radio with Windows Media Player.

2. To listen to a station on your preset list, double-click the station.

3. You can also search for stations by format, band (AM or FM), language, location, call sign, frequency, or keyword. Double-click a station name to play that station.

It's easy to create a list of presets for your favorite Internet radio stations. To add a station to your list of presets, select the station and then click the **Add** button. Your preset stations are displayed on the left side of the screen.

## Listening with RealAudio

Another popular program for playing back Internet radio is RealOne Player (available at www.real.com). Since the majority of Web sites use Real Networks' RealAudio format to deliver their streaming audio content, the RealOne Player is an extremely popular program. When you go to a Web site and click the link to start streaming audio or video playback, chances are that RealOne Player (or its predecessor, RealPlayer) will launch automatically—it's probably already installed on your PC.

Even though RealOne Player and WMP are somewhat incompatible, they both operate in pretty much the same fashion. As you can see in Figure 28.2, the main RealOne window has a row of transport controls (Play, Pause, Stop, and so on) along the top, underneath the main menu bar. There's a big window on the right to display video broadcasts, and the My Channels pane on the left displays your favorite Internet radio stations.

**note**

You might need to have both Windows Media Player and RealOne Player installed on your system. This is because Internet radio streamed in one format often can't be played on the competing player.

To use RealOne Player to listen to Internet radio broadcasts, follow these steps:

1. From the RealOne Player, select **View**, **Radio**; this opens a separate Radio window below the main player window, as shown in Figure 28.2.

2. Either browse through the available genres, or search for a specific station.

3. To go directly to your favorite station, select the **My Stations** tab.

4. To begin playback, click the link for a specific station.

**FIGURE 28.2**

The main RealOne Player window.

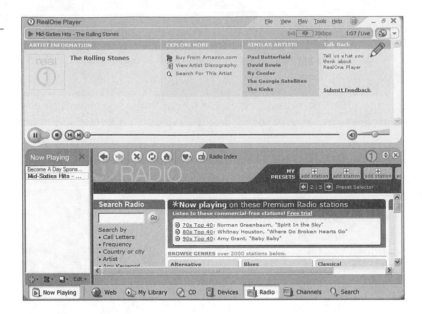

## Finding an Internet Radio Station

When you're looking for Internet radio broadcasts (of which there are thousands, daily), you need a good directory of available programming. Here's a list of sites that offer links to either traditional radio simulcasts or original Internet programming:

- Live@ (www.live-at.com)
- Radio Broadcast Network (www.radiobroadcast.net)
- Radio-Locator (www.radio-locator.com)
- RadioMOI (www.radiomoi.com)
- SHOUTcast (yp.shoutcast.com)
- Web-Radio (www.web-radio.com)

# Watching Webcasts

When you add pictures to an Internet radio broadcast, you get Internet television—or what some people call *Webcasts*. Just as Internet radio broadcasts use streaming audio technology, Webcasts use streaming video to deliver both prerecorded and real-time pictures direct to your PC.

There are actually three formats for streaming video over the Internet. Each format requires a different type of media player program, which means you will probably have to download and install all three programs on your PC.

## Using Windows Media Player

You're familiar with Windows Media Player (WMP) because we've used it to perform a number of activities in this book. You should have a copy of WMP already installed on your PC; it comes free of charge as part of Microsoft Windows.

When you're using WMP to watch a Webcast, it's easy to change the size of the video display. Just pull down the **View** menu, select **Zoom**, and then choose from **50%**, **100%**, **200%**, or **Fit to Window**. You can also display the video full-screen by pulling down the **View** menu and selecting **Full Screen**.

## Using RealOne Player

Using RealOne Player to watch RealMedia-format Webcasts is almost identical to using it to listen to Internet radio broadcasts. In addition, you can change the size of RealOne Player's video display by using the Zoom control. Just click the **Zoom** button and select from **Original Size**, **Double Size**, or **Full Screen**.

## Using QuickTime Player

Apple's QuickTime Player is a media player similar to WMP and RealOne Player, used primarily for playing QuickTime-format movies and video clips. You can download a copy of the player from `www.apple.com/quicktime/`.

QuickTime Player, shown in Figure 28.3, is a little different from RealPlayer or WMP in that if you open multiple movies at the same time, multiple viewing windows are displayed. You can change the size of the viewing window by pulling down the **Movie** menu and then selecting from **Normal Size**, **Double Size**, or **Full Screen**.

**FIGURE 28.3**

Watching movies with QuickTime Player.

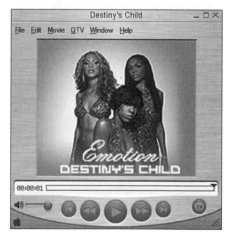

## Finding Webcasts on the Internet

Many different sites offer different types of Webcast programming. Most Webcasts are simulcasts of traditional television programs or sporting events. There are also a variety of live concerts and special events broadcast in real-time over the Web.

To find a Webcast, check out the following sites:

- Feedroom (www.feedroom.com)
- InterneTV (www.internetv.com)
- LikeTelevision (www.liketelevision.com)
- mediaontap.com (www.mediaontap.com)
- RealGuide (realguide.real.com)
- Yahoo! Broadcast (broadcast.yahoo.com)

In addition, most of the major news sites offer Internet television broadcasts of the latest news clips and headlines directly from their home pages. You can also find streaming video of selected sporting events at the major Web sports sites.

**tip**

You really need a broad-band Internet connection to watch Webcasts. A normal dial-up connection simply isn't add fast enough to watch high-bandwidth streaming video programming.

# THE ABSOLUTE MINIMUM

Here are the key points to remember from this chapter:

- Live audio broadcast over the Web is called Internet radio; live video broadcasts are called Webcasts.
- Internet radio and Webcasts both use streaming technology to funnel their broadcasts to your PC.
- To listen to or watch a streaming broadcast over the Internet, you use a media player program—such as Windows Media Player or RealOne Player.
- While Internet radio works well over a traditional dial-up connection, you probably need a broadband connection to view Webcasts at an acceptable quality level.

## IN THIS CHAPTER

- Understanding Digital Audio
- Finding Digital Music to Download
- Swapping Files with Other Users
- Playing Digital Music on Your PC
- Making Copies of Your Favorite Songs

**29**

# DOWNLOADING AND PLAYING DIGITAL MUSIC

Downloading music from the Web is a big deal. Originally popularized by college students (with fast university Internet connections), users of all ages are now using the Internet for at least part of their music listening.

If you're a music lover, digital music—in the form of MP3 files—is a really cool thing. Want to check out the latest single from a new band you've been hearing about? Then download it. Want your own copy of a big top forty hit from your teenage years? Download it. Or how about digging up an obscure album track from some long out-of-print vinyl LP? Chances are, you can download that, too.

There's a wealth of music available online that you can download and then play back on your PC. You can even copy your downloaded files to a portable digital music player, and take your MP3s with you on the go. It's like having the world's biggest jukebox available to you, over the Internet.

So read on—and learn more about the world of digital audio!

# Understanding Digital Audio

Anyone with a personal computer—and the right software—can make digital copies of music from CDs, and then store these copies on their computer's hard disk. These digital audio files can also be traded with other users, over the Internet.

There are many different ways to make a digital recording, which results in many different file formats for digital audio. The two most popular file formats are MP3 and WMA (Windows Media Audio).

## MP3 Audio

MP3 is the most popular digital audio format because it was the first widely accepted format that combined near-CD quality sound with reasonably small file sizes. Before MP3, a CD's worth of music took up 600MB or more on your hard disk. With MP3 (and competing formats), the same amount of music might only use 60MB of hard disk space.

Most audio player programs—such as Windows Media Player—can play back files recorded in either MP3 or WMA formats.

File size is important not just because smaller files take up less space on your hard drive, but also because they take less time to download over the Internet. With a normal 56.6Kbps dial-up connection, a 3MB song takes about five minutes to download. This same song, uncompressed (as it originally appeared on CD), is a 32MB file—which would take more than a half-hour to download.

## Windows Media Audio

MP3 isn't the only digital audio file format in use today. Microsoft is waging a strong campaign for its Windows Media Audio (WMA) format, which offers similar quality to MP3, but with slightly smaller files.

WMA also offers something that you might not want—copy protection. Files encoded in the WMA format can be configured to play back only on the system that recorded the files. This means you might find WMA files that were recorded on other computers and won't play back on your computer—or were recorded on your computer, but won't play back on your portable audio player.

So, while the music industry likes the fact that WMA protects its copyrights, most users prefer the MP3 format, which doesn't impose any copy protection on users.

# Finding Digital Music to Download

In recent years there has been a flood of digital audio files available on the Internet. Some of these files are official versions, supplied by artists and record labels; other files are created by normal users who record songs from their own CD collections.

There are a number of both "official" and "unofficial" digital audio archive sites and services on the Web. The official sites typically charge some sort of subscription fee to download a certain number of songs per month; the unofficial sites offer an unlimited selection of music for free.

To find files to download, fire up Internet Explorer and navigate to one of the following Web sites:

- AMPCAST.COM (www.ampcast.com)
- ARTISTdirect (www.artistdirect.com)
- BeSonic (www.besonic.com)
- EMusic (www.emusic.com)
- Launch (launch.yahoo.com)
- Lycos Music (music.lycos.com)
- Buymusic.com (www.buymusic.com)
- iTunes (www.apple.com/itunes/)
- Napster 2.0 (www.napster.com)
- RealOne (www.real.com)
- sonicnet.com (www.sonicnet.com)

Figure 29.1 shows the new Napster 2.0 software. As with many of these services, Napster requires you to download a proprietary music player program; you can then access a library of more than 500,000 songs for downloading. Napster, like most of the other paid services, charges 99 cents per song, or $9.99 per album. You can also pay $9.95 per month for unlimited streaming audio.

**FIGURE 29.1**

Downloading individual songs from the new Napster.

# Swapping Files with Other Users

In addition to these archives of digital music, there are also services that let you swap digital audio files directly with other users. These file-swapping services help you find other users who have the songs you want. You then connect directly to the user's computer and copy the file you want from that computer to yours.

Among the most popular of these file-sharing services are

- Gnutella (www.gnutelliums.com)
- KaZaA Media Desktop (www.kazaa.com)
- MusicCity Morpheus (www.musiccity.com)

Most of these services require you to download a copy of their software and then run that software whenever you want to download. You use their software to search for the songs you want; the software then generates a list of users who have that file stored on their computers. You select which computer you want to connect to, and then the software automatically downloads the file from that computer to yours.

> **note**
>
> It works the other way, also. When you register with one of these services, other users can download digital audio files from *your* computer, as long as you're connected to the Internet.

# Playing Digital Music on Your PC

After you've downloaded a fair number of MP3- or WMA-format digital audio files, you probably want to listen to them. Just as you need a CD player to play your compact discs, you need a digital audio player program to play MP3 and WMA files on your computer.

## Choosing a Media Player

There are a number of digital audio players available, most for free and almost all downloadable over the Internet. The most popular audio player programs include

- RealOne Player (www.real.com)
- Sonique Media Player (sonique.lycos.com) )
- UltraPlayer (www.ultraplayer.com) )
- WinAmp (www.winamp.com) )

Aside from these popular programs, there's another digital audio player you might want to consider—because it's probably already installed on your PC. This player is the Windows Media Player (WMP), and we'll examine how to use WMP to manage all your digital audio files.

**note**

The original MP3 file-sharing service was Napster. Due to an ongoing series of copyright-infringement lawsuits, Napster is no longer in business.

**caution**

Downloading or copying copyrighted material without permission is against the law and deprives musicians of their hard-earned income. Let your conscience be your guide.

## Playing Digital Audio Files

Whichever audio player you use, you follow the same general steps to play an MP3 or WMA file. You start by launching the program; then, you pull down the **File** menu and select **Open**. (Some players have an **Open** button you can use, instead.) Select the file you want to play, and then use the player's transport controls to play, pause, and stop playback.

Some players let you create *playlists* of songs to play, one after another. You can create playlists from the files you have stored on your hard disk, in any order you want.

## Using Windows Media Player

If you've read the previous two chapters, you already know Windows Media Player. It's a versatile media player that's included free with Microsoft Windows, and is probably already installed on your PC.

To play back an MP3 or WMA file with WMP, you follow these steps:

1. Select the **Now Playing** tab.

2. Select **File**, **Open**.

3. Select the file you want to play; the file you selected will start playing automatically.

WMP stores your favorite files in what it calls the Media Library (shown in Figure 29.2). To add a file to the Media Library, select **File**, **Add to Library**, then select either **Add Currently Playing Track**, **Add File** (to add a file from your hard disk), or **Add URL** (to add a file from the Web) .

**FIGURE 29.2**

Store your favorite MP3 files in WMP's Media Library.

## Create a Playlist of Your Favorite Songs

Files in your WMP Media Library can be combined into *playlists*. This way you can play all your favorite songs in a single operation—just like listening to a radio station's playlist.

To create a new playlist, follow these steps:

1. Select the **Media Library** tab.
2. Click the **New Playlist** button (shown in Figure 29.3) to display the New Playlist dialog box.
3. Enter a name for the playlist and click **OK**.

**FIGURE 29.3**

Use these buttons to create a new playlist and add songs to an existing playlist.

To add a file to a playlist, follow these steps:

1. Select the **Media Library** tab.
2. Select the file from the title listing.
3. Click the **Add to Playlist** button (shown in Figure 29.4), and select **Additional Playlists**; this displays the Playlist dialog box.
4. Select the playlist you want to copy to.
5. Click **OK**.

Playing an entire playlist is a simple operation. Just follow these steps:

1. Select the **Now Playing** tab.
2. Pull down the **Playlist** list (in the top right-hand corner of the WMP window) and select a playlist.

The playlist should start playing automatically. If not, all you have to do is click the **Play** button. All the tracks in your playlist will play, one at a time, in the order listed.

# Making Copies of Your Favorite Songs

If you have a decent compact disc collection and a CD-ROM drive in your computer system, you can make your own MP3 or WMA files from the

**tip**

You can play the songs in your playlist in random order by clicking the **Turn Shuffle On** button (or selecting **Play, Shuffle**) .

songs on your CDs. You can then listen to these files on your computer, download the files to a portable audio player for listening on the go, share them with other users via a file-swapping service, or use these files to burn your own custom mix CDs.

This process of copying files from a CD to your hard disk, in either MP3 or WMA format, is called *ripping*. You use an audio encoding program, such as Windows Media Player or MusicMatch Jukebox, to rip your files.

The ripping process is fairly simple. You start by inserting the CD you want to copy from into your PC's CD-ROM drive. Then you launch your encoder program and select which songs on your CD you want to rip. You'll also need to select the format for the final file (MP3 or WMA) and the *bit rate* you want to use for encoding; the higher the bit rate, the better the sound quality. (And the larger the file size!) After you've set everything up, click the appropriate button to start the encoding process.

After you start encoding, the song(s) you selected will be played from your PC's CD drive, processed through the encoder program into a WAV-format file, encoded into an MP3- or WMA-format file (your choice), and then stored on your hard disk.

## Ripping with Windows Media Player

Windows Media Player (WMP) not only plays back digital audio files, it can also create those files from the songs on a compact disc. The only drawback about using WMP to encode digital audio is that, by default, it doesn't encode in the MP3 format. While WMP can play back both MP3 and WMA files, it can encode only in the WMA format.

> **caution**
>
> After you've started the encoding process, do *not* use your computer to do anything else while encoding; doing so runs the risk of adding "skips" to your MP3s.

You can, however, add MP3-format encoding to WMP. You do this via an add-on software utility called the MP3 Creation Pack. This add-on pack is available (for about $30) in three versions, each using a different MP3 encoder. The three versions are marketed by CyberLink (www.gocyberlink.com), InterVideo (www.intervideo.com), and Sonic CinePlayer (www.cineplayer.com); one version is as good as the other.

### Setting the Format and Quality Levels

Before you begin copying, you first have to tell WMP what format you want to use for your ripped files—and which quality level you want to record at.

You do this by following these steps:

1. Select **Tools**, **Options** to display the Options dialog box.
2. Select the **Copy Music** tab.

3. Go to the Copy Settings section of the dialog box, pull down the **File Format** list, and select either **Windows Media Audio** or **MP3**. (If you haven't installed the MP3 Creation Pack, you won't have a choice here—your only option will be **Windows Media Audio**.)

4. Use the **Copy Music at This Quality** slider to set the bit rate for your ripped files. Move the slider to the left for smaller files and lower sound quality. Move the slider to the right for larger files and higher sound quality.

5. Click **OK** when done.

**tip**

When you're copying in the WMA format, either the 96Kbps or 128Kbps level should be a good compromise between file size and sound quality. When you're copying in the MP3 format, the 128Kbps rate is recommended—although higher bit rates produce noticeably better-sounding files.

### Ripping the Files

After your settings are set, it's time to start ripping. Follow these steps:

1. Insert the CD you want to rip into your PC's CD-ROM drive.

2. Connect to the Internet; this lets WMP download track names and CD cover art for the songs you're ripping.

3. In WMP, select the **Copy from CD** tab to show the contents of the CD.

4. Put a check mark by the tracks you want to copy.

5. When you've selected which tracks to rip, click the **Copy Music** button.

WMP now begins to copy the tracks you selected, in the format you selected, and at the quality level you selected. Unless you specify otherwise in the Options dialog box, the tracks are recorded into your My Music folder, into a subfolder for the artist, and within that in another subfolder for this particular CD.

## Ripping with MusicMatch Jukebox

MusicMatch Jukebox is the most popular MP3 encoding program because it's so easy to use—

**note**

You can download a free copy of MusicMatch Jukebox from `www.musicmatch.com`.

practically the entire process is automated. It also has MP3 encoding built in, so you don't have to buy or install any "add-on" software like you do with Windows Media Player.

To rip a CD with MusicMatch Jukebox, follow these steps:

1. Connect to the Internet, then launch the MusicMatch software, shown in Figure 29.4.

**FIGURE 29.4**

Use MusicMatch Jukebox to convert a CD to digital audio files.

2. From MusicMatch Jukebox, click the **Record** button; this starts the encoder program.

3. Insert the CD you want to copy from into your PC's CD-ROM drive. MusicMatch will now synch up (over the Internet) with CDDB, an online database, to obtain track information.

4. To set the bit rate and format for recording, select **Options**, **Recorder**, **Settings**; when the next dialog box appears, select the **Settings** tab. In the Recording Quality section, select the desired bit rate and format, then click **OK**.

5. Back in the main window, check the boxes next to the tracks you want to copy.

6. When you've selected which tracks to rip, click the **Record** button.

MusicMatch now copies the selected files from your CD to the My Music folder on your hard disk.

# The Absolute Minimum

Here are the key points to remember from this chapter:

- Music can be converted to digital audio files in either the MP3 or WMA file formats.

- Both MP3 and WMA files compress music files to about one-tenth the file size they occupy on an audio CD.

- You can use any audio player program—such as Windows Media Player—to play back digital audio files.

- There are a number of sites that offer MP3 files for downloading over the Internet; some of the "official" sites" require a paid subscription, while most unofficial sites are free.

- You can also swap MP3 files with other users, using a file-swapping service like KaZaA.

- To convert songs from an audio CD to MP3 format (called "ripping"), use an audio encoding program like MusicMatch Jukebox.

## IN THIS CHAPTER

- How to Burn a CD
- Burning CDs with Windows Media Player
- Creating CD Labels

**30**

# BURNING YOUR OWN CDS

One of the great things about having a recordable/rewritable CD (CD-R/RW) drive in your computer system is that you can make your own audio mix CDs. You can take any combination of songs on your hard disk (in either MP3 or WMA format) and "burn" them onto a blank CD—and then play that CD in your home, car, or portable CD player.

And, although the big record labels discourage it, you can also use your CD burner to make copies of other CDs in your collection. That way you can have keep the original for your home audio system, and take the copy with you to play back in your car.

You might think that burning a CD is a complicated high-tech procedure. It isn't. Burning a CD is almost as easy as copying files from one folder to another—and much less complicated than making an old-fashioned mix cassette tape!

# How to Burn a CD

Unlike CD ripping, CD burning doesn't require you to set a lot of format options. That's because whatever format the original file is in, when it gets copied to CD it gets encoded into the CD Audio (CDA) format. All music CDs use the CDA format, so whether you're burning an MP3 or WMA file, your CD burner software translates it to CDA before the copy is made.

There are no quality levels to set, either. All CDA-format files are encoded at the same bit rate. So you really don't have any configuration to do—other than deciding which songs you want to copy.

The easiest way to burn a CD full of songs is to copy an entire playlist. Assemble the playlist beforehand (in your audio player program) to get the timing right, and then send the entire playlist to your CD. You can record up to 74 minutes or 650MB worth of music, whichever comes first.

After you've decided which songs to copy, load a blank CD-R disc into your computer's CD-R/RW drive, launch your CD burner software, and then follow the program's instructions to start translating and copying the song files. After the ripping begins, the MP3 files on your hard drive are converted and copied onto a blank CD-R in standard CD Audio format.

**tip**

To play your new CD in a regular (non-PC) CD player, record in the CD-R format and use a blank CD-R disc specifically labeled for audio use. (CD-RW discs will not play in most CD players.)

# Burning CDs with Windows Media Player

Because most CD burner software works in pretty much the same fashion, you might as well use Windows Media Player (WMP) to burn your CDs. (It's already installed on your PC, after all.)

To use WMP to burn a music CD, follow these steps:

1. Insert a blank CD-R disc into your computer's CD-R/RW drive.
2. From within WMP, select the **Media Library** tab.

**tip**

MusicMatch Jukebox (www.musicmatch.com) is another popular CD burner program.

3. Create a playlist of the songs you want to burn. (You learned how to create a WMP playlist in Chapter 29, "Downloading and Playing Digital Music.")

4. Select the **Copy to CD** or **Device** tab; this displays the Music to Copy list, shown in Figure 30.1.

5. Click the **Music to Copy** section to display all your playlists.

6. Select the playlist or album you want to copy.

7. Select your CD-R/RW drive from WMP's Music on Device list.

8. Click the **Copy Music** button.

**FIGURE 30.1**

Preparing to copy a complete playlist to CD.

WMP now inspects the files you want to copy, converts them to CDA format, and copies them to your CD. When the entire process is done, WMP displays a Closing Disk message for the last track on your playlist. The burning is complete when this message is displayed.

## Creating CD Labels

When you burn a custom CD, it's a good idea to create a label for the new CD—and maybe even a track listing for the CD jewelbox.

**tip**

You can find round labels specially made for compact discs at your local computer or office supply store.

There are many label-creation programs available. If you have Microsoft Works Suite on your system, Microsoft Picture It! Photo lets you create some great-looking CD picture labels. (See Figure 30.2 for an example.) You should also check out some of the many inexpensive third-party label maker software, including:

- cdrLabel (www.ziplabel.com)
- My CD Labeler (www.elibrium.com/mysoftware/)
- Neato CD Labeler Kit (www.neato.com)

**FIGURE 30.2**

A CD picture label, created with Microsoft Picture It! Photo.

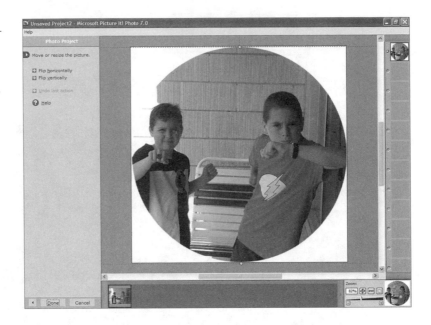

# THE ABSOLUTE MINIMUM

Here are the key points to remember from this chapter:

- The process of copying digital audio files to an audio CD is called "burning."
- To make your own music CDs, you need a digital audio player program that supports CD burning—such as Windows Media Player.
- Burning a music CD is as simple as assembling a playlist of songs, and then copying those songs onto a blank CD-R disc, in CD Audio format.
- Once you've burned your CD, use a label maker program to create round CD labels and jewelbox inserts.

## IN THIS CHAPTER

- Connecting and Configuring Your System for Video Editing
- Understanding Windows Movie Maker
- Importing Your Source Material
- Editing Your Video
- Adding Transitions
- Working with Audio
- Saving—and Watching—Your Movie

31

# EDITING YOUR OWN HOME MOVIES

If you have a camcorder and make your own home movies, you can use your computer system to make those movies a lot more appealing. With the right hardware and software, you can turn your PC into a video editing console—and make your home movies look a *lot* more professional.

PC-based video editing software performs many of the same functions as the professional editing consoles you might find at your local television station. You can use video editing software to cut entire scenes from your movie, rearrange scenes, add fancy transitions between scenes, add titles (and subtitles), and even add your own music soundtrack. The results are amazing!

And the neat thing is, you probably don't have to buy anything extra to do your video editing. If you're using Windows XP and have one of the latest digital video recorders, all you have to do is hook up a few cables and start editing!

# Connecting and Configuring Your System for Video Editing

Windows XP includes its own video editing software, called Windows Movie Maker (WMM). While there are more sophisticated programs available, WMM includes all the features you need to do basic home video editing.

Preparing your PC for video editing is fairly simple. All you have to do is connect your camcorder or VCR to your PC system unit. How you do this depends on what type of camcorder or VCR you have.

If you have a VHS, VHS-C, SVHS, 8mm, or Hi8 recorder, you'll need to buy and install an analog-to-digital video capture card in your PC. (You can buy one at most computer stores.) You'll plug your recorder into the jacks in this card (typically using standard RCA connectors), and it will convert the analog signals from your recorder into the digital audio and video your computer understands.

If you have one of the latest digital video (DV) recorders in the Digital8 or MiniDV formats, you don't need a video capture card. What you do need is an IE1394 FireWire interface, which is included with many new PCs. This type of the connection is fast enough to handle the huge stream of digital data pouring from your DV recorder into your PC.

**tip**

If you need a more sophisticated video editing program, check out either Adobe Premiere (www.adobe.com) or Ulead MediaStudio (www.ulead.com/msp/).

**tip**

For best results, you should strive for a completely digital chain. Start with digital video shot on Digital8 or MiniDV, edit the video digitally with Windows Movie Maker, and then output the completed movie to a CD or DVD in WMV format.

# Understanding Windows Movie Maker

Windows Movie Maker works by dividing your home movie into scene segments it calls *clips*. You can then rearrange and delete specific clips to edit the flow of your movie.

The basic WMM window is divided into four parts, as shown in Figure 31.1. All the clips you can use appear in the Clips area in the middle of the screen. The movie you assemble from these clips appears in the Workspace at the bottom of the screen. You can view your movie-in-progress in the Monitor area.

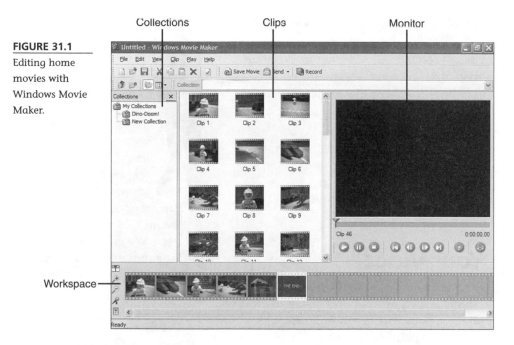

Collections          Clips          Monitor

Workspace

**FIGURE 31.1**
Editing home
movies with
Windows Movie
Maker.

# Importing Your Source Material

The first step in editing your movie is to import
your original home movie into Windows Movie
Maker. Follow these steps:

1. Connect your camcorder or VCR to
   your PC.

2. Launch Windows Movie Maker.

3. Select **File**, **Record** to display the Record
   dialog box.

4. After you have your camcorder or VCR
   connected, pull down WMM's **File** menu
   and select **Record** to display the Record
   dialog box.

5. Pull down the **Record** list and select the type of source material you want to
   record, then pull down the **Setting** list and select the level of recording quality you want.

6. Still within the Record dialog box, check the **Record Time Limit and
   Create Clips** options, and click the **Record** button.

## tip

For most purposes,
Medium Quality represents a
good compromise between
audio/video quality and file
size.

7. Move to your VCR or camcorder and click the unit's **Play** button.

8. Recording will now start and continue until you click WMM's **Stop** button (or two hours elapse, whichever comes first).

9. When recording is stopped, the Save Windows Media File dialog box appears; enter a name and location for this file, and then click **Save**.

The new clips you create now appear in the Clips area of the WMM window.

# Editing Your Video

You create your movie by dragging clips into the Workspace area. You can insert clips in any order, and more than once if you want. After the clips are in the Workspace, you can drag them around in a different order. This is how you edit the flow of your movie.

Working with Movie Maker's clips is fairly intuitive. Just drag things into place and move them around as you like, and you have 90% of it mastered.

## Add a Clip

To add a clip to your project, use your mouse to drag it into position in the Workspace. You can add a clip more than once, to repeat it in different sections of your movie.

## Move a Clip

To move a clip from one position to another, grab it with your mouse and drag it to the new position. The surrounding clips will be rearranged when the clip is dropped into its new position.

**tip**

While most of your projects will consist primarily of movies recorded from videotape, you can also use other types of source material—including movie clips you download from the Internet, songs you rip from your favorite CDs, or title slides you create in a graphic editing program. Just select **File**, **Import**, then navigate to and select the file you want to import. The files you import will appear as one or more clips in the Clips panel.

**tip**

By default, the Workspace is shown in Storyboard view. This view is easiest for seeing how all your clips fit together. When you get the basic flow of your movie in place, you can switch the Workspace to Timeline view (by clicking the **Timeline/Storyboard** button at the upper-left of the workspace). In this view you see the timing of each segment and can overlay background music and narration.

## Remove a Clip

If you end up with a clip that you no longer want to include, just select it and then select **Edit**, **Delete**.

## Trim a Clip

Sometimes a clip contains more footage than you really want. You can remove excess parts from a clip by *trimming* it from the beginning or end.

You trim a clip by setting its *trim points*. There's a start trim point and an end trim point, and everything outside these two points will be trimmed.

The easiest way to set the trim points is to display the Workspace in Timeline view and then select the clip to trim. Two trim handles appear above the selected clip (as shown in Figure 31.2), and you can use your mouse to move the handles to make your trim.

**FIGURE 31.2**
Adjust the trim handles with your mouse when you're in Timeline view.

You can also trim a clip in real time by playing the clip on the Monitor. While the clip is playing, select **Clip**, **Set Start Trim Point** to set the beginning of the area to be trimmed. Select **Clip**, **Set End Trim Point** to set the end of the area to be trimmed.

## Split a Clip

As you start to edit your movie, you'll probably find that the cuts and edits you want to make sometimes fall in the middle of a clip. When this is the case, you can split the clip in two and then work with each half of the clip separately.

**tip**

Trim handles are easier to work with when you expand the Timeline by clicking the **Zoom In** button.

To split a clip, follow these steps:

1. From the Clips area, select the clip you want to split and begin playing it on the Monitor.

2. When you reach the point where you want to make the split, click the **Pause** button. (You can then reverse and forward the clip to find the exact split point.)

3. Select **Clip**, **Split**.

You've now created two separate clips. The first clip retains the name of the original clip. The second clip has the original name with the number one in parentheses: (1).

### Combine Multiple Clips

You may want to combine two or more contiguous clips into a single clip, to make them easier to work with in the Workspace. To do this, select the clips (by holding down **Ctrl** while clicking each clip) and then select **Clip**, **Combine**. The combined clip retains the name of the first clip you selected.

## Adding Transitions

Once you've assembled all your clips, you can see how your movie plays by selecting all the clips and playing them on the Monitor. What you'll see is the "rough cut" of your movie, with very abrupt cuts between clips.

To make a more pleasing movie, you can add professional cross-fade transitions between scenes, where the last frames in the first clip fade out as the initial frames of the second clip fade in.

To create a transition, the Workspace must be in Timeline view. Then all you have to do is drag the second clip so that it overlaps the first clip. The shaded area indicates the length of the transition.

## Working with Audio

Most of your video clips will also have accompanying audio. You can overlay additional audio on top of the original audio by inserting audio clips into the timeline.

**tip**

You can change the length of the transition by dragging the second clip left or right in small increments. If you drag the second clip far enough to the right, you remove the transition.

You insert an audio clip the same way you insert a video clip. The difference is that the audio clip is displayed below the video clip in the Workspace, in what is called the audio bar.

When you insert an audio clip, it plays simultaneously with the audio from the current video clip. Actually, the audio is mixed 50/50 (original/inserted audio). You can even insert overlapping audio clips —as long as the two clips do not start and stop at precisely the same points. Again, the sound from each clip will be equally mixed.

If you don't like the automatic level mixing, you can adjust the sound levels for each clip manually, by selecting **Edit**, **Audio Levels** to display the Audio Levels dialog box. From here you can set your audio clip for background music or ambient sound, and set your video clip for foreground dialog.

If you have a microphone connected to your computer, you can add a personal narration to your movie. Just put the Workspace into Timeline view and select **File**, **Record Narration**. This opens the Record Narration dialog box; adjust the Record Level slider, click the **Record** button, and start narrating!

**note**

To work with audio clips, the Workspace must be in Timeline mode.

**tip**

Choosing the right quality level is important. The higher the quality, the larger the file size. (And movie files can get really big, really fast!) You can create smaller files by lowering the quality— but if the quality is too low, viewers might not be able to fully enjoy the movie.

# Saving—and Watching—Your Movie

When you're done editing, you save your project by selecting **File**, **Save Project**. This does not save a movie file, however—it only saves the component parts of your project.

When your project is absolutely, positively finished you actually make the movie. Pull down the **File** menu and select **Save Movie** to display the Save Movie dialog box. From here you have to select the playback quality, enter a title, and click **OK**. Windows Movie Maker then creates your movie and saves it as a WMV-format file, which can be viewed with the Windows Media Player.

# THE ABSOLUTE MINIMUM

Here are the key points to remember from this chapter:

- Windows Movie Maker is a digital video editing program, included with Windows XP, that you can use to edit your home movies originally recorded on videotape.

- For the best results, stay all-digital throughout the entire process; this means recording your original movie in Digital8 or MiniDV format.

- You can import audio files, still images, and other video files to supplement your original videotaped home movie.

- The bits and pieces of your project are called *clips*; you put together your movie by dragging clips into the Workspace area at the bottom of the Movie Maker window.

- When saving your project as a movie file, choose a high quality setting if you intend to distribute the movie via CD or DVD—or a lower setting if you want to send it across the Internet.

# PART Vi

# Protecting and Maintaining Your System

32  Protecting Yourself and Your Kids
    Online . . . . . . . . . . . . . . . . . . . . . 309

33  Adding New Hardware . . . . . . . . . . . 319

34  Setting Up a Home Network . . . . . . . . 325

35  Performing Routine Maintenance . . . . . 333

36  Dealing with Common Problems . . . . . 341

## IN THIS CHAPTER

- Protecting Against Inappropriate Content
- Dealing with Email Spam
- Protecting Your System from Computer Viruses
- Protecting Against Other Forms of Computer Attack

# 32

# PROTECTING YOURSELF AND YOUR KIDS ONLINE

When you connect your PC to the Internet, you open up a whole new world of adventure and information for you and your family. Unfortunately, you also open up a new world of potential dangers.

The Internet is full of lots of good stuff, and a fair amount of bad stuff, as well. While the good stuff definitely outnumbers the bad stuff, it's still prudent to take appropriate precautions—to protect you and your family from inappropriate content and outside attack.

Don't let the few bad apples on the Internet spoil all your fun. Read on to learn about the annoyances and dangers you might find online—and how to protect against them.

# Protecting Against Inappropriate Content

The Internet contains an almost limitless supply of information on its billion-plus Web pages. While most of these pages contain useful information, it's a sad fact that the content of some pages can be quite offensive to some people—and that there are some Internet users who prey on unsuspecting youths.

As a responsible parent, you want to protect your children from any of the bad stuff (and bad people) online, while still allowing access to all the good stuff. How do you do this?

While there are programs and services you can use to filter out inappropriate content, the most important thing you can do, as a parent, is to create an environment that encourages *appropriate* use of the Internet. Nothing replaces traditional parental supervision, and, at the end of the day, you have to take responsibility for your children's online activities. Provide the guidance they need to make the Internet a fun and educational place to visit—and your entire family will be better for it.

That said, there are some guidelines you can follow to ensure a safer surfing experience for your family:

- Make sure your children know never to give out any identifying information (home address, school name, telephone number, and so on) or to send their photos to other users online.

- Provide each of your children with an online pseudonym so they don't have to use their real names online.

- Don't let your children arrange face-to-face meetings with other computer users without parental permission and supervision. If a meeting is arranged, make the first one in a public place and be sure to accompany your child.

- Teach your children that people online might not always be who they seem; just because someone says that she's a 10-year-old girl doesn't necessarily mean that she really is 10 years old, or a girl.

- Consider making Internet surfing an activity you do together with your younger children—or turn it into a family activity by putting your kids' PC in a public room (like a living room or den) rather than in a private bedroom.

- Set reasonable rules and guidelines for your kids' computer use. Consider limiting the number of minutes/hours they can spend online each day.

- Monitor your children's Internet activities. Ask them to keep a log of all Web sites they visit; oversee any chat sessions they participate in; check out any files they download; even consider sharing an email account (especially with younger children) so that you can oversee their messages.

■ Don't let your children respond to messages that are suggestive, obscene, belligerent, or threatening—or that make them feel uncomfortable in any way. Encourage your children to tell you if they receive any such messages, and then report the senders to your ISP.

■ Install content-filtering software on your PC, and set up one of the kid-safe search sites (discussed later in this section) as your browser's start page.

■ Subscribe to America Online. AOL offers great filtering options for younger users; you can set up your kids' email accounts so that they can't receive files or pictures in their messages. AOL's filtering options can also be configured to keep younger users away from chat rooms and other inappropriate content both on AOL and the Web.

Teach your children that Internet access is not a right; it should be a privilege earned by your children and kept only when their use of it matches your expectations.

## Using Content Filtering Software

If you can't trust your children to always click away from inappropriate Web content, you can choose to install software on your computer that performs filtering functions for all your online sessions. These safe-surfing programs guard against either a pre-selected list of inappropriate sites or a pre-selected list of topics—and then block access to sites that meet the selected criteria. Once you have the software installed, your kids won't be able to access the really bad sites on the Web.

The most popular filtering programs include

■ BrowseSafe (www.browsesafe.com)

■ Cybersitter (www.cybersitter.com)

■ FamilyConnect (www.familyconnect.com)

■ Net Nanny (www.netnanny.com)

■ Norton Internet Security (www.symantec.com)

■ SurfControl (www.surfcontrol.com/products/)

**tip**

If you're an America Online subscriber, check out AOL's built-in (and very effective) Parental Controls feature. (Select **Settings**, **Parental Controls**; when the AOL Parental Controls window opens, select **Set Parental Controls**.) You can select different filtering options for different AOL screen names, and choose from four age-rated categories—**Kids Only (12 and under)**, **Young Teen (13-15)**, **Mature Teen (16-17)**, and **General Access (18+)**.

## Content Filtering with Internet Explorer

The Internet Explorer Web browser includes its own built-in content filtering via the Content Advisor, which can be used to block access to sites that meet specified criteria. Content Advisor enables you to set your own tolerance levels for various types of potentially offensive content and then blocks access to sites that don't pass muster.

To activate and configure Content Advisor, follow these steps:

1. Launch Internet Explorer, then select **Tools**, **Internet Options** to display the Internet Options dialog box.

2. Select the **Content** tab.

3. To enable the Content Advisor, click the **Enable** button. When prompted for your Supervisor Password, enter your Windows password and click **OK**.

4. To adjust the tolerance level for different types of questionable content (such as language, nudity, sex, and violence), click the **Settings** button in the Content Advisor section to display the Content Advisor dialog box.

5. Click the **Ratings** tab and select a category.

6. Adjust the **Rating** slider to the right to increase the tolerance for this type of content; leaving the slider all the way to the left is the least tolerant level.

7. Click **OK** when done.

> **caution**
>
> Turning on Content Advisor (especially at the highest levels) is likely to block access to a lot of sites you're used to visiting on a normal basis. To disable Content Advisor, return to the Internet Options dialog box and click the **Disable** button.

## Kid-Safe Searching

If you don't want to go to all the trouble of using content filtering software, you can at least steer your children to some of the safer sites on the Web. The best of these sites offer kid-safe searching, so that all inappropriate sites are filtered out of the search results.

The best of these kid-safe search sites include:

- AltaVista—AV Family Filter (www.altavista.com; click the Family Filter link)
- Apple Learning Interchange (ali.apple.com/ali/resources.shtml)
- Ask Jeeves for Kids (www.ajkids.com)
- Fact Monster (www.factmonster.com)
- Google SafeSearch (www.google.com; select the Preferences link then choose a SafeSearch Filtering option)

- OneKey (www.onekey.com)
- Yahooligans! (www.yahooligans.com)

# Dealing with Email Spam

Whenever you check your email, you have to deal with *spam*—those unsolicited, unauthorized, and unwanted marketing messages that clog your inbox every day. Junk email is the online equivalent of the junk mail you receive in your postal mailbox, and it's becoming a huge problem.

While it's probably impossible to do away with 100% of the spam you receive (you can't completely stop junk mail, either), there are steps you can take to reduce the amount of spam you have to deal with.

## Protecting Your Email Address

Spammers accumulate email addresses via a variety of methods. Some use high-tech methods to harvest email addresses listed on public Web pages and Usenet newsgroup postings. Others use the tried-and-true approach of buying names from list brokers. Still others automatically generate addresses using a "dictionary" of common names and email domains.

One way to reduce the amount of spam you receive is to limit the public use of your email address. It's a simple fact: the more you expose your email address, the more likely it is that a spammer will find it–and use it.

To this end, you should avoid putting your email address on your Web page, or your company's Web page. You should also avoid including your email address in any postings you make to Web-based message boards or Usenet newsgroups. In addition, you should most definitely not include your email address in any signatures you attach to IRC, chat room, or instant messaging messages.

**tip**

Kid-safe search sites are often good to use as the start page for your children's browser, since they are launching pads to guaranteed safe content.

**tip**

If you do have to leave your email address in a public forum, you can insert a *spamblock* into your address—an unexpected word or phrase that, while easily removed, will confuse the software spammers use to harvest addresses. For example, if your email address is john-jones@myisp.com, you might change the address to read johnSPAMBLOCKjones@myisp.com. Other users will know to remove the SPAMBLOCK from the address before emailing you, but the spam harvesting software will be foiled.

Another strategy is to actually use *two* email addresses. Take your main email address (the one you get from your ISP) and hand it out only to a close circle of friends and family; do *not* use this address to post any public messages, or to register at any Web sites. Then obtain a second email address (you can get a free one at www.hotmail.com) and use that one for all your public activity. When you post on a message board or newsgroup, use the second address. When you order something from an online merchant, use the second address. When you register for Web site access, use the second address. Over time, it's the second address that will attract the spam; your first email address will remain private and relatively spam-free.

## Blocking Addresses in Outlook Express

You can manually block messages from known spammers by using the Blocked Senders List feature in Outlook Express. When you receive a spam message in your inbox, just tell Outlook Express to ignore all future messages from this spammer. It works like this:

1. From the Outlook Express inbox, select the message from the sender you want to block.

2. Select **Message**, **Block Sender**.

Outlook Express doesn't actually block any email messages; the messages are still received by your computer, but sent immediately to the Delete folder—where they can still be viewed, until you delete the contents of the folder.

## Using Anti-Spam Software

As a last resort, you can take more drastic measures—in the form of anti-spam software. Most anti-spam software uses some combination of spam blocking or content filtering to keep spam messages from ever reaching your inbox; their effectiveness varies, but they will decrease the amount of spam you receive, to some degree.

The most popular anti-spam software includes

- ANT 4 MailChecking (ant4.com)
- Email Chomper (www.sarum.com/echomp.html)
- MailWasher (www.mailwasher.net)
- RoadBlock (www.roadblock.net)
- Spambam (www.epage.com.au/spambam/)
- SpamEater (www.hms.com/spameater.asp)
- SpamKiller (www.mcafee.com)

# Protecting Your System from Computer Viruses

Spam isn't the only menace waiting for you in your email inbox. Some email messages can also carry *computer viruses*—rogue computer programs designed to wreak havoc on your computer system.

Computer viruses can infect program files, the macro code found in some Office documents, or the HTML code used to create a Web page. Plain-text email messages are not capable of being infected—although HTML email and email attachments *can* contain viruses.

## How to Catch a Virus

Whenever you share data with another computer or computer user, you risk exposing your computer to potential viruses. There are many ways you can share data and many ways a virus can be transmitted:

- Sharing a floppy disk with another computer user
- Sharing a computer file with someone else on your network
- Opening a file downloaded from the Internet
- Opening a file attached to an email message

## Signs of Infection

How do you know whether your computer system has been infected with a virus?

In general, whenever your computer starts acting somehow different than normal, it's possible that you have a virus. You might see strange messages or graphics displayed on your computer screen or find that normally well-behaved programs are acting erratically. You might discover that certain files have gone missing from your hard disk or that your system is acting sluggish—or failing to start at all. You might even find that your friends are receiving emails from you (that you never sent) that have suspicious files attached.

If your computer exhibits one or more of these symptoms—especially if you've just downloaded a file or received a suspicious email message—the prognosis is not good. Your computer is probably infected.

## Practicing Safe Computing

Because you're not going to completely quit doing any of these activities, you'll never be 100% safe from the threat of computer viruses. There are, however, some steps you can take to reduce your risk:

- Don't open email attachments from people you don't know—or even from people you *do* know, if you aren't expecting them.
- Share disks and files only with users you know and trust.
- Download files only from reliable Web sites.
- Don't execute programs you find in Usenet newsgroups.
- Use antivirus software.

These precautions—especially the first one, about not opening email attachments—should provide good insurance against the threat of computer viruses.

## Using an Antivirus Program

Antivirus software programs are capable of detecting known viruses and protecting your system against new, unknown viruses. These programs check your system for viruses each time your system is booted and can be configured to check any programs you download from the Internet.

The most popular antivirus programs include

- Command AntiVirus (www.commandsoftware.com)
- Kaspersky Anti-Virus Personal (www.kaspersky.com)
- McAfee VirusScan (www.mcafee-at-home.com)
- Norton AntiVirus (www.symantec.com)
- PC-cillin (www.antivirus.com/pc-cillin/)

Whichever antivirus program you choose (Norton AntiVirus is shown in Figure 32.1), you'll need to go online periodically to update the virus definition database the program uses to look for known virus files. As new viruses are created every week, this file of known viruses must be updated accordingly.

**FIGURE 32.1**

Use Norton AntiVirus to protect against computer viruses.

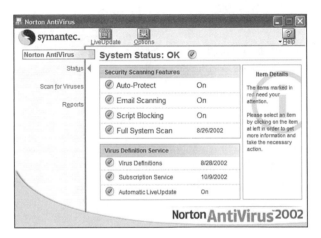

# Protecting Against Other Forms of Computer Attack

Connecting to the Internet is a two-way street—not only can your PC access other computers online, but other computers can also access *your* PC. Which means that, unless you take proper precautions, malicious hackers can read your private data, damage your system hardware and software, and even use your system (via remote control) to cause damage to other computers.

**caution**

The risk of outside attack is even more pronounced if you have an always-on connection, like that offered with DSL and cable modems.

You protect your system against outside attack by blocking the path of attack with a *firewall*. A firewall is a software program that forms a virtual barrier between your computer and the Internet. The firewall selectively filters the data that is passed between both ends of the connection and protects your system against outside attack.

## Using the Windows XP Internet Connection Firewall

If you're running Windows XP, you already have a firewall program installed on your system. You can make sure that Windows' Internet Connection Firewall is activated by following these steps:

1. Click the Windows **Start** button to display the **Start** menu.
2. Select **Connecting**, **Show All Connections** to open the Network Connections folder.
3. Right-click the connection you use for your ISP and select **Properties** from the pop-up menu; this displays the Properties dialog box.
4. Select the **Advanced** tab.
5. Make sure that the **Internet Connection Firewall** option is checked.

## Using Third-Party Firewall Software

There are also a number of third-party firewall programs available for purchase. The best of these programs include

- BlackICE PC Protection (www.iss.net/solutions/home_office/)
- Kerio Personal Firewall (www.kerio.com) /)
- McAfee Personal Firewall (www.mcafee.com) /)
- Norton Personal Firewall (www.symantec.com) /)
- Sygate Personal Firewall (www.sygate.com) /)

# THE ABSOLUTE MINIMUM

Here are the key points to remember from this chapter:

- To protect against inappropriate content on the Internet, install content filtering software—and make sure your children use a kid-safe search site.

- To reduce the amount of email spam you receive, try to keep your email address as private as possible, then install an anti-spam software program.

- Avoid computer viruses by not opening any unsolicited email attachments you receive, and by using an antispam software program.

- Protect your computer from Internet-based attack by using a firewall software program.

## IN THIS CHAPTER

- Most Popular Peripherals
- Understanding Ports
- Adding New External Hardware
- Adding New Internal Hardware
- Using the Add Hardware Wizard

33

# ADDING NEW HARDWARE

If you just purchased a brand-new, right-out-of-the-box personal computer, it probably came equipped with all the components you could ever desire—or so you think. At some point in the future, however, you might want to expand your system—by adding a second printer, or a scanner, or a PC camera, or something equally new and exciting.

Adding new hardware to your system is relatively easy, if you know what you're doing.

That's where this chapter comes in.

# Most Popular Peripherals

When it comes to adding stuff to your PC, what are the most popular peripherals? Here's a list of hardware you can add to or upgrade on your system:

- **Video card**—To display a higher-resolution picture on your computer monitor, provide smoother playback with visually demanding PC games, or add a second monitor for some high-end programming or development activities.

- **Monitor**—To upgrade to a larger viewing area or a flatter, more space-saving monitor.

- **Sound card**—To improve the audio capabilities of your systems; this is particularly important if you're listening to high-quality MP3 files, watching surround-sound DVD movies, playing PC games with so-called 3D sound, or mixing and recording your own digital audio.

- **Speakers**—To upgrade the quality of your computer's sound system. (Speaker systems with subwoofers are particularly popular.)

- **Keyboard**—To upgrade to a more ergonomic or wireless model.

- **Mouse**—To upgrade to a different type of controller (such as a trackball), a more fully featured unit, or a wireless model.

- **Joystick or other game controller**—To get better action with your favorite games.

- **Modem**—In case your PC doesn't have a state-of-the-art 56.6Kbps model, or if you're upgrading to broadband DSL or cable service.

- **CD-ROM drive**—In case your computer doesn't have one.

- **CD-R/RW drive**—To add recordable/rewritable capabilities to your system.

- **DVD**—To add DVD capability to your system.

- **Hard drive**—To add more storage capacity to your system (can be either external or internal).

- **Removable drive (such as a Zip drive)**—To add more removable storage capacity to your system.

- **Scanner**—So you can scan photographs and documents into a digital format to store on your computer's hard drive.

- **Digital still camera**—So you can transfer images from your digital camera to your computer's hard drive.

- **PC camera**—So you can send real-time video to friends and family or create your own Webcam on the Internet.

- **Portable digital audio player**—So you can download MP3 audio files to listen to on the go.

- **Network card**—So you can connect your computer to other computers in a small home network.

# Understanding Ports

Everything that's hooked up to your PC is connected via some type of *port*. A port is simply an interface between your PC and another device—either internally (inside your PC's system unit) or externally (via a connector on the back of the system unit).

Internal ports are automatically assigned when you plug a new card into its slot inside the system unit. As for external ports, many types are available—each optimized to send and receive specific types of data. Different types of hardware connect via different types of ports.

The most common types of external ports include

- **Serial**—A *serial* port is an interface that enables communication one bit at a time, in one direction at a time. Serial ports are used to connect modems, printers, mice, and similar peripherals.

- **Parallel**—A *parallel* port is an interface that can handle communications going in two directions at once. Parallel ports typically are used to connect printers and are often referred to as *printer ports*.

- **USB**—A *Universal Serial Bus (USB)* port is a newer, faster, more intelligent type of serial port. USB devices can be added while the computer is still running, which you can't do with other types of connections. You can use USB ports to connect just about any type of device, including printers, scanners, modems, CD-ROM/DVD drives, hard drives, Zip drives, PC cameras, digital still cameras, keyboards, mice, and joysticks.

- **FireWire**—*FireWire* (also called IEEE 1394) is an interface that enables hot-pluggable, high-speed data transmission. It's typically used to connect digital video camcorders, external hard drives, and CD burners.

- **SCSI**—The *small computer system interface* (*SCSI*, pronounced "scuzzy") port is a high-speed parallel interface. You use SCSI ports to connect hard disks, CD-ROM and DVD drives, Zip drives, tape backups, and other mass storage media—as well as some scanners and printers.

- **PCMCIA**—The Personal Computer Memory Card International Association (PCMCIA) established the standard for the PC Card interface used on most of today's portable PCs. On a portable PC, the PC Card slot can be used to connect everything from modems, miniature hard disks, and additional system memory.

Most computer peripherals today connect through the USB port, although other ports are still used for specific applications.

# Adding New External Hardware

Perhaps the easiest way to add new devices to your system is to add them via an external port; this way, you don't have to open your PC's case.

When attaching new devices to most ports, you should turn off your system first, connect the new device, and then restart your system. However, if you're connecting a device to a USB or FireWire port, you don't have to turn off your system to add new peripherals; the peripherals are *hot swappable*. That means you can just plug the new device into the port, and Windows will automatically recognize it in real-time. And, no matter how you're connecting, you should make sure to read the installation instructions for the new hardware, and follow the manufacturer's instructions and advice.

Follow these steps to attach a new external device to your system:

1. For all connections *except* USB and FireWire, close Windows, and turn off your computer.

2. Find an open port on the back of your system unit, and connect the new peripheral.

3. For all connections *except* USB and FireWire, restart your system.

4. As Windows starts, it should recognize the new device and either install the proper drivers automatically or ask you to supply the device drivers (via CD-ROM or disk). If you have a USB or FireWire device, Windows should recognize it automatically without rebooting.

5. Windows installs the drivers and finishes the startup procedure. Your new device should now be operational.

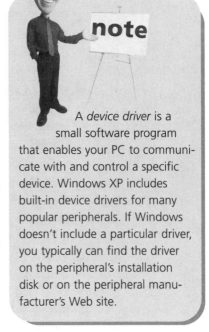

A *device driver* is a small software program that enables your PC to communicate with and control a specific device. Windows XP includes built-in device drivers for many popular peripherals. If Windows doesn't include a particular driver, you typically can find the driver on the peripheral's installation disk or on the peripheral manufacturer's Web site.

# Adding New Internal Hardware

Adding an internal device— usually through a plug-in card—is slightly more difficult than adding an external device, primarily because you have to use a screwdriver and get "under the hood" of your system unit. Other than the extra screwing and plugging, however, the process is pretty much the same as with external devices.

Follow these steps to add a new card to your system:

1. Turn off your computer, and unplug the power cable.

2. Take the case off your system unit, per the manufacturer's instructions.

3. If the new card has switches or jumpers that need to be configured, do this before inserting the card into your system unit.

4. Find an open card slot inside the system unit, and insert the new card according to the manufacturer's instructions.

5. After the card is appropriately seated and screwed in, put the case back on the system unit, plug back in the power, and restart your system.

6. After Windows starts, it should recognize the new device and automatically install the appropriate driver.

> **caution**
>
> You probably want to see whether the new component configures properly and works fine before you close your system unit back up. For that reason, you might want to leave the case off until you're convinced everything is working okay and you don't need to do any more fiddling around inside your PC.

# Using the Add Hardware Wizard

In most cases, both your system and Windows will recognize the new card without any manual prompting. If, however, Windows doesn't recognize your new device, you can install it manually via the Add Hardware Wizard. To use the Add Hardware Wizard, follow these steps:

1. Click the **Start** button to display the **Start** menu.

2. Select **Control Panel** to open the Control Panel folder.

3. Select **Add Hardware** to open the Add Hardware Wizard, shown in Figure 33.1.

4. Click the **Next** button.

5. Windows now evaluates your system and displays a list of installed devices. To add a new device, select **Add a New Hardware Device** from the list, and click the **Next** button.

6. When the next screen appears, select **Search For and Install the Hardware Automatically**; then click **Next**.

**FIGURE 33.1**

Use the Add
Hardware
Wizard to add
new hardware
to your com-
puter system.

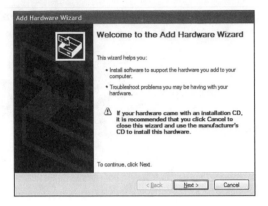

7. Windows now looks for new plug-and-play hardware. If it can identify the new hardware, the wizard continues with the installation. If it can't find a new device, it tells you so. If this is your situation, click **Next** to begin a manual installation.

8. Select the type of device you want to install, and then click **Next**.

9. On the next screen, select the manufacturer and specific device. If you want to install the drivers that came with the device, click the **Have Disk** button. To use a built-in Windows driver, click the **Next** button.

10. When the necessary files have been loaded, follow the onscreen instructions to complete the installation.

Note, however, that in most cases new hardware is detected automatically by Windows, thus eliminating the need for this somewhat more complicated procedure.

# The Absolute Minimum

Here's what you need to know if you're adding new equipment to your computer system:

■ If you connect a new component via the USB or FireWire ports, you don't have to turn off your PC first.

■ Connecting through any other port requires you to turn off your computer, connect the new component, and then restart your system.

■ When you're installing an internal card, make sure you turn off your PC before you open the system unit's case!

■ In most cases, Windows automatically recognizes your new hardware and automatically installs all the necessary drivers.

■ If Windows doesn't recognize the new piece of hardware, run the Add Hardware Wizard.

## IN THIS CHAPTER

- Understanding Home Networks
- Different Ways to Connect
- Setting Up a Home Network

**34**

# SETTING UP A HOME NETWORK

When you connect multiple computers like this, you're creating a *network*. A *local area network (LAN)* is a network of computers that are geographically close together; a *wide area network (WAN)* is a network with computers not all in the same place. The Internet is the widest-area network today, connecting computers and computer networks from all around the world.

Why would you want to connect two computers together? Maybe you want to transfer files from one computer to another. Maybe you want to share an expensive piece of hardware (such as a printer) instead of buying one for each PC. Maybe you want to connect all your computers to the same Internet connection.

Whatever your reasons, Windows XP makes it easy to create simple home networks. Read on to learn how!

# Understanding Home Networks

When you need to share files, or printers, or an Internet connection, you need to hook all your computers together into a network—similar to the one shown in Figure 4.1.

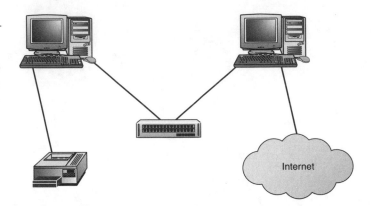

**FIGURE 34.1**

Connect two computers in a network to share a printer and an Internet connection.

Connecting multiple computers is actually fairly simple. For each computer in the network, you need to install and configure a *network interface card (NIC)*. If you're connecting more than two computers in your network, each network card then has to be connected to a *hub*, which is a simple device that functions like the hub of a wheel and serves as the central point in your network. Then, each computer has to be configured to function as part of the network and to share designated files, folders, and peripherals.

You can find everything you need to create your network in a preassembled networking kit. These kits typically contain all the cards, cables, and hubs you need to create your network, along with easy-to-follow instructions. (And if you don't want to open up your computer, you can even find kits that include external network "cards" that connect via USB ports!)

The configuration part of setting up a network is handled by Windows XP's Network Setup Wizard. You run the wizard on each PC that's connected to the network and tell it about anything else you have connected—such as a printer or an Internet connection you want to share.

The wizard does all the hard work, and when it's done, your network is up and running and ready to use.

# Different Ways to Connect

When it comes to physically connecting your network, you have a handful of choices. Here's a brief overview of the major types of networks to consider.

## Ethernet Networks

An *Ethernet network* is a traditional wired network. You install Ethernet cards in each PC and connect the cards via Ethernet cable. Although this type of network is very easy to set up and probably the lowest-cost alternative, you must deal with all that cable—which can be a hassle if your computers are in different areas of your house. Data is transferred at either 10Mbps or 100Mbps, depending on what equipment you install.

A 100Mbps Ethernet network is called *Fast Ethernet*. Some cards and hubs are labeled 10/100 because they can handle either 10Mbps or 100Mbps data transmission, depending on the capability of the other equipment on the network.

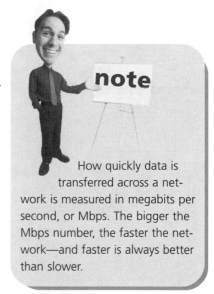

How quickly data is transferred across a network is measured in megabits per second, or Mbps. The bigger the Mbps number, the faster the network—and faster is always better than slower.

## Wireless Networks

A *wireless network* uses radio frequency (RF) signals to connect one computer to another. The big advantage of wireless, of course, is that you don't have to run any cables—a big plus if you have a large house with computers on either end.

Windows XP supports the IEEE 802.11b wireless networking standard, which is capable of speeds up to 11Mbps. This is the same type of wireless network used in large corporations, and it's very stable and robust.

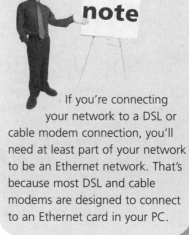

If you're connecting your network to a DSL or cable modem connection, you'll need at least part of your network to be an Ethernet network. That's because most DSL and cable modems are designed to connect to an Ethernet card in your PC.

## Phone Line Networks

When you don't want to run cables but also don't want the high cost of an 802.11b wireless network, consider connecting your network via your home's telephone lines.

A *phone line network* provides a similar level of convenience as a wireless network, but with higher data transfer rates and greater reliability. With telephone line networking (commonly referred to as *HomePNA*, based on the specifications developed by the Home Phone Networking Alliance), you connect each computer to an adapter that plugs into a standard phone jack. Data signals are sent from your computer through the adapter into your home phone line and received by another adapter and PC elsewhere on the network.

Many HomePNA products are available on the market, the most popular of which is Intel's AnyPoint Home Network kit. The standard AnyPoint adapter plugs into a parallel or USB port on your PC and then connects to the nearest phone line. (No hub is necessary.)

Where the earliest HomePNA networks transferred data at just 1Mbps, most current phone line networks offer 10Mbps transfer rates. So, if you need decent speed without the hassle of running lots of cable, this might be the way to go.

The official marketing name for 802.11b wireless networking is *WiFi*, for *wired fidelity*. WiFi lets you connect to wireless network access points up to 150 feet away from your PC.

# Setting Up a Home Network

Setting up a network is as easy as installing a few pieces of equipment, connecting a few cables, and then running Windows XP's Network Setup Wizard. Windows is smart enough to recognize which devices are installed where and does almost all the configuration for you. You have to answer a question or two—and you still have to plug in all the cards and cables, of course—but that's about it.

Because each adapter on a HomePNA network sends its signal at a different frequency, your computer network can share the phone line with other voice and data traffic.

## Choosing the Right Equipment

Begin by making a list of all the hardware and cables you'll need to purchase. Use Table 34.1 to determine what you'll need for each PC for your specific type of network.

**TABLE 34.1**  Equipment Needed for Each Type of Network

| Type of Network | Host PC | Client PCs |
|---|---|---|
| Ethernet | Ethernet network cards (2) Ethernet network hub (1 for the entire network) Modem (dial-up or broadband) | Ethernet network card (1) |
| Wireless | Wireless network adapter (1) Ethernet network card (1) Modem (dial-up or broadband) | Wireless network adapter (1) |
| Phone line | HomePNA network adapter (1) Ethernet network card (1) Modem (dial-up or broadband) | HomePNA network adapter (1) |

If you're connecting an Ethernet network, you'll also need one Ethernet cable to go from the hub to the host computer and additional cables to connect each of your other PCs to the hub. If you're connecting a phone-line network, you'll need telephone cables to connect each PC (including the host) to the nearest telephone jack. And, no matter which type of networking you're installing, if you're connecting a cable or DSL modem, you'll need an Ethernet cable to run from the modem to your host PC.

**note**

The main computer on your network—the one connected directly to your Internet connection—is designated the *host* PC. The other computers on the network are called *clients*.

## Setting Up the Network

After you've made the requisite trip to the computer store, it's time to install all that new hardware—including the network cards in each PC. This is normally as easy as turning off your PC, installing the card, and then turning your PC back on again. Windows should recognize the new card and install the appropriate drivers automatically.

Next, power down and turn off all your computers and printers. With the power off, run all the cables you need to run and connect them to each computer and hub in your network. After all the computers are connected, you can power them back on again—and run the Network Setup Wizard.

# Running the Network Setup Wizard

After you've physically connected your computers together, Windows XP's Network Setup Wizard guides you through setting up your home network. This wizard must be run on each computer on your network.

## Configuring the Host PC

You start by running the wizard on your host computer, by clicking the Windows **Start** button and then selecting **All Programs**, **Accessories**, **Communications**, **Network Setup Wizard** (shown in Figure 34.2).

When the wizard launches, proceed through the screens, reading all the onscreen information carefully and making the appropriate selections. When you come to the Select a Connection Method screen, be sure to select the first option, **This Computer Connects Directly to the Internet—The Other Computers in My Home Network Connect to the Internet Through This Computer**. Continue through the following screens to complete the host PC's configuration.

> **tip**
>
> For simple two- or three-PC networks, you can probably find all the equipment you need in a commercial "home networking kit" at your local computer store. These kits contain all the cards, cables, and hubs you'll need to set up a typical network—typically with step-by-step instructions and installation disks, and at a discounted price.

**FIGURE 34.2**

Use the Network Setup Wizard to configure each of the PCs on your network.

## Configuring Client PCs

After you've run the Network Setup Wizard on your host PC, you have to run it on all the other PCs on your network. If a computer is running Windows XP, you can run the wizard as previously described. If a computer is running Windows 98,

Windows Me, or Windows 2000, you need to run the wizard from the Windows XP installation CD. (Insert the CD and then, after the main screen appears, select **Use Windows Support Tools**; then select **Tools, Network Setup Wizard**.)

When you run the wizard on a client PC, you should select the **This Computer Connects to the Internet Through Another Computer in My Home Network** option. Then, follow the onscreen instructions and let XP finish the network configuration for you.

After all your computers are configured, your network is now fully functional.

## Sharing Files and Folders

To share files with other users on your network, you have to enable Windows XP's file sharing. You do this by following these steps:

1. Use My Computer to navigate to the folder or file you want to share.

2. Right-click the folder or file icon and select **Sharing and Security** from the pop-up menu; this displays the Properties dialog box.

3. Select the **Sharing** tab, shown in Figure 34.2.

4. Check the **Share This Folder on the Network** option.

5. Click **OK** when done—then repeat this procedure for every folder or file you want to share on every computer connected to your network.

**FIGURE 34.3**

Enable file sharing so other computers can access a particular file or folder.

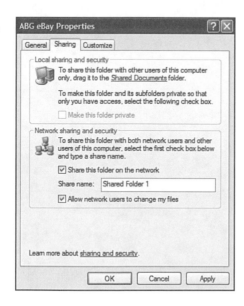

# THE ABSOLUTE MINIMUM

Here are the key things to remember about networking and the Internet:

- To share information or hardware between two or more computers, you have to connect them in a network.

- There are three basic types of networks—wired, wireless (using radio frequencies), and phone line.

- The quickest, easiest, and cheapest way to put together a home network is to use a commercial home networking kit.

- Once you have all the networking hardware installed and connected, use Windows XP's Network Setup Wizard to configure all the PCs on your network.

- To share folders between computers on your network, enable Windows XP's file sharing feature.

# 35

# PERFORMING ROUTINE MAINTENANCE

"An ounce of prevention is worth a pound of cure."

That old adage might seem trite and clichéd, but it's also true—especially when it comes to your computer system. Spending a few minutes a week on preventive maintenance can save you from costly computer problems in the future.

To make this chore a little easier, Windows XP includes several utilities to help you keep your system running smoothly. You should use these tools as part of your regular maintenance routine—or if you experience specific problems with your computer system.

# Cleaning Up Unnecessary Files

Even with today's humongous hard disks, you can still end up with too many useless files taking up too much hard disk space. Fortunately, Windows XP includes a utility that identifies and deletes unused files tool to use when you want to free up extra hard disk space for more frequently used files. To use Disk Cleanup, follow these steps:

1. Click the **Start** button to display the **Start** menu.

2. Select **All Programs**, **Accessories**, **System Tools**, **Disk Cleanup**.

3. Disk Cleanup starts and automatically analyzes the contents of your hard disk drive.

4. When Disk Cleanup is finished analyzing, it presents its results in the Disk Cleanup dialog box, shown in Figure 35.1.

**FIGURE 35.1**

Use Disk Cleanup to delete unused files from your hard disk.

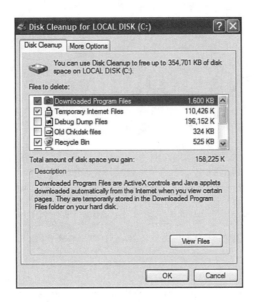

5. Select the **Disk Cleanup** tab.

6. You now have the option of permanently deleting various types of files: downloaded program files, temporary Internet files, deleted files in the Recycle Bin, setup log files, temporary files, WebClient/Publisher temporary files, and catalog files for the Content Indexer. Select which files you want to delete.

7. Click **OK** to begin deleting.

# Defragging Your Disk

If you think that your computer is taking longer than usual to open files or notice that your hard drive light stays on longer than usual, you might need to *defragment* your hard drive.

File fragmentation is sort of like taking the pieces of a jigsaw puzzle and storing them in different boxes along with pieces from other puzzles. The more dispersed the pieces are, the longer it takes to put the puzzle together. Spreading the bits and pieces of a file around your hard disk occurs whenever you install, delete, or run an application, or when you edit, move, copy, or delete a file.

note

You can safely choose to delete all these files *except* the setup log and Content Indexer files.

If you notice your system takes longer and longer to open and close files or run applications, it's because these file fragments are spread all over the place. You fix the problem when you put all the pieces of the puzzle back in the right boxes—which you do by defragmenting your hard disk.

You use Windows XP's Disk Defragmenter utility to defragment your hard drive. Follow these steps:

1. Click the **Start** button to display the **Start** menu.
2. Select **All Programs**, **Accessories**, **System Tools**, **Disk Defragmenter** to open the Disk Defragmenter utility, shown in Figure 35.2.
3. Select the drive you want to defragment, typically drive C:.
4. Click the **Defragment** button.

**FIGURE 35.2**

Use Windows XP's Disk Defragmenter to make your hard drive run faster.

Defragmenting your drive can take awhile, especially if you have a large hard drive or your drive is really fragmented. So, you might want to start the utility and let it run while you are at lunch.

# Performing a Hard Disk Checkup with ScanDisk

Any time you run an application, move or delete a file, or accidentally turn the power off while the system is running, you run the risk of introducing errors to your hard disk. These errors can make it harder to open files, slow down your hard disk, or cause your system to freeze when you open or save a file or an application.

caution

You should close all applications—including your screensaver—and stop working on your system while Disk Defragmenter is running.

Fortunately, you can find and fix most of these errors directly from within Windows XP. All you have to do is run the built-in ScanDisk utility.

To find and fix errors on your hard drive, follow these steps:

1. Click the **Start** button to display the **Start** menu.
2. Select **My Computer** to open the My Computer folder.
3. Right-click the icon for the drive you want to scan, then select the **Properties** option from the pop-up menu; this displays the Properties dialog box.
4. Select the **Tools** tab.
5. Click the **Check Now** button to display the Check Disk dialog box, shown in Figure 35.3.
6. Check both the options (**Automatically Fix File System Errors** and **Scan for and Attempt Recovery of Bad Sectors**).
7. Click **Start**.

**FIGURE 35.3**

Use ScanDisk to check your hard disk for errors.

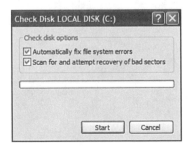

Windows now scans your hard disk and attempts to fix any errors it encounters.

# Backing Up Important Files

If your files are important to you—and they should be, or else why did you create them in the first place?—then you need to protect against any loss or damage to them. If, heaven forbid, your hard disk or system unit goes kablooey, do you want to completely lose all your data and documents—or do you want to be able to somehow recover from such a disaster?

The best way to protect yourself against catastrophic data loss is to make backup copies of all your important files. That means all your Word and Works documents, Money financial records, MP3 audio files, digital photographs, and so on—everything you have stored on your hard disk that you can't (or don't want to) create from scratch.

Once you get in the habit of doing it, it's relatively easy to make backup copies of these files. All you need is a file backup program (such as Microsoft Backup, included free with Windows) and some sort of backup media. This type of storage needs to be large (because you'll be backing up *lots* of files) and relatively inexpensive. Many users prefer removable tape cartridges, although Zip disks and rewritable CDs are also popular. (Floppy disks work as long as you're not backing up a lot of data; most users need to back up 100MB or more of data at a time, which would take a *lot* of 1.44MB floppy disks!)

How often you need to back up your files depends on how often the files change and how critical the changes are. For many users, once a month is often enough. If your system crashes, you'll lose some information, but nothing you can't reproduce with a little time and

> **tip**
>
> Windows XP includes a Scheduled Tasks utility that lets you automatically run essential system maintenance tasks while you're away from your computer. To use this utility, click the **Start** button; then select **All Programs**, **Accessories**, **System Tools**, **Scheduled Tasks**. When the Scheduled Tasks window opens, click the icon for a specific task to display its scheduling dialog box. Click the **Schedule** tab, and then select how often you want to run the task. Click **OK** to schedule the task.

> **tip**
>
> Make sure you keep your backup copies in a safe place—and, ideally, in a *different* place from your computer. This way, if your computer is damaged as part of a larger disaster (fire, flood, or something similarly dire), your backup data will still be safe.

effort. If you store critical information that changes rapidly, however, you should consider backing up more regularly—even daily.

## Making a Backup

Windows comes with the Microsoft Backup utility pre-installed. You use Microsoft Backup to back up your personal files and settings. The entire operation is run from the Backup or Restore Wizard, which makes this somewhat dull task just a little easier.

Microsoft Backup lets you store your backup files on floppy disks, backup tapes, Zip disks, or CD-R/RW discs. If you ever happen to have a hard drive crash, you can also use Microsoft Backup to restore your backed-up files from your backup copies, and thus minimize your data loss.

To back up your data with Microsoft Backup, follow these steps:

1. Click the **Start** button to display the **Start** menu.

2. Select **My Computer** to open the My Computer folder.

3. Right-click the drive you want to back up, then select **Properties** from the pop-up menu; this displays the Properties dialog box.

4. Select the **Tools** tab.

5. Click the **Backup Now** button to launch the Backup or Restore Wizard.

6. Click the **Next** button.

7. Check the **Back Up Files and Settings** option and click **Next** to display the What to Back Up screen, shown in Figure 35.4.

8. Select the files you want to back up: your personal documents and settings, everybody's documents and settings, all data on this computer, or specific files that you select (the **Let Me Choose What to Back Up** option). Most users back up either their own personal data or (if they've configured your system for multiple users) everyone's data. Click **Next** when you're done selecting.

9. Select the specific backup device, then click **Next**.

10. You'll now be prompted to insert the appropriate backup media; follow the balance of the onscreen instructions to complete the backup.

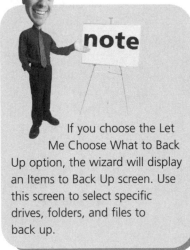

If you choose the Let Me Choose What to Back Up option, the wizard will display an Items to Back Up screen. Use this screen to select specific drives, folders, and files to back up.

**FIGURE 35.4**

Use the Microsoft Backup utility to determine which files you back up from your hard drive.

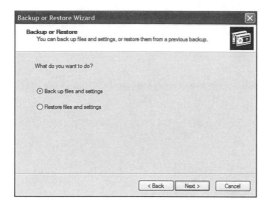

## Restoring Files from a Backup

If you ever need to restore files from a backup, you do it from the same Backup or Restore Wizard. In this instance, when you get to the second screen, select the **Restore Files and Settings** option.

The wizard will now display the What to Restore screen. Select which files and folders you want to restore, and then click the **Next** button. You'll be prompted to insert your backup copies; follow the onscreen instructions to copy your backup files back to their original locations.

**caution**

The files you restore from a backup might not be the most recent versions of those files, especially if the original files were used anytime after your most recent backup. Still, recovering a slightly older version of a file is better than not having any version of that file at all.

# THE ABSOLUTE MINIMUM

Here are the key points to remember from this chapter:

- Dedicating a few minutes a week to PC maintenance can prevent serious problems from occurring in the future.
- To delete unused files from your hard disk, use the Disk Cleanup utility.
- To defragment a fragmented hard disk, use the Disk Defragmenter utility.
- To find and fix hard disk errors, use the ScanDisk utility.
- To protect your most valuable data, use the Microsoft Backup utility to back up the data to a removable storage medium.

## IN THIS CHAPTER

- What to Do When Windows Freezes
- Dealing with a Major Crash
- Undoing the Damage with System Restore
- How to Troubleshoot Computer Problems

**36**

# DEALING WITH COMMON PROBLEMS

Computers aren't perfect. It's possible—although unlikely—that at some point in time, something will go wrong with your PC. It might refuse to start, it might freeze up, it might crash and go dead.

Like I said, it's possible.

When something goes wrong with your computer, there's no need to panic. (Even though that's what you'll probably feel like doing!) Most PC problems have easy-to-find causes, and simple solutions. The key thing is to keep your wits about you, and attack the situation calmly and logically—following the advice you'll find in this chapter!

# What to Do When Windows Freezes

Probably the most common computer trouble is the freeze-up. That's what happens when your PC just stops dead in its tracks. The screen looks normal, but nothing works—you can't type onscreen, you can't click any buttons, nothing's happening.

If your system happens to freeze up, the good news is that there's probably nothing wrong with your computer hardware. The bad news is that there's probably something funky happening with your operating system.

This doesn't mean your system is broken. It's just a glitch. And you can recover from glitches. Just remember not to panic and to approach the situation calmly and rationally.

## What Causes Windows to Freeze?

What causes Windows to freeze? There can be many different causes of a Windows freeze, including the following:

- You might be running an older application that isn't compatible with Windows XP. If so, upgrade the program.
- You might not have enough memory installed on your system. Upgrade the amount of memory in your PC.
- A memory conflict might exist between applications, or between an application and Windows itself. Try running fewer programs at once, or running problematic programs one at a time to avoid potential memory conflicts.
- You might not have enough free hard disk space on your computer. Delete any unnecessary files from your hard drive.
- Your hard disk might be developing errors or bad sectors. Check your hard disk for errors. (See the ScanDisk section in Chapter 35, "Performing Routine Maintenance.")

If your system only freezes once and then starts working again, don't worry about it. Shut down your computer (you might have to press **Ctrl+Alt+Del** a few times to do this) and start it up again. Chances are everything will be working just fine.

If your system crashes or freezes frequently, however, you should call in a pro. These kinds of problems can be tough to track down by yourself when you're dealing with Windows.

## Dealing with Error Messages

Sometimes Windows displays an error message when it freezes up. These messages are just nice ways to say that something (who knows what) has bombed.

More often than not, it's just your current program that has frozen, and not all of Windows. In this case you get a `Program Not Responding` error message. Try pressing **Ctrl+Alt+Del** to bring up the Windows Task Manager; select the **Applications** tab, select the unresponsive program, and then click the **End Task** button.

## Freezes Without Error Messages

Sometimes Windows freezes without displaying an error message. If this is the case, one of two things has happened:

■ Windows itself has locked up,

or

■ Your current Windows application has locked up.

In either case, the solution is the same: Press **Ctrl+Alt+Del**.

If Windows itself has frozen, either nothing will happen or you'll start hearing a beep every time you press a key on your keyboard. If this happens, you'll need to press **Ctrl+Alt+Del** again to fully reboot, or you might have to turn off your PC at the **On/Off** button (or at the power source).

If, on the other hand, it's an errant program that freezes up, see "Dealing with Application Freezes," next.

## Dealing with Application Freezes

Sometimes Windows works fine but it's an individual piece of software that freezes. Fortunately, Windows XP is an exceptionally safe environment. When an individual application crashes or freezes, it seldom messes up your entire system. You can use the Windows Task Manager to close the problem application without affecting other Windows programs.

When a Windows application freezes or crashes, press **Ctrl+Alt+Del**. When the Windows Task manager opens, select the **Applications** tab, and then select the frozen application from the list. Now click the **End Task** button. After a few seconds, a Wait/Shutdown window appears; confirm that you want to shut down the selected application; then, click the **End Task** button.

This closes the offending application and lets you continue your work in Windows.

If you have multiple applications that crash on a regular basis, the situation probably can be attributed to insufficient memory. See your computer dealer about adding more RAM to your system.

# Dealing with a Major Crash

Perhaps the worst thing that can happen to your computer system is that it crashes—completely shuts down, without any warning. If this happens to you, start by not panicking. Stay calm, take a few deep breaths, and then get ready to get going again.

You should always wait about 60 seconds after a computer crashes before you try to turn your system on again. This gives all the components time to settle down and—in some cases—reset themselves. Just sit back and count to 60 (slowly), then press your system unit's "on" button.

Nine times out of ten, your system will boot up normally, as if nothing unusual has happened. If this is what happens for you, great! If, on the other hand, your system doesn't come back up normally, you'll need to start troubleshooting the underlying problem, as discussed later in this chapter.

Even if your system comes back up as usual, the sudden crash might have done some damage. A system crash can sometimes damage any software program that was running at the time, as well as any documents that were open when the crash occurred. You might have to reinstall a damaged program or recover a damaged document from a backup file.

# Undoing the Damage with System Restore

Perhaps the best course of action when your system crashes is to use Microsoft's System Restore utility. This Windows XP utility can automatically restore your system to the state it was in before the crash occurred—and save you the trouble of rein-stalling any damaged software programs.

Think of System Restore as a safety net for your essential system files. It isn't a backup program per se because it doesn't make copies of your personal files. (You still need to use Microsoft Backup for that, as described in Chapter 35.) It simply keeps track of all the system-level changes that are made to your computer and (when activated) reverses those changes.

## Setting System Restore Points

System Restore works by monitoring your system and noting any changes that are made when you install new applications. Each time it notes a change, it automati-cally creates what it calls a *restore point*. A restore point is basically a "snapshot" of key system files just before the new application is installed.

Just to be safe, System Restore also creates a new restore point after every 10 hours of system use. You can also choose to manually create a new restore point at any moment in time. It's a good idea to do this whenever you make any major change to your system, such as installing a new piece of hardware.

To set a manual restore point, follow these steps:

1. Click the **Start** button to display the **Start** menu.

2. Select **All Programs**, **Accessories**, **System Tools**, **System Restore** to open the System Restore window.

3. Select **Create a Restore Point** and click **Next**.

4. You'll now be prompted to enter a description for this new restore point; do this.

5. Click the **Create** button.

That's all you have to do. Windows notes the appropriate system settings and stores them in its System Restore database.

## Restoring Your System

If something in your system goes bad, you can run System Restore to set things right. Pick a restore point before the problem occurred (such as right before a new installation), and System Restore will then undo any changes made to monitored files since the restore point was created. This restores your system to its preinstallation—that is, *working*—condition.

To restore your system from a restore point, follow these steps:

1. Click the **Start** button to display the **Start** menu.

2. Select **All Programs**, **Accessories**, **System Tools**, **System Restore** to open the System Restore window.

3. Select **Restore My Computer to an Earlier Time** option, then click **Next**.

4. When the Select a Restore Point screen appears, you'll see a calendar showing the current month, as shown in Figure 36.1; any date highlighted in bold contains a restore point. Select a restore point, and then click the **Next** button.

5. When the confirmation screen appears, click **Next**.

Windows now starts to restore your system. You should make sure that all open programs are closed because Windows will need to be restarted during this process.

**FIGURE 36.1**

**FIGURE 36.1**

Use the System Restore utility to restore damaged programs or system files.

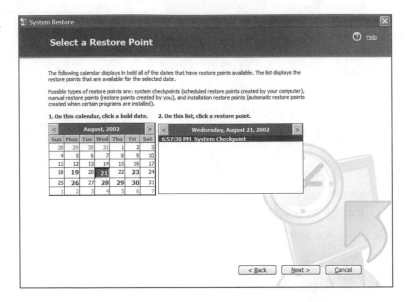

When the process is complete, your system should be back in tip-top shape. Note, however, that it might take a half-hour or more to complete a system restore—so you'll have time to order a pizza and eat dinner before the operation is done!

# How to Troubleshoot Computer Problems

No matter what kind of computer-related problem you're experiencing, there are seven basic steps you should take to track down the cause of the problem. Work through these steps calmly and deliberately, and you're likely to find what's causing the current problem—and then be in a good position to fix it yourself:

1. **Don't panic!**—Just because there's something wrong with your PC is no reason to

**tip**

System Restore will help you recover any damaged programs and system files, but it won't help you recover any damaged documents or data files. If you made a backup of your data files (as described in Chapter 35), you can recover a damaged file by restoring its backup copy. You'll lose any work you did to the file since the backup, of course, but this option is probably preferable to starting completely from scratch.

fly off the handle. Chances are there's nothing seriously wrong. Besides, getting all panicky won't solve anything. Keep your wits about you and proceed logically, and you can probably find what's causing your problem and get it fixed.

2. **Check for operator errors**—In other words, something *you* did wrong. Maybe you clicked the wrong button, or pressed the wrong key, or plugged something into the wrong jack or port. Retrace your steps and try to duplicate your problem. Chances are the problem won't recur if you don't make the same mistake twice.

3. **Check that everything is plugged into the proper place and that the system unit itself is getting power**—Take special care to ensure that all your cables are *securely* connected—loose connections can cause all sorts of strange results!

> **tip**
>
> If you're technically able, consider using third-party software utilities, such as Norton Utilities (www.symantec.com) or McAfee Utilities (www.macafee.com) to help diagnose your PC problems.

4. **Make sure you have the latest versions installed for all the software on your system**—While you're at it, make sure you have the latest versions of device drivers installed for all the peripherals on your system.

5. **Try to isolate the problem by *when* and *how* it occurs**—Walk through each step of the process to see if you can identify a particular program or driver that might be causing the problem.

6. **When all else fails, call in professional help**—If you think it's a Windows-related problem, contact Microsoft's technical support department. If you think it's a problem with a particular program, contact the tech support department of the program's manufacturer. If you think it's a hardware-related problem, contact the manufacturer of your PC or the dealer you bought it from. (And don't rule out where you purchased the computer—many computer dealers have helpful tech support departments.) The pros are there for a reason—when you need technical support, go and get it!

## Using Windows Troubleshooters

Windows XP includes several interactive utilities that can help you diagnose and fix common system problems. These utilities are called Troubleshooters, and they walk you step-by-step through a series of questions. All you have to do is answer the questions in the Troubleshooter, and you'll be led to the probable solution to your problem.

To run a Troubleshooter, follow these steps:

1. Click the **Start** button to display the **Start** menu.
2. Select **Help and Support** to open the Help and Support Center.
3. Click **Fixing a Problem** in the **Pick a Help Topic** column.
4. When the next screen appears, click the link for the type of problem you're having, and then click the link to start a specific Troubleshooter.

All you have to do now is follow the interactive directions to troubleshoot your particular hardware problem.

## Troubleshooting in Safe Mode

If you're having trouble getting Windows to start, it's probably because some setting is set wrong or some driver is malfunctioning. The problem is, how do you get into Windows to fix what's wrong, when you can't even start Windows?

The solution is to hijack your computer before Windows gets hold of it and force it to start *without* whatever is causing the problem. You do this by watching the screen as your computer boots up and pressing the **F8** key just before Windows starts to load. This displays the Windows startup menu, where you select Safe mode.

*Safe mode* is a special mode of operation that loads Windows in a very simple configuration. Once in Safe mode, you can look for device conflicts, restore incorrect or corrupted device drivers, or restore your system to a prior working configuration (using the System Restore utility, discussed previously).

Depending on the severity of your system problem, Windows might start in Safe mode automatically.

# THE ABSOLUTE MINIMUM

Here are the key points to remember from this chapter:

- If something strange happens to your computer system, the first thing to do is *not panic!*

- Most so-called computer problems are actually caused by operator error, so backup and do whatever it is you did one more time—carefully, this time.

- You can shut down frozen programs from the Windows Task Manager, which you display by pressing **Ctrl+Alt+Del**.

- Press **Ctrl+Alt+Del** a second time to reboot your computer.

- Some problems can be fixed from Windows Safe mode; to enter Safe mode, restart your computer and press **F8** before the Windows start screen appears.

- If your system misbehaves after installing new software or hardware, use the System Restore utility to return your system to its pre-installation state.

# Index

## Symbols

(*) asterisk character, 200

## A

AARP Webplace Web site, 207

ABC News Web site, 203

About.com Web site, 202

accessory programs (Windows), 57

Account List button, 149

accounts
email, 222
ISPs, setting up, 186-187
Money, 149
MSN Bill Pay, 157

AccuWeather Web site, 204

activity pane, defined, 54

Add Favorite dialog box, 195

Add Hardware Wizard, 323-324

Add or Remove Programs dialog box, 103

Add or Remove Programs utility, 101-102

Address book (email), 107, 227
adding contacts, 228-229
emailing contacts, 230
editing contacts, 229
sorting contacts, 229

addresses (email), 313-314

Adobe GoLive Web site, 251

Adobe Photoshop Elements Web site, 261

Adobe Premiere Web site, 300

Adventure Workshop Web site, 166

advertising online auctions, eBay, 218

algebraic operators, 131-132

All Games Free Web site, 175

AllTheWeb Web site, 202

AltaVista Web site, 202, 312

America Online (AOL), 184

AMP.CAST.COM Web site, 285

AngelFire Web site, 248

ANT 4 MailChecking Web site, 314

antivirus software, 316

AnyWho Web site, 203

AOL (America Online), 184

AOL Hometown Web site, 249

AOL Instant Messenger Web site, 232

Apple, Windows compatibility, 13

Apple Learning Interchange Web site, 312

applications. See also programs; software
defined, 12
troubleshooting, freeze-ups, 343

ArcadeTown Free Web site, 175

archives, downloading files from, 244-245

articles
defined, 238
newsgroups, 239-240

ARTISTdirect Web site, 285

Ask Jeeves for Kids Web site, 312

Ask Jeeves! Web site, 202

asterisk character (*), 200

AT&T WorldNet Web site, 184

attachments (email), 225
attaching to messages, 225
opening, 226
viruses, 227

auctions, online, 215-216
bids, 216-217
eBay, 216-219
advertising on, 218
confirmations on, 219
payments on, 218-219
selling on, 218
payments, 217
seller feedback, 217
shipments, 219

audio
digital, 283-284
downloading, 285
MP3, 284
MusicMatch Jukebox, 291-292
playing files, 287
playing on PCs, 287-289
swapping files, 286-287
WMA, 284
WMP, 284, 288-291
Internet broadcasts, 277
playing DVDs, 274
streaming, 278
video editing, 304-305

Auto-By-Tel Web site, 212

automatic software installation, 100

AutoNation.com Web site, 212

AutoSite Web site, 212

AutoSum function, 133

Autoweb Web site, 212

## B

Back button, 194

backgrounds, desktops, 73-74

backup files, 337-339

Backup or Restore Wizard, 338-339

Backup utility, 338

banking (Money), 152
   checkbook balances, 153-154
   Internet use, 154, 157-158
   transactions, 152-153

Barnes and Noble.com Web site, 211

Battle.net Web site, 176

Bcc (blind carbon copy), 230

BeSonic Web site, 285

bids, online auctions, 216-217

bill paying services online (Money), 157-158

Billpoint Web site, 219

Bills & Deposits button, 155-156

BlackICE PC Protection Web site, 317

blocking email addresses (Outlook Express), 314

Blue Mountain, 162, 164

booting, 35

booting up, 35

BoxerJam.com Web site, 175

broadband connections, 181, 184

broadcast Internet connections, Webcasts, 282

browsers, Web, 191

BrowseSafe Web site, 311

Budget button, 151

Budget Planner (Money), 151-152

burning CDs, 295
   labels, 297
   WMP, 296-297

buttons
   Account List, 149
   Back, 194
   Bills & Deposits, 155-156

Budget, 151
Categories, 149
Change or Remove Programs, 103
Copy, 89
Customize, 78
Defragment, 335
Effects, 75
Favorites, 195
Filter, 144
History, 196
Home, 194
Insert, 126, 134
Internet Explorer toolbar, 193-194
Money Home page buttons, 151
New Chart, 136
Print, 121, 196
Record Payment, 156-157
Save, 118
Start, 78
Start (Windows XP), 43
Turn Off Computer, 53
Views, 84

Buy.com Web site, 211

bytes, defined, 19

## C

cable connections, 32

cameras
   digital, 255-256
      adding special effects to pictures, 263
      connections, 256
      creating photo albums, 264
      cropping pictures, 263
      defined, 12
      emailing pictures, 266
      editing pictures, 261-264
      modifying pictures, 258
      photo-processing sites, 267-268
      printing pictures, 264-267
      scanning pictures, 259-260
      software, 258
      storing pictures, 260-261
      touching up pictures, 262
      transferring pictures to PCs, 257-258
   digital still, 320
   PC, 12, 320

Cars.com Web site, 212

cases, system units, 15

categories (Money), 149

Categories button, 149

CBS Marketwatch Web site, 205

CBS News Web site, 203

CBS SportsLine Web site, 204

Cc (carbon copy), 230

CD-R/RW drives, 295, 320

CD-ROM (compact disc-read-only memory), 21
   disk drives, 21, 270, 320
   disks, 21

CDNow.com Web site, 211

cdrLabel Web site, 298

CDs
   burning, 295
      labels, 297
      WMP, 296-297
   playing, 269
      CD-ROM drives, 270
      WMP, 270-272

cells, 128-129
   active, 128
   defined, 128
   spreadsheets, 130
      formulas, 132
      sorting cells, 134-135

central processing units (CPUs), 17

Change or Remove Programs button, 103

charts, 135-136

chatting online, 234
   chat sites, 236
   Internet Relay Chat (IRC), 236
   Yahoo!, 235-236

CheatStation Web site, 176

checkbook balances, electronic banking (Money), 153-154

checks, printing (Money), 156-157

children, Internet security, 310-311
   filtering software, 311-312
   kid-safe searching, 312-313

ChineseNow! Web site, 167

chips, microprocessor, 17-18

ClearType (Windows XP), 73

clients, 188-189

Clip Art Gallery, 125-126

clips, 302-303

closed captions, DVDs, 274

closing
 Notepad, 65
 windows, 46-47

Club Photo Web site, 267

CNET Internet Services Web site,
 252

CNN Web site, 203

CNN.com Web site, 196

CNN/Money Web site, 205

CNN/Sports Illustrated Web site,
 204

colors, desktops, 75

columns, spreadsheets, 130-131

Command Antivirus Web site,
 316

compact disc-read-only memory.
 *See* CD-ROM

compatibility, Apple and
 Windows, 13

components
 PCs, 12
 system, connections, 33
 Works Suite, 106

composing email messages
 (Outlook Express), 223

compressing files, 93

computer administrator user
 accounts, 36-37

computer files, downloading
 archives, 244-245
 Internet, 243
 online, 244
 Web pages, from, 245-246

computer hardware, 11-14
 system units, 14-16
  *cases, 15*
  *CD-ROM disk drives, 21*
  *connectors, 15*
  *DVD disk drives, 22*

 *hard disk drives, 20*
 *keyboards, 22*
 *memory, 19*
 *microprocessors, 17-18*
 *modems, 24*
 *monitors, 25-27*
 *motherboards, 16*
 *mouse, 23-24*
 *printers, 27*
 *removable disk drives, 20-21*
 *sound cards, 24*
 *speakers, 24*
 *vertical, 14*
 *video cards, 25-27*

computer software, 12-13

computer viruses, 227, 315-316

computers. *See also* PCs
 booting up, 35
 clients, 188-189
 hosts, 188-189
 personal. *See* PCs
 rebooting, 35
 setting up, 32
  *cable connections, 32*
  *first-time startup, 34-35*
  *power, 34-36*
  *startup, 35-36*
  *system component connec-*
   *tions, 33*
  *users, 36-38*
 troubleshooting, 346-347
  *crashing, 344-346*
  *error messages, 342-343*
  *freeze-ups, 342-343*
  *Safe mode, 348*
  *Windows Troubleshooters,*
   *348*
 turning off, 52-53, 69

configuration utilities, 55-56

configuring
 clients, 189
 hosts, 188-189
 Money, 148
  *accounts, 149*
  *categories, 149*
  *Setup Assistant, 148-149*
 non-Windows XP PCs, 189

Confirm File Delete dialog box,
 93

connecting
 AOL, 184
 ISPs, 183

connections
 broadband, 181-184
 cables, 32
 digital cameras, 256
 Internet, 180-184
  *broadband, 181-184*
  *dial-up, 184*
  *game playing, 175*
  *initiating, 190*
  *ISPs, 180*
  *networks, 188*
  *sharing, 187-190*
  *speed, 181*
 networks, 327
  *Ethernet networks, 327*
  *phone line networks,*
   *327-328*
  *wireless networks, 327*
 scanners, 259
 system component, 33

connectors, system units, 15

continuing education software,
 167

Control Panel utility, 55-56

Copy button, 89

Copy Items dialog box, 89

copying files, 89-90

Corel WordPerfect Productivity
 Pack, 106

CorelDRAW Essentials Web site,
 261

CPUs (central processing units), 17

crashing, 344-346

Create Database dialog box, 140

creating
 charts in spreadsheets, 136
 database reports, 145-146
 databases, 140-141
 folders, 88
 greeting cards (Word), 160
 newsgroup articles, 240
 Web pages, 247
  *hosting services, 251-252*
  *software programs, 251*
  *Yahoo! GeoCities, 248-250*
 Word documents, 117

cropping digital pictures, 263

Crutchfield Web site, 211

Curious George Downtown
 Adventure Web site, 166

*How can we make this index more useful? Email us at indexes@quepublishing.com*

**cursors, 23-24**

**Customize button, 78**

**Customize Start Menu dialog box, 78**

**customizing**
databases, 140-141
desktops, 71-76
file displays, 84
mouse clicking, 77-78
Start menu, 78-79
Windows desktops, 77

**Cyber Ed Chemistry Web site, 167**

**CyberLink Web site, 290**

**Cybersitter Web site, 311**

# D

**damages, computers, 14**

**data**
databases
*adding, 142*
*filtering, 143-144*
*sorting, 143*
spreadsheets, 129

**databases, 139.** *See also* **Works Database**
creating, 140-141
data
*filtering, 143-144*
*sorting, 143*
editing, 142
preformatted applications, 140
reports, 144
*printing lists, 144-145*
*ReportCreator tool, 145-146*
viewing, 141

**Date and Time Properties dialog box, 82**

**Date and Time tab, 82**

**Defragment button, 335**

**defragmenting**
files, 335
hard drives, 335-336

**deleting**
columns into spreadsheets, 130
files, 91-92
rows into spreadsheets, 130

**Deposit tab, 153**

**desktops**
dialog boxes, 49-50
menus, 47-48
moving windows, 45-47
scrolling through windows, 47
sizing windows, 45-47
toolbars, 48
Windows
*backgrounds, 73-74*
*ClearType, 73*
*customizing, 71-77*
*elements, 73-74*
*sizing, 72-73*
*themes, 73*
Windows XP, 43-44
*colors, 75*
*fonts, 75*
*mouse clicking, 77-78*
*navigating, 43*
*screen savers, 80*
*special effects, 75-77*
*Start menu, 78-80*
*system sounds, 81*
*time and date, 82*

**Details view, 85**

**device drivers, 322**

**dial-up Internet connections, 180-184**

**dialog boxes, 144**
Add Favorite, 195
Add or Remove Programs, 103
Confirm File Delete, 93
Copy Items, 89
Create Database, 140
Customize Start Menu, 78
Date and Time Properties, 82
Disk Cleanup, 334
Display Properties, 72
Email, 266
Easy Calc, 132
Edit, 152
Effects, 75
Folder Options, 77, 86
Format Picture, 126
Function, 134
Insert Function, 134
Insert Picture, 126
Modify Category, 149
Modify Style, 123

Move Items, 91
New Chart, 136
Newsgroups, 239
Paragraph, 122
Performance Options, 76
Print, 49, 121
Properties, 67
Record, 301
Record Payment, 156
Report Name, 145
ReportCreator, 145
Run, 100
Save As, 118
Save Movie, 305
System Properties, 18, 76-77
Templates, 117
Turn Off Computer, 53
Windows, 49-50

**digital audio, 283-284**
downloading, 285
files
*playing, 287*
*swapping, 286-287*
MP3, 284
MusicMatch Jukebox, ripping, 291-292
playing on PCs, 287-289
WMA, 284
WMP, 284, 288
*playlists, 288-289*
*ripping, 290-291*
*song copies, 289-290*

**digital cameras, 255-256**
connections, 256
defined, 12
pictures
*cropping, 263*
*emailing, 266*
*editing, 261-264*
*modifying, 258*
*photo albums, 264*
*photo-processing sites, 267-268*
*printing, 264-267*
*scanners, 259-260*
*software, 258*
*special effects, 263*
*storing, 260-261*
*touching up, 262*
*transferring to PCs, 257-258*
still, 320

**digital picture files, 255**

**digital video (DV) recorders, 300**

**digital video discs.** *See* **DVDs**

**Digital8 format, 300**

**directories (Web), 199-201**
- financial information searches, 205
- Google, 202
- medical information searches, 205-207
- news searches, 203
- people searches, 202-203
- physician information searches, 207
- search sites, 202
- senior citizen searches, 207
- sports headline searches, 204
- weather report searches, 204
- white pages, 203
- Yahoo!, 201

**Disk Cleanup, 334-335**

**Disk Cleanup dialog box, 334**

**Disk Cleanup tab, 334**

**Disk Defragmenter utility, 335**

**diskettes, 20-21**

**disks**
- CD-ROM, 21
- DVD, 22
- floppy, 20-21
- formatted, 20
- removable, 20-21

**Disney Interactive Web site, 166**

**Display Properties dialog box, 72**

**displaying Word documents, 115-116**

**documents**
- viewing, 66
- Word
  - *creating, 117*
  - *defined, 116*
  - *displaying, 115-116*
  - *formatting, 122-123*
  - *opening, 118*
  - *outlines, 124-125*
  - *pictures, 125-126*
  - *printing, 121*
  - *reviewing before printing, 121*
  - *saving, 118*
  - *text, 119-120*

**dotPhoto Web site, 267**

**double-clicking (mouse), 44**

**Download.com Web site, 245**

**downloading**
- digital audio, 285
- files
  - *archives, 244-245*
  - *from Internet, 243*
  - *from Web pages, 245-246*
  - *online, 244*

**dragging and dropping (mouse), 45**

**Dreamweaver Web site, 251**

**drives**
- CD-R/RW, 295, 320
- CD-ROM, 270, 320
- DVD-ROM, 272
- hard, 320
  - *defragmenting, 335-336*
- removable, 320

**DVDs (digital video disc), 22, 320**
- disk drives, 272
  - *storage, 22*
- disks, 22
- menus, 274
- playing, 269-272
  - *audio options, 274*
  - *closed captions, 274*
  - *subtitles, 274*
  - *WMP, 273*

## E

**EA.com Web site, 176**

**Earth's Dynamic Surface Web site, 166**

**Earthlink Web site, 184**

**Easy Calc dialog box, 132**

**Easy Language Deluxe Web site, 167**

**eBay, 216**
- advertising, 218
- confirmations, 219
- payments, 218-219
- selling, 218
- shipments, 219

**eBay.com Web site, 215**

**Eddie Bauer Web site, 211**

**Edit dialog box, 152**

**editing**
- databases, 142
- digital pictures, 261-264
- text (Word), 119
- video, 299
  - *audio, 304*
  - *clips, 302-304*
  - *software, 300*
  - *transitions, 304*
  - *WMM imports, 301-302*
  - *Workspace, 302-305*

**Edmunds.com Web site, 212**

**educational software, 165**
- types, 166
  - *continuing education, 167*
  - *electronic encyclopedia, 168*
  - *elementary, 166-167*
  - *high school, 167*
  - *Microsoft Encarta, 168*
  - *preschool, 166*

**Effects button, 75**

**Effects dialog box, 75**

**electronic encyclopedia educational software, 168**

**electronic greeting cards, online sites, 162**
- Blue Mountain, 162-164
- Yahoo! Greetings, 162-164

**electronically banking (Money), 152**
- checkbook balances, 153-154
- Internet use, 154-158
- transactions, 152-153

**elementary educational software, 166-167**

**elements, desktops, 73-74**

**email, 181**
- accounts, 222
- Address Book, 227
  - *adding contacts, 228-229*
  - *emailing contacts, 230*
  - *editing contacts, 229*
  - *sorting contacts, 229*
- defined, 11
- message boards, 11
- instant messaging, 231
  - *contact lists, 233*
  - *receiving, 232-234*
  - *sending, 232-234*
  - *sending messages, 232*

mailing lists, 242
messages
*email viruses, 227*
*file attachments, 225-226*
*Outlook Express, 223-225*
PCs, 11
receiving, 221
sending, 221
*Address Book contacts, 230*
*Bcc (blind carbon copy), 230*
*Cc (carbon copy), 230*
*Outlook, 221*
*Outlook Express, 221*
spam, 313
*anti-spam software, 314*
*blocking addresses, 314*
*protecting addresses,*
*313-314*
viruses, 315
*antivirus software, 316*
*exposure to, 315*
*infection signs, 315*
*preventing, 315*

**Email Chomper Web site, 314**

**Email dialog box, 266**

**emailing digital pictures, 266**

**EMusic Web site, 285**

**Encarta (Microsoft), 168-169**

**Encarta Encyclopedia (Microsoft),**
**108**

**Encarta Web site, 168**

**Encyclopedia Britannica Web site,**
**168**

**eRealty.com Web site, 213**

**error messages, system freeze-**
**ups, 342-343**

**ESPN.com Web site, 204**

**e-tailers, 209**

**Ethernet network, 327**

**Excite Message Boards Web site,**
**242**

**Excite Super Chat Web site, 236**

**Excite Web site, 202**

**Expedia Web site, 214**

**extensions, file, 89**

**external hardware, 322**

**external ports, 321-322**

**extracting files, 94**

**Extraction Wizard, 94**

**Extreme Gamers Web site, 176**

**ezboard Web site, 242**

## F

**Fact Monster Web site, 312**

**FamilyConnect Web site, 311**

**Fast Ethernet network, 327**

**Favorites button, 195**

**Favorites list (Internet Explorer),**
**195**

**Feedroom Web site, 282**

**fees, online auctions, 218**

**fields**
databases, adding, 142
defined, 139
formats, 141

**Fields tab, 145**

**file attachments (email), 225-226**
viruses, 227

**file extensions, 89**

**File Transfer Protocol (FTP), 182**

**files**
backing up, 337-338
defined, 53
defragmenting, 335
digital audio
*playing, 287*
*swapping, 286-287*
digital pictures, 255
Disk Cleanup, 334-335
downloading
*archives, 244-245*
*from Internet, 243*
*online, 244*
*Web pages, from, 245-246*
folders, 53
networks, sharing, 331
Notepad, saving, 65
overview, 53
restoring backups, 339
ripping, 290
Windows XP
*compressing, 93*
*copying, 89-90*
*deleting, 91-92*

*displaying, 84*
*extracting, 94*
*grouping, 85*
*moving, 90-91*
*naming, 88-89*
*restoring deleted files, 92-93*
*sorting, 85*
*viewing, 84*

**Files and Folders Tasks panel, 55**

**Filter button, 144**

**Filter dialog box, 144**

**Filter tab, 145**

**filtering data in databases,**
**143-144**

**final value fees (online auctions),**
**218**

**finances, PCs, 10.** *See also* **Money**

**financial centers (Money),**
**150-151**

**financial information searches**
**(Web), 205**

**firewalls, 317**

**Firewire, 321**

**FireWire ports, 321**

**flame wars, 238**

**Flipside.com Web site, 175**

**floppy disks, 20-21**

**Flying Colors Web site, 166**

**Folder Options dialog box, 86**

**folders**
defined, 53
My Computer, 54
*viewing hard disk, 67*
My Documents, 55
*viewing documents, 66*
sub-folders, 55
Windows XP
*compressed, 93-94*
*creating, 88*
*grouping, 85*
*naming, 88-89*
*navigating, 87*
*saving settings, 86*
*sorting, 85*
*viewing, 84*

**Folders Option dialog box, 77**

**fonts, desktops, 75**

**Form view, 141-142**

**Format menu, 123**

**Format Picture dialog box, 126**

**formats, defined, 141**

**formatted disks, 20**

**formatting**
  pictures (Word), 126
  spreadsheets, 129
    *cell contents, 130*
    *number formats, 129*
  text (Word), 120
  Word documents, 122
    *headings, 123*
    *paragraphs, 122*
    *styles, 122-123*

**formulas, spreadsheets, 131**
  algebraic operators, 131-132
  AutoSum function, 133
  cells, 132

**FotoTime Web site, 267**

**Fox News Web site, 203**

**FOXSports Web site, 204**

**Free Games Net Web site, 173**

**freeze-ups, 342-343**

**FrenchNow! Web site, 167**

**FSBO.com Web site, 213**

**FTP (File Transfer Protocol), 182**

**Function dialog box, 134**

**functions, spreadsheets, 133-134**

**Future Games network Web site, 176**

## G

**games**
  PCs, 10
  playing, 171
    *Internet connections, 175*
    *online, 174-175*
    *players, 175-176*
    *requirements, 172*
  software, installing, 173
  Windows, playing, 60-62

**Games Arena Web site, 175**

**Games.com Web site, 175**

**GameSpot Web site, 173**

**GeoCities (Yahoo!), creating Web pages, 248-250**

**gigahertz (GHz), 18**

**Gnutella Web site, 286**

**Google directories, 202**

**Google Groups Web site, 240**

**Google SafeSearch Web site, 312**

**Google Web site, 197, 202**

**grammar checking (Word), 120**

**graphic links (Web), 192**

**graphics**
  inserting files into Word documents, 125
  Web, 192

**graphics editing software, 13**

**greeting cards**
  online sites, 162-164
  sending electronically, 162
  Word, 160

**Grolier Web site, 168**

**grouping files/folders 85**

**Grouping tab, 145**

**groups, defined, 242**

**guest user accounts, 36**

## H

**hackers, 317**

**hard copies, 27**

**hard disk drives, 20**

**hard disks, viewing, 67**

**hard drives, 320**
  defragmenting, 335-336

**hardware, 319**
  adding to PCs
    *Add Hardware Wizard, 323-324*
    *external, 322*
    *internal, 322-323*
  computer, 11-14
    *CD-ROM disk drives, 21*
    *DVD disk drives, 22*
    *hard disk drives, 20*
    *keyboards, 22*
    *memory, 19*
    *microprocessors, 17*

    *modems, 24*
    *monitors, 25-27*
    *mouse, 23-24*
    *printers, 27*
    *removable disk drives, 20-21*
    *sound cards, 24*
    *speakers, 24*
    *system units, 14-19*
    *video cards, 25-27*
  external, 322
  internal, 322-323
  networks
    *installing, 329*
    *setting up, 328*
  peripherals, 320-321

**headings, Word documents, 123**

**healthAtoZ.com Web site, 206**

**help (Windows XP), 57**

**Help and Support Center, launching, 57**

**high school educational software, 167**

**history, Web pages, 196**

**History button, 196**

**History page (Task Launcher), 109**
  launching old documents, 111-112

**Home button, 194**

**home movies. *See* video**

**home networks, 326**
  connecting, 327
    *Ethernet networks, 327*
    *phone line networks, 327-328*
    *wireless networks, 327*
  NIC, 326
  setting up, 328-330
    *client PC configuration, 330*
    *equipment, 328*
    *host PC configuration, 330*
  sharing files/folders, 331

**Home page (Task Launcher), 108**

**home pages**
  creating
    *hosting services, 251-252*
    *software programs, 251*
    *Yahoo! GeoCities, 248-250*
  defined, 192
  Internet Explorer, 194

*How can we make this index more useful? Email us at indexes@quepublishing.com*

home PCs, 10

home publishing software, 160-161

HomePNA networks, 328

homes, online shopping, 213

Homes.com Web site, 213

HomeScape.com Web site, 213

HomeSite Web site, 251

Hoovers Online Web site, 205

HostIndex.com Web site, 252

hosting services, creating Web pages, 251-252

hosts, 188-189

HostSearch Web site, 252

HotBot Web site, 202

hotmail Web site, 314

Hotwire Web site, 214

hovering (mouse), 45

HTML (Hypertext Markup Language), 247

hubs, 326

hypertext links (Web), 192

Hypertext Markup Language (HTML), 247

**I**

icons
    defined, 49
    Recycle Bin, 92
    shortcut (Windows XP), 44
    Start menu, displaying, 79

ICQ Web site, 232

IE. *See* Internet Explorer (IE)

IEEE 1394, 321

IGN Guides Web site, 176

iHomeowner.com Web site, 213

IM (Instant Messaging), 181

indexes (Web), 202

InfoSpace Web site, 203

inkjet printers, 27

input devices
    keyboards, 22
    mouse, 23-24
    video cards, 27

Insert button, 126, 134

Insert Function dialog box, 134

Insert Picture dialog box, 126

inserting
    columns into spreadsheets, 130
    rows into spreadsheets, 130

insertion fees (online auctions), 218

Inspiration Web site, 167

installing
    game software, 173
    software, 99
        built-in programs, 100
        from Internet, 101-102
        manual, 101

instant messaging (email), 11, 231
    contact lists, 233
    MSN Messenger, 232
    receiving, 232-234
    sending, 232
    sending messages, 234
    Windows Messenger, 232

Instant Messaging (IM), 181

Intensive Phonics Web site, 166

InterActivities (Microsoft Encarta), 169

interfaces (Task launcher), 105

internal hardware, 322-323

Internet. *See also* online; Web
    audio broadcasts, 277
    connections, 180-184
        broadband, 181-184
        dial-up, 184
        initiating, 190
        ISPs, 180
        networks, 188
        sharing, 187-190
        speed, 181
    downloading computer files, 243
    electronic banking (Money), 154-158
    greeting cards, 162-164
    installing programs from, 101-102
    overview, 180
    PCs, 11

security, 310-311
    filtering software, 311-312
    kid-safe searching, 312-313
services, 181
    email, 181
    FTP (File Transfer Protocol), 182
    IM (Instant Messaging), 181
    Internet radio, 182
    IRC (Internet Relay Chat), 182
    MP3, 182
    Usenet newsgroups, 182
    WWW (World Wide Web), 181
video broadcasts, 277

Internet Chess Web site, 175

Internet Connection Firewall, 189

Internet Explorer (IE), 191
    Favorites list, 195
        adding to Web pages, 195
        viewing, 195
    home pages, 194
    Internet content filtering, 312
    launching, 192
    surfing the Web, 196-198
    toolbar buttons, 193-194
    Web pages, 196

Internet Park Web site, 175

Internet radio, 182, 277
    locating stations, 280
    RealAudio, 279
    streaming audio, 278
    WMP, 278-279

Internet Relay Chat (IRC), 182, 236

Internet service providers. *See* ISPs

Internet TeleCafe Web site, 236

Internet television, 280
    broadband Internet connections, 282
    locating sites, 282
    QuickTime Player, 281
    RealOne Player, 281
    WMP, 281

Internet Time tab, 82

Internet utility (Windows XP), 57

InterneTV Web site, 282

InterVideo Web site, 290

Investing view, 150

iOwn Web site, 213

IRC (Internet Relay Chat), 182, 236

ISPs (Internet service providers), 180
   accounts, setting up, 186-187
   choosing, 184
   connecting, 183
   Internet connections, 180
   modems, 180
   signing up, 185

IT Pro Downloads Web site, 245

iVillage Web site, 242

**J**

J.Jill Web site, 211

joysticks, 12, 320

Jumbo Web site, 245

JumpStart Series Web site, 166

**K**

Kahn Web site, 176

Kali Web site, 176

Kaplan Web site, 167

Kaspersky Anti-Virus Personal Web site, 316

KaZaA Media Desktop Web site, 286

Kerio Personal Firewall Web site, 317

keyboards, 22, 320

keywords, 200

Kid Performer Web site, 166

kid-safe searching (Internet), 312-313

kidsDoctor Web site, 206

Kidspiration Web site, 166

kilobytes, defined, 19

**L**

L.L. Bean Web site, 212

labels, CDs, 297

Land's End Web site, 212

LANs (local area networks), 325

laptops, 27-28

laser printers, 27

Launch Web site, 285

launching
   Help and Support Center, 57
   Internet Explorer, 192
   Microsoft Encarta, 168-169
   Money, 148
   Money Budget Planner, 151-152
   MSN Messenger, 232
   Notepad, 63
   Picture It! Photo (Microsoft), 261
   programs (Windows), 51
   Windows Messenger, 232
   Works Database, 140
   Works Suite, 108
      *History page, 111-112*
      *Programs page, 109*
      *Task Launcher, 108-109*
      *Tasks page, 110*

Layout tab, 126

Learn to Speak Spanish Web site, 167

LikeTelevision Web site, 282

limited user accounts, 36

links
   graphic, 192
   hypertext, 192
   Money Home page, 150

List view, 141

List Web site, The, 184

lists (databases), printing, 144-145

Live@ Web site, 280

local area networks (LANs), 325

LookSmart Web site, 202

Lycos Chat Web site, 236

Lycos Gamesville Web site, 175

Lycos Music Web site, 285

Lycos Web site, 202, 242

**M**

mailing lists (email), 242

MailWasher Web site, 314

manual software installation, 101

Math Advantage Web site, 167

Math Blaster Web site, 166

Mavis Beacon Teaches Typing Web site, 167

maximizing windows, 46-47

McAfee Personal Firewall Web site, 317

McAfee Utilities Web site, 347

McAfee VirusScan Web site, 316

MedExplorer Web site, 206

Media Center (Windows XP), 42

media players, 287

mediaontap Web site, 282

medical information searches (Web), 205-207

MedicineNet Web site, 206

megabytes, 19

memory, 19-21

Menu bar (Word), 114

menus
   DVDs, 274
   Format, 123
   Outline, 124
   Start
      *adding programs, 80*
      *customizing, 78-79*
      *displaying icons, 79*
      *displaying programs, 79*
      *Windows XP, 43*
   Start (Windows)
      *launching programs, 51*
      *navigating, 51*
      *switching programs, 52*

menus (Windows), 47-48

message boards, 11, 240
   types, 241-242
   Yahoo!, 240-241

*How can we make this index more useful? Email us at indexes@quepublishing.com*

**messages**
email
*email viruses, 227*
*file attachments, 225-226*
*Outlook Express, 223-225*
instant messaging (email),
231
*contact lists, 233*
*receiving, 232-234*
*sending, 232-234*

**Messenger contact lists
(Windows Messenger), 233**

**metasearchers Web sites, 202**

**Micrografx Picture Publisher Web
site, 261**

**microprocessor chips, speed,
17-18**

**microprocessors, 17**

**Microsoft Encarta, 168-169**

**Microsoft Encarta Encyclopedia,
108**

**Microsoft FrontPage Web site,
251**

**Microsoft Internet Explorer.** *See*
**Internet Explorer (IE)**

**Microsoft Money.** *See* **Money**

**Microsoft Network (MSN), 184**

**Microsoft Outlook.** *See* **Outlook;
Outlook Express**

**Microsoft Picture It! Photo, 107,
261**

**Microsoft Plus! Web site, 73**

**Microsoft Streets & Trips, 108**

**Microsoft Web site, 156**

**Microsoft Windows.** *See*
**Windows**

**Microsoft Word.** *See* **Word**

**Microsoft Works Suite.** *See*
**Works Suite**

**mini-towers, defined, 14**

**MiniDV format, 300**

**minimizing windows, 46-47**

**mIRC Web site, 236**

**modems, 24, 180, 320**

**Modify Category dialog box, 149**

**Modify Style dialog box, 123**

**Money (Microsoft), 107, 147**
banking electronically, 152
*checkbook balances, 153-154*
*Internet use, 154-158*
*transactions, 152-153*
checks, printing, 156-157
configuring, 148-149
launching, 148
recurring payments, 155-156
Setup Assistant, 148-149

**Money Budget Planner, 151-152**

**Money Home page, 150**

**monitors, 25-27, 320**

**motherboards, 16-18**

**Motley Fool Web site, 205**

**mouse, 24, 320**
clicking, customization,
77-78
cursors, 23-24
defined, 23
double-clicking, 44
dragging and dropping, 45
hovering, 45
pointing and clicking, 44
right-clicking, 44

**Move Items dialog box, 91**

**movies.** *See* **video**

**moving files, 90-91**

**MP3, 182**
digital audio, 284

**MP3.com Web site, 285**

**MSN (Microsoft Network), 184**

**MSN Bill Pay accounts, 157**

**MSN CarPoint Web site, 212**

**MSN Chat Web site, 236**

**MSN Gaming Zone Web site,
175-176**

**MSN HomeAdvisor Web site, 213**

**MSN Messenger, 232-233**

**MSN Messenger Web site, 232**

**MSN MoneyCentral Web site, 205**

**MSN Photos Web site, 267**

**MSN Web Communities Web site,
242**

**MSNBC Web site, 203**

**MusicCity Morpheus Web site,
286**

**MusicMatch Jukebox, 290-292**

**MusicMatch Jukebox Web site,
291**

**Musicseek Web site, 285**

**My Cd Labeler Web site, 298**

**My Computer folder, 54, 67**

**My Computer utility, 54**

**My Documents folder, 55, 66**

**My Documents utility, 55**

# N

**names, newsgroups, 239**

**naming files/folders, 88-89**

**National Library of Medicine
Web site, 206**

**National Weather Service Web
site, 204**

**NBC Sports Web site, 204-205**

**Neato CD Labeler Kit Web site,
298**

**Net Nanny Web site, 311**

**netiquette, 238**

**network cards, 321**

**network interface card (NIC), 326**

**Network Setup Wizard, 189, 326,
330**

**networks, 12, 326**
defined, 325
Ethernet, 327
Fast Ethernet, 327
HomePNA, 328
Internet connections, 188
NIC, 326
phone line, 327-328
setting up, 328-329
*client PC configuration, 330*
*equipment, 328*
*host PC configuration, 330*
*Network Setup Wizard, 330*
sharing files/folders, 331
wireless, 327

**New Category Wizard, 149**

**New Chart button, 136**

**New Chart dialog box, 136**

**New Connection Wizard, 186**

**New York Times Web site, 203**

**NewHomeNetwork.com Web site, 213**

**news searches (Web), 203**

**newsgroups, 238-240**

**Newsgroups dialog boxes, 239**

**newsreader programs, 238**

**NIC (network interface card), 326**

**non-Windows XP PCs, configuring, 189**

**Nordstrom Web site, 212**

**Normal view, 115**

**Norton AntiVirus Web site, 316**

**Norton Internet Safety Web site, 311**

**Norton Personal Firewall Web site, 317**

**Norton Utilities Web site, 347**

**notebooks, 27-28**

**Notepad, 63**
closing, 65
launching, 63
printing notes, 64
saving files, 65
writing notes, 64

**numbers, spreadsheets, 129**

## O

**Ofoto Web site, 267**

**OneKey Web site, 313**

**online.** *See also* **Internet; Web**
chatting, 234
*chat sites, 236*
*Internet Relay Chat (IRC), 236*
*Yahoo!, 235-236*
digital photos, printing, 267
downloading computer files, 244
electronic banking (Money), 154-158
game playing, 174-175
retailing, 209
rules, 238
shopping, 210
*homes, 213*
*online auctions, 215-219*

*reservations, 214*
*retail sites, 211-212*
*safety, 210*
*vehicles, 212*
*virtual malls, 212*

**Open Directory Web site, 202**

**opening**
file attachments (email), 226
Word documents, 118

**operating systems**
Apple, 13
defined, 13, 42
Windows, 13, 42

**operations (Windows), 44**
desktop windows, 45-47
dialog boxes, 49-50
double-clicking, 44
dragging and dropping, 45
hovering, 45
menus, 47-48
mouse, 44-50
pointing and clicking, 44
right-clicking, 44
toolbars, 48

**operators, algebraic, 131-132**

**Orbitz Web site, 214**

**Outbox (email), 226**

**Outline view, 116, 124**

**outlines, Word documents, 124-125**

**Outlook (Microsoft), 221**

**Outlook Express (Microsoft), 221**
Address Book, 227
*adding contacts, 228-229*
*emailing contacts, 230*
*editing contacts, 229*
*sorting contacts, 229*
blocking email addresses, 314
email accounts, 222
email messages
*composing, 223-224*
*reading, 224*
*replying, 225*
file attachments, 226-227

**Outlook Express window, 223**

## P

**panes**
activity, 54
Styles and Formatting, 123
task, 54

**Paragraph dialog box, 122**

**paragraphs, Word documents, 122-123**

**parallel ports, 321**

**passwords**
email accounts, 222
user accounts, 37-38

**paying recurring payments (Money), 156**

**payments**
Money
*paying, 156*
*scheduling, 155*
online auctions, 217-219

**PayPal Web site, 219**

**PC cameras, 12, 320**

**PC-cillin Web site, 316**

**PCMCIA (Personal Computer Memory Card International Association), 321**

**PCMCIA ports, 321**

**PCs, 10.** *See also* **computers**
clients, configuring, 189
components, 12
computer hardware, 11-14
*CD-ROM disk drives, 21*
*DVD disk drives, 22*
*hard disk drives, 20*
*keyboards, 22*
*memory, 19*
*microprocessors, 17*
*modems, 24*
*monitors, 25-27*
*mouse, 23-24*
*printers, 27*
*removable disk drives, 20-21*
*sound cards, 24*
*speakers, 24*
*system units, 14-19*
*video cards, 25-27*
computer software, 12-13
damaging, 14
digital pictures, transferring from cameras, 257-258

email, 11
finances, 10
games, 10
hardware, 319-321
home, 10
hosts, configuring, 188-189
Internet, 11
networks, 12
non-Windows XP, configuring, 189
overview, 10
portable, 27-28
ports, 321-322
Windows XP, 11

**Pencil Pal Preschool Web site,
166**

**people searches (Web), 202-203**

**Performance Options dialog box,
76**

**peripherals, hardware, 320-321**

**Personal Computer Memory Card
International Association (PCM-
CIA), 321**

**personal computers.** *See* **PCs**

**phone line networks, 327-328**

**photo albums, digital pictures,
264**

**Photo Printing Wizard, 265**

**photo-processing sites, digital
pictures, 267-268**

**PhotoAccess Web site, 267**

**PhotoFun.com Web site, 267**

**photos.** *See* **pictures**

**PhotoSuite Web site, 261**

**PhotoWorks Web site, 267**

**physician information searches
(Web), 207**

**picture files, downloading from
Web pages, 245-246**

**Picture It! Photo (Microsoft), 107,
261**

**pictures**
digital
*cropping, 263*
*emailing, 266*
*editing, 261-264*
*modifying, 258*
*photo albums, 264*

*photo-processing sites,
267-268*
*printing, 264-267*
*scanning, 259-260*
*special effects, 263*
*storing, 260-261*
*touching up, 262*
*transferring from cameras to
PCs, 257-258*
Word documents, 125
*Clip Art Gallery, 125-126*
*formatting, 126*

**pixels, 26**

**Planet Wellness Web site, 206**

**players, game playing, 175-176**

**playing**
CDs, 269
*CD-ROM drives, 270*
*WMP, 270-272*
digital audio on PCs,
287-289
DVDs, 269, 272
*audio options, 274*
*closed captions, 274*
*subtitles, 274*
*WMP, 273*
games, 171
*Internet connections, 175*
*online, 174-175*
*players, 175-176*
*requirements, 172*

**playlists, 287-290**

**Playsite Web site, 175**

**Pogo.com Web site, 175**

**pointing and clicking (mouse), 44**

**portable digital audio players,
321**

**portable PCs, 27-28**

**ports, 15, 321-322**

**preschool educational software,
166**

**pressplay Web site, 285**

**preventing computer viruses, 315**

**previewing Word document print
jobs, 121**

**Priceline Web site, 214**

**Print button, 121, 196**

**Print dialog box, 49, 121**

**Print Layout view, 116**

**printers**
defined, 12
digital photos, 264-265
inkjet, 27
laser, 27
overview, 27

**printing**
checks (Money), 156-157
database reports, 144-145
digital pictures, 264
*from programs, 265*
*online, 267*
*printers, 264-265*
Notepad notes, 64
Web pages, 196
Word documents, 121

**PrintMaster, 161**

**PrintRoom Web site, 267**

**programs.** *See also* **applications;
software**
accessory (Windows), 57
digital photos, printing from,
265
firewalls, 317
launching (Windows), 51
newsreader, 238
spreadsheet, defined, 13
Start menu
*adding, 80*
*displaying, 79*
switching between
(Windows), 52
WinZip, 94

**Programs page (Task Launcher),
109**

**Properties dialog box, 67**

**pull-down menus (Windows),
47-48**

## Q-R

**Quattro Pro, 106, 127**

**queries (Web), 200**

**QuickTime Player, Webcasts, 281**

**radio**
Internet, 182, 277
*locating stations, 280*
*RealAudio, 279*

*streaming audio, 278*
*WMP, 278-279*

**Radio Broadcast Network Web site, 280**

**Radio-Locator Web site, 280**

**RadioMOI Web site, 280**

**RAM (random access memory), 19**

**Reader Rabbit Web site, 166**

**reading email messages (Outlook Express), 224**

**Reading Blaster Web site, 166**

**RealAudio, 279**

**RealGuideWeb site, 282**

**RealOne Player, 279**
*Webcasts, 281*

**RealOne Player Web site, 279, 287**

**RealOne Web site, 285**

**Realty.com Web site, 213**

**rebooting, defined, 35**

**receiving**
*email, 221*
*instant messages, 232-234*

**Record dialog box, 301**

**Record Payment button, 156-157**

**Record Payment dialog box, 156**

**recordable/rewritable CD (CD-R/RW) drives, 295**

**recorders, digital video (DV), 300**

**records**
*databases, adding, 142*
*defined, 139*

**recurring payments (Money), 155-156**

**Recycle Bin**
*restoring deleted files, 92-93*
*Windows XP, 44*

**Recycle Bin icon, 92**

**removable disk drives, storage, 20-21**

**removable disks, 20-21**

**removable drives, 320**

**removing software, 102-103**

**renaming files, 88-89**

**replying to email messages (Outlook Express), 225**

**Report Name dialog box, 145**

**ReportCreator dialog box, 145**

**ReportCreator tool, 145-146**

**reports, databases, 144-146**

**requirements**
*game playing, 172*
*Setup Assistant (Money), 148-149*

**reservations, online, 214**

**reserve prices (online auctions), 216**

**resolution, 26**
*desktop sizing, 72*
*pixels, 27*

**restore points, 344-345**

**restoring**
*backup files, 339*
*computer systems, 344-346*
*deleted files, 92-93*

**retail sites, online shopping, 211-212**

**retailing online, 209**

**right-clicking (mouse), 44**

**ripping (files), 290**
*MusicMatch Jukebox, 291-292*
*WMP, 290-291*

**RoadBlock Web site, 314**

**rows, spreadsheets, 130**

**rulers (Word), 115**

**rules, online, 238**

**Run dialog box, 100**

---

# S

**Safe mode, 348**

**safety, online shopping, 210**

**Save As dialog box, 118**

**Save button, 118**

**Save Movie dialog box, 305**

**saving**
*folder settings, 86*
*Notepad files, 65*

video movies, 305
Word documents, 118

**ScanDisk utility, 336-337**

**Scanner and Camera Wizard, 257**

**scanners, 320**
defined, 12
digital pictures, 259-260

**Scheduled Tasks utility, 337**

**scheduling recurring payments (Money), 155**

**screen resolution, desktop sizing, 72**

**screen savers, 80**

**Screentip, 116**

**scroll bars**
Windows, 47
Word, 115

**scrolling through windows, 47**

**SCSI (small computer system interface), 321**

**SCSI ports, 321**

**search box, 200**

**search button, 200**

**search engines, 199**

**searching**
newsgroup articles, 239-240
Web, 199. *See also* surfing, Web
*directories, 199-202*
*financial information searches, 205*
*indexes, 202*
*keywords, 200*
*medical information searches, 205-207*
*news searches, 203*
*people searches, 202-203*
*physician information searches, 207*
*queries, 200*
*search box, 200*
*search button, 200*
*search engines, 199*
*search sites, 202*
*senior citizen searches, 207*
*sports headline searches, 204*
*weather report searches, 204*
*wildcards, 200*

secure servers, 210

security, Internet, 310-311
   filtering software, 311-312
   kid-safe searching, 312-313

selling, online auctions (eBay), 218

sending
   email, 221
      Address Book contacts, 230
      Bcc (blind carbon copy), 230
      Cc (carbon copy), 230
      Outlook, 221
      Outlook Express, 221
   electronic greeting cards, 162-164
   instant messages, 232-234

senior citizen searches (Web), 207

Senior Information Network Web site, 207

Senior Surfers Web site, 207

Senior Women Web Web site, 207

serial ports, 321

servers, secure, 210

services (Internet), 181
   email, 181
   FTP (File Transfer Protocol), 182
   IM (Instant Messaging), 181
   Internet radio, 182
   IRC (Internet Relay Chat), 182
   MP3, 182
   Usenet newsgroups, 182
   WWW (World Wide Web), 181

Sesame Street Web site, 166

setting up
   computers, 32
      cable connections, 32
      first-time startup, 34-35
      power, 34-36
      startup, 35-36
      system component connections, 33
      users, 36-38
   ISP accounts, 186-187

Setup Assistant (Money), 148-149

shareware, 243

sharing Internet connections, 187-190

shipments, online auctions (eBay), 219

shopping online, 210
   homes, 213
   online auctions, 215-219
   reservations, 214
   retail sites, 211-212
   safety, 210
   vehicles, 212
   virtual malls, 212

shortcut icons (Windows XP), 44

SHOUTcast Web site, 280

Shutterfly Web site, 268

shutting down Windows, 52-53, 69

signing up, ISPs, 185

sizing desktops, 72-73

small computer system interface (SCSI), 321

Snapfish Web site, 268

software. See also applications; programs
   anti-spam, 314
   antivirus, 316
   computer, 12-13
   digital cameras, 258
   educational, 165-168
   filtering Internet content, 311
      Internet Explorer, 312
      kid-safe searching, 312-313
   games, installing, 173
   graphics editing, 13
   home publishing, 160-161
   installing, 99
      built-in programs, 100
      from Internet, 101-102
      manual, 101
   removing, 102-103
   video editing, 300
      WMM imports, 301-302
   Web pages, creating, 251

Sonic CinePlayer Web site, 290

sonicnet.com Web site, 285

Sonique Media Player Web site, 287

sorting
   data in databases, 143
   files, 85
   folders, 85

Sorting tab, 145

sound, Windows systems, 81

sound cards, 24, 320

spam, 313-314

Spambam Web site, 314

spamblock, 313

SpamEater Web site, 314

SpamKiller Web site, 314

SpanishNow! Web site, 167

speakers, 24, 320

special effects
   desktops, 75-77
   digital pictures, 263

speed
   Internet connections, 181
   microprocessor chips, 17-18

spell checking (Word), 120

splitting (video clips), 303

Sporting News Web site, The, 204

sports headline searches (Web), 204

spreadsheet programs, defined, 13

spreadsheets. See also Works Spreadsheet
   cells, 128-129
      sorting, 134-135
   charts, 135-136
   columns
      column width, 131
      deleting, 130
      inserting, 130
   creating, 129
   data, entering, 129
   defined, 127
   formatting, 129
      cell contents, 130
      number formats, 129
   formulas, 131
      algebraic operators, 131-132
      AutoSum function, 133
      cells, 132

functions, 133-134
rows, 130

**Start button, 78**

**Start button (Windows XP), 43**

**Start menu**
adding programs, 80
customizing, 78-79
displaying icons, 79
displaying programs, 79
Windows XP, 43
Windows
*launching programs, 51*
*navigating, 51*
*switching between programs,*
*52*

**startup, computers, 34-36**

**Status bar (Word), 115**

**storage (memory), 19**
CD-ROM disk drives, 21
DVD disk drives, 22
hard disk drives, 20
removable disk drives, 20-21

**storing digital pictures, 260-261**

**streaming audio, 278**

**Streets & Trips (Microsoft), 108**

**StudyWorks Web site, 167**

**Styles and Formatting pane, 123**

**sub-folders, 55**

**subscribing to ISPs, 183**

**subtitles, DVDs, 274**

**Summary tab, 145**

**SuperKids Web site, 166**

**SurfControl Web site, 311**

**surfing Web, 191.** *See also*
**searching, Web**
overview, 194
steps, 196-198

**surge suppressors, 32**

**Switchboard Web site, 203**

**Sygate Personal Firewall Web**
**site, 317**

**system component connections,**
**33**

**system configuration, 35**

**System Properties dialog box, 18,**
**76-77**

**System Restore utility, 344-346**

**system tray (Windows XP), 43**

**system units, 16**
cases, 15
CD-ROM disk drives, 21
connectors, 15
defined, 14
DVD disk drives, 22
hard disk drives, 20
memory, 19
microprocessors, 17-18
motherboards, 16
removable disk drives, 20-21
vertical, 14

# T

**tabs**
Date and Time, 82
Deposit, 153
Disk Cleanup, 334
Fields, 145
Filter, 145
Grouping, 145
Internet Time, 82
Layout, 126
Sorting, 145
Summary, 145
Time Zone, 82
Title, 145
Withdrawal, 153

**Task Launcher, 106**
component software,
106-107
linking to pages, 108
*History page, 109*
*Home page, 108*
*Programs page, 109*
*Tasks page, 109*

**Task Launcher interface, 105**

**task pane, defined, 54**

**Task Pane (Word), 115**

**taskbar (Windows XP), 43**

**Tasks page (Task Launcher),**
**109-110**

**television, Internet, 280**
broadband Internet connections, 282
locating sites, 282
QuickTime Player, 281

RealOne Player, 281
WMP, 281

**templates (Word), defined, 117**

**Templates dialog box, 117**

**text, Word documents, 119**
editing, 119
entering, 119
formatting, 120-122
headings, 123
paragraph styles, 122-123
spelling and grammar check,
120

**themes, desktops, 73**

**ThemeWorld.com Web site, 73**

**ThirdAge Web site, 207**

**Thumbnails view, 85**

**Tiles view, 85**

**time and date, Windows sys-**
**tems, 82**

**Time Zone tab, 82**

**Title bar (Word), 114**

**Title tab, 145**

**toolbars**
Windows, 48
Word, 114

**tools**
ReportCreator, 145-146
Windows XP, 57

**TopHosts.com Web site, 252**

**towers, 14**

**transactions, electronic banking**
**(Money), 152-153**

**transitions, video editing, 304**

**TravelNow.com Web site, 214**

**Travelocity Web site, 214**

**trim points, 303**

**trimming (video clips), 303**

**Trip.com Web site, 214**

**Tripod Web site, 248**

**Troubleshooters (Windows), 348**

**troubleshooting**
applications, freeze-ups, 343
computers, 346-347
*crashing, 344-346*
*error messages, 342-343*
*freeze-ups, 342-343*

*How can we make this index more useful? Email us at indexes@quepublishing.com*

*Safe mode, 348*
*Windows Troubleshooters, 348*

**Tucows Games Web site, 173**

**Tucows Web site, 245**

**Turn Off Computer button, 53**

**Turn Off Computer dialog box, 53**

**turning off computers, 52-53**
Windows shut down, 69

**turning on computers, 34**
first-time startup, 34-35
startup, 35-36

**types**
dialog boxes (Windows), 50
educational software, 166
*continuing education, 167*
*electronic encyclopedia, 168*
*elementary, 166-167*
*high school, 167*
*Microsoft Encarta, 168*
*preschool, 166*
home publishing software, 160-161
message boards, 241-242

## U

**Ulead MediaStudio Web site, 300**

**UltraPlayer Web site, 287**

**uniform resource locator (URL), 192**

**Universal Serial Bus (USB), 321**

**URL (uniform resource locator), 192**

**USA Today Web site, 203**

**USB (Universal Serial Bus), 321**

**USB ports, 321**

**Usenet newsgroups, 182, 238**

**user accounts, defined, 36**
computer administrator, 36-37
guest, 36
limited, 36
passwords, 37-38

**User Accounts utility, 37**

**users, computers, 36-38**

**utilities**
Add or Remove Programs, 101-102
Backup, 338
configuration, 55-56
Control Panel, 55-56
Disk Defragmenter, 335
Internet (Windows XP), 57
My Computer, 54
My Documents, 55
ScanDisk, 336-337
Scheduled Tasks, 337
System Restore, 344-346

## V

**vehicles, online shopping, 212**

**versions**
Windows, 13, 42-43
Word, 115
Works Suite, 106

**vertical system units, 14**

**video**
editing, 299
*audio, 304*
*clips, 302-304*
*software, 300*
*WMM imports, 301-302*
*Workspace, 302-305*
*Workstransitions, 304*
Internet broadcasts, 277
saving, 305

**video cards, 25-27, 320**

**View buttons (Word), 115**

**View menu, 124**

**viewing**
databases, 141
documents, 66
Favorites list (Internet Explorer), 195
files, 84
folders, 84
hard disks, 67

**views**
Details, 85
Form, 141-142
Investing, 150
List, 141
Normal, 115
Outline, 116, 124

Print Layout, 116
Thumbnails, 85
Tiles, 85
Web Layout, 116
Word documents, 115-116

**Views button, 84**

**virtual malls, online shopping, 212**

**viruses**
computer, 315
*antivirus software, 316*
*exposure to, 315*
*infection signs, 315*
*preventing, 315*
email, 227
file attachments (email), 227

## W-X

**WANs (wide area networks), 325**

**weather report searches (Web), 204**

**Weather Underground Web site, 204**

**Weather.com Web site, 204**

**Web. *See also* Internet; online**
graphic links, 192
graphics, 192
hypertext links, 192
overview, 192
searching, 199
*directories, 199-202*
*financial information searches, 205*
*indexes, 202*
*keywords, 200*
*medical information searches, 205-207*
*news searches, 203*
*people searches, 202-203*
*physician information searches, 207*
*queries, 200*
*search box, 200*
*search button, 200*
*search engines, 199*
*search sites, 202*
*senior citizen searches, 207*
*sports headline searches, 204*
*weather report searches, 204*
*wildcards, 200*

surfing, 191
  *overview, 194*
  *steps, 196-198*

**Web addresses**
  CNN.com, 196
  Google, 197

**Web browsers, 191**

**Web Layout view, 116**

**Web pages, 192**
  creating, 247
    *software programs, 251*
    *Yahoo! GeoCities, 248-250*
  downloading files from,
    245-246
  history, 196
  printing, 196

**Web-radio Web site, 280**

**Webcasts, 277-280**
  broadband Internet connec-
    tions, 282
  locating sites, 282
  QuickTime Player, 281
  RealOne Player, 281
  WMP, 281

**WebHosters.com Web site, 252**

**WebMD Health Web site, 206**

**white pages directories (Web),
  203**

**WhitePages.com Web site, 203**

**WhoWhere Web site, 203**

**wide area networks (WANs), 325**

**WiFi (wired fidelity), 328**

**wildcards, 200**

**WinAmp Web site, 287**

**Windows, 13. *See also* Windows
  XP**
  accessory programs, 57
  Apple, compatibility, 13

**windows**
  closing, 46-47
  maximizing, 46-47
  menus, 47-48
  minimizing, 46-47
  moving, 45-47
  Outlook Express, 223
  scrolling through, 47
  sizing, 45-47
  WMM, 300
  WMP, 270-272

**Windows**
  desktops
    *backgrounds, 73-74*
    *customizing, 71-77*
    *elements, 73-74*
    *sizing, 72-73*
    *themes, 73*
  documents, viewing, 66
  files
    *folders, 53*
    *navigating, 53-55*
  folders, navigating, 54-56
  games, playing, 60-62
  hard disk, viewing, 67
  Notepad, 63
    *closing, 65*
    *launching, 63*
    *printing notes, 64*
    *saving files, 65*
    *writing notes, 64*
  operations, 44
    *desktop windows, 45-47*
    *dialog boxes, 49-50*
    *double-clicking, 44*
    *dragging and dropping, 45*
    *hovering, 45*
    *menus, 47-48*
    *mouse, 44-50*
    *pointing and clicking, 44*
    *right-clicking, 44*
    *toolbars, 48*
  overview, 42
  shutting down, 52-53
  shutting down systems, 69
  versions, 13, 42-43

**Windows configuration, 35**

**Windows Media Audio (WMA),
  284**

**Windows Media Player. *See* WMP**

**Windows Messenger, 232**
  launching, 232
  Messenger contact lists, 233

**Windows Messenger Web site,
  232**

**Windows Movie Maker (WMM),
  300-302**

**Windows Notepad. *See* Notepad**

**Windows product activation, 34**

**Windows Recycle Bin, 44**

**Windows registration, 35**

**Windows Troubleshooters, 348**

**Windows XP, 42-43. *See also*
  Windows**
  ClearType, 73
  desktops, 43-44
    *colors, 75*
    *fonts, 75*
    *mouse clicking, 77-78*
    *navigating, 43*
    *special effects, 75-77*
  digital photo-processing sites,
    268
  files
    *compressing, 93*
    *copying, 89-90*
    *deleting, 91-92*
    *displaying, 84*
    *extracting, 94*
    *grouping, 85*
    *moving, 90-91*
    *naming, 88-89*
    *restoring deleted files, 92-93*
    *sorting, 85*
    *viewing, 84*
  firewalls, 317
  folders
    *compressed, 93-94*
    *creating, 88*
    *grouping, 85*
    *naming, 88-89*
    *navigating, 87*
    *saving settings, 86*
    *sorting, 85*
    *viewing, 84*
  help features, 57
  Internet connections, 189
  Internet utilities, 57
  networks, 326
    *client PC configuration, 330*
    *connecting, 327-328*
    *host PC configuration, 330*
    *NIC, 326*
    *setting up, 328-330*
    *sharing files/folders, 331*
  PCs, 11
  screen savers, 80
  Start menu
    *adding programs, 80*
    *customizing, 78-79*
    *displaying icons, 79*
    *displaying programs, 79*
  system sounds, 81
  system tools, 57
  time and date, 82

*How can we make this index more useful? Email us at indexes@quepublishing.com*

**Windows XP Control Panel, 55-56**

**Windows XP Internet Connection Firewall, 317**

**Windows XP Media Center, 42**

**WinZip program, 94**

**wired fidelity (WiFi), 328**

**wireless networks, 327**

**Withdrawal tab, 153**

**wizards**
　　Add Hardware, 323-324
　　Backup or Restore, 338-339
　　Extraction, 94
　　Network Setup, 189, 326,
　　　330
　　New Category, 149
　　New Connection, 186
　　Photo Printing, 265
　　Scanner and Camera, 257

**WMA (Windows Media Audio),
284**

**WMM (Windows Movie Maker),
300-302**

**WMM window, 300**

**WMP (Windows Media Player),
270**
　　burning CDs, 296-297
　　digital audio, 284, 288
　　　*playlists, 288-289*
　　　*ripping, 290-291*
　　　*song copies, 289-290*
　　Internet radio, 278-279
　　playing CDs, 272
　　playing DVDs, 273
　　ripping files, 290-291
　　Webcasts, 281

**WMP Media Library, 288-289**

**WMP window, 270-272**

**Word (Microsoft), 113**
　　displaying documents,
　　　115-116
　　documents
　　　*formatting, 122-123*
　　　*outlines, 124-125*
　　　*pictures, 125-126*
　　　*previewing before printing,
　　　　121*
　　　*printing, 121*
　　　*text, 119-120*
　　greeting cards, 160

Task Pane, 115
templates, defined, 117
versions, 115
workspace
　　*documents, 115*
　　*Menu bar, 114*
　　*rulers, 115*
　　*scroll bars, 115*
　　*Status bar, 115*
　　*Title bar, 114*
　　*toolbars, 114*
　　*View buttons, 115*

**Word (Microsoft), 107**

**word processors, 113**

**WordPerfect, 106**

**Works Calendar, 107**

**Works Database, 107, 139.** *See
also* **databases**
　　creating customized databas-
　　　es, 140-141
　　data, 143-144
　　editing, 142
　　launching, 140
　　preformatted applications,
　　　140
　　reports, 144
　　　*printing lists, 144-145*
　　　*ReportCreator tool, 145-146*
　　viewing databases, 141

**Works Spreadsheet, 106, 128.** *See
also* **spreadsheets**
　　cell operations, 132
　　cells, 128-129
　　　*sorting, 134-135*
　　charts, 135-136
　　creating spreadsheets, 129
　　formulas, AutoSum function,
　　　133
　　functions, 133-134
　　operators, 131-132

**Works Suite, 105-106**
　　Address Book, 227
　　　*adding contacts, 228-229*
　　　*emailing contacts, 230*
　　　*editing contacts, 229*
　　　*sorting contacts, 229*
　　launching, 108
　　　*History page, 111-112*
　　　*Programs page, 109*
　　　*Task Launcher, 108-109*
　　　*Tasks page, 110*

Task Launcher, 106-107
versions, 106

**Workspace, video editing, 302**
　　audio, 304-305
　　clips, 302-303
　　transitions, 304

**workspace (Word)**
　　documents, 115
　　Menu bar, 114
　　rulers, 115
　　scroll bars, 115
　　Status bar, 115
　　Title bar, 114
　　toolbars, 114
　　View buttons, 115

**World Book Web site, 168**

**World Wide Web (WWW), 181**

**writing Notepad notes, 64**

# Y-Z

**Yahoo!**
　　chatting online, 235-236
　　directories, 201

**Yahoo! Broadcast Web site, 282**

**Yahoo! Chat, 235**

**Yahoo! Games Web site, 175**

**Yahoo! GeoCities Web pages,
creating, 248-250**

**Yahoo! GeoCities Web site, 248**

**Yahoo! Greetings, 162-164**

**Yahoo! Groups Web site, 242**

**Yahoo! Message Boards, 240-241**

**Yahoo! Messenger Web site, 232**

**Yahoo! Web site, 201, 235**

**Yahooligans! Web site, 313**


**ZDNet Downloads Web site, 245**

**zooming, Word documents, 116**